"Marketing professionals can benefit greatly from this book. Its engaging style and numerous research-based takeaways make it a standout in the field."
Robert Cialdini, author of *Influence* and *Pre-Suasion*

"A tour de force. The most intelligent marketing book I have read in years."
Mark Schaefer, author of *Marketing Rebellion*

"Using the latest behavioral science research, Nancy Harhut has created a clear and actionable guide to how customers' brains really work. Every marketer who wants to attract and retain more customers needs this book."
Roger Dooley, author of *Brainfluence* and *Friction*

"An actionable and comprehensive guide to neuromarketing from an industry veteran—get it before your competitors do!"
Tim Ash, author of *Unleash Your Primal Brain*, keynote speaker, executive marketing advisor

"Nancy has one of the most brilliant marketing minds I have ever come to know. If you follow even one of the principles outlined in this book it will change the course of your business forever!"
Paul Chambers, CEO and Co-Founder, Subscription Trade Association (SUBTA)

"Nancy has created a straightforward, well-researched, easy-to-use guide for how behavioral insights can improve your marketing strategy and results. It is a gift."
Jeff Kreisler, co-author of *Dollars and Sense*, Founding Editor of PeopleScience.com, Head of Behavioral Science, JP Morgan Chase

"Nancy's book is like a brain tell-all, revealing all the secrets, biases, and weird brain science fueling human decisions. P.S. Chapter 14 is my favorite."
Ann Handley, WSJ bestselling author of *Everybody Writes* and Chief Content Officer at MarketingProfs

"This is the most important book on marketing in many years. Every page includes valuable and often counterintuitive information you can put to use right away. If you like Dan Ariely, Robert Cialdini and other behavioral scientists, you're going to love Nancy Harhut."
Alan Rosenspan, President, Alan Rosenspan & Associates, author of *Confessions of a Control Freak*

"Is it too late to steal this manuscript and tell everyone I wrote it? The world is frustrated with what marketing can't accomplish for their businesses. What Nancy Harhut has here is the fix. Don't read this book. Implement it."
Chris Brogan, envious author and keynote speaker

"Tried and tested principles are at the heart of Nancy's book. Bringing in behavioral techniques such as temporal landmarks, instant gratification and bridging the gap between our present and future selves, this is the type of practical book needed now as we take behavioral science out of the lab and into our working business practices."
Louise Ward, 42 Courses and Co-Host of Behavioural Science Club

"A valuable playbook for using mental shortcuts to speed up the decision-making process. One of the most worthwhile marketing books you'll ever read!"
Kerry O'Shea Gorgone, Senior Editor and Writer at Appfire, Consigliere and Showrunner at Chris Brogan Media

"Marketers have a must-read with *Using Behavioral Science in Marketing*. Nancy provides both thoughtful research and insight into how to better connect with the behaviors of consumers."
Kenneth "Shark" Kinney, Professional Speaker / Marketing Strategist / Shark Diver / Host of *A Shark's Perspective* podcast

"Clear, concise, and most importantly, damn interesting. If you can't see her on stage, you're holding the next best thing."
Damian Francis, Managing Partner, Unmade and former Head of Content at Mumbrella

"You'll use these tactics in your next marketing campaign, but you'll also use them in your next marketing meeting. Yes, this book will help you win support for your ideas in the conference room. I apply what I've learned from Nancy in marketing, in sales and even in management."
Andy Crestodina, Co-Founder/Chief Marketing Officer, Orbit Media Studios, and author of *Content Chemistry*

"Through continuous testing, direct marketers have long understood that they could motivate a response from prospects using various methods like urgency and social proof. But they never understood exactly why people respond the way they do. At last, Nancy Harhut has harnessed modern neuroscience to explain the reasons behind human response, and help us apply the science to our campaigns. A must for every marketer's bookshelf."
Ruth P. Stevens, B2B marketing consultant and educator, author of *B2B Data-Driven Marketing*, Adjunct Professor at NYU Stern

"Nancy has an incredible ability to help marketers uncover why people respond and how to capture that interest. This is a must read for anyone who wants to drive engagement, sales, and growth."
Jay Schwedelson, Founder, SubjectLine.com, and President and CEO, Worldata Group

"*Using Behavioral Science in Marketing* does a fantastic job of taking a weighty and complex topic like behavioral science and making it practical and easy for anyone to apply. On top of that, it is a fun and engaging read! The book moves along at a pleasing pace, with short chapters that give you a mix of great stories balanced with science and Nancy's proven tips. A must-read for every marketer who wants to be competitive in the age of behavioral science (which has already begun)."
Melina Palmer, author of *What Your Customer Wants and Can't Tell You* and host of *The Brainy Business* podcast

"Have you ever wished someone would read all the books you've been meaning to read, highlight the best parts, and then figure out the best ways to put those parts into practice with the specific work you do? That's what Nancy Harhut does with this absolute gift of a book. With *Using Behavioral Science in Marketing*, Nancy Harhut has created a must-have manual for marketers who want to make sure their work actually works."
Tamsen Webster, author of *Find Your Red Thread*

"Mind. Blown. Nancy has reverse-engineered buyer behavior to help you know EXACTLY how to connect and engage with your audience based on behavioral science."
Tom Shapiro, CEO Stratabeat, author of *Rethink Lead Generation* and *Rethink Your Marketing*

"Nancy Harhut is unquestionably one of the sharpest, most knowledgeable and experienced authorities on consumer psychology in the marketing world. Both hyper-effective and supported by data science, the strategies she outlines in her book, *Using Behavioral Science in Marketing*, will have an immediate impact on your marketing campaigns and a massive impact on your bottom line."
Jeffry Pilcher, CEO/President, The Financial Brand

"In an era of media abundance and attention scarcity, we as marketers have to make the most of every moment we happen to get with a prospective consumer. Nancy's practical application of such a wide variety of behavioral science principles will help any brand ensure these valuable moments aren't wasted. An amazing collection of case studies with proven outcomes that will inspire smarter, more effective work and offer readers a distinct competitive edge."
Josh Blacksmith, Senior Director—Global Consumer Relationships and Engagement, Kimberly-Clark

"A great read for today's results-now marketers. Practical and specific, this is how to actually increase response."
Brian Whipple, CEO Accenture Interactive, 2010–2021

Using Behavioral Science in Marketing

Drive Customer Action and Loyalty by Prompting Instinctive Responses

Nancy Harhut

KoganPage

First published in Great Britain and the United States in 2022 by Kogan Page Limited

2nd Floor, 45 Gee Street	8 W 38th Street, Suite 902	4737/23 Ansari Road
London	New York, NY 10018	Daryaganj
EC1V 3RS	USA	New Delhi 110002
United Kingdom		India
www.koganpage.com		

Kogan Page books are printed on paper from sustainable forests.

ISBNs

Hardback	978 1 3986 0668 5
Paperback	978 1 3986 0648 7
Ebook	978 1 3986 0667 8

British Library Cataloguing-in-Publication Data

A CIP record for this book is available from the British Library.

Library of Congress Control Number

2022939080

Typeset by Integra Software Services, Pondicherry
Print production managed by Jellyfish
Printed and bound by CPI Group (UK) Ltd, Croydon CR0 4YY

To Cathy, who always encouraged me to write a book.

To my colleagues and clients, who made so much of this possible.

And to Alissa, who one day may write a book of her own.

CONTENTS

ACKNOWLEDGMENTS

You don't write a book like this without a lot of help. While most of the people on this list knew nothing of my project, they are why I came to write it. It is either their collaboration, counsel, encouragement, or inspiration that I want to gratefully acknowledge. And for many, the results-generating work we did together.

Some are agency types that I was lucky enough to work with over the years. Others are the clients who chose to work with us. And others, still, are people I've met throughout my career who in one way or another left their mark, and in so doing, left me better. Sprinkled among them are people who asked me when I'd write a book, as well as a couple who hunted down assets for me when I finally decided to do it.

So, many thanks to: Tim Ash, Dan Ariely, Jaclyn Agy, Megan Allinson, Jean Alexander, Neal Boornazian, Michael Bronner, Carla Baratta, Chris Brogan, Sue Burton, Edward Boches, Catherine Bartholow, Kim Borman, Michelle Bottomley, Darren Bult, Cassie Bagshaw, Robert Cialdini, Keith Clark, Andy Crestodina, Sean Cunningham, Jamie Condon, Debbie Cavalier, Jessica Cross, Roger Dooley, Nichole Dickinson, Andy Doucette, Jeremey Donovan, Arnon Dreyfuss, Melissa Dietrich, Pete Doucette, Mark Emond, M. Valentina Escobar-Gonzalez, Najla Frayha, Tommy Fiorito, Greg Faucher, Greg Gordon, Kerry O'Shea Gorgone, Mitch Glazier, Joe Grimaldi, Christopher Graves, Chris Geraghty, Joanie Golden, Bill Gustat, Cara Gresser, Heidi Green, Amy Hunt, Ann Handley, David Hussong, Colin Heward, Gary Hennerberg, Ben Hall, Joe Harr, Anne Louise Hanstad, Burr Johnson, Kat Jaibur, Karen Kaplan, Cat Kolodij, Kenneth Kinney, Jean Keller, Mike King, Matt Kaiser, Greg Long, Mitch Lunsford, Chris Lee, Jim Mullen, Mark Mylan, Michelle Martineau, Sharon Martin, Ed Marino, Brennan Mullin, Mary Kubitskey, Matt Kaiser, Brian Massey, Shawn McNulty, Cheryl Morrison Deutsch, Chris McConaughey, Greg Ng, Dan Nearing, Julie Nichols, Mat Nelson, Chey Ottoson, Frank Parrish, Chris Plehal, Pat Peterson, Peter Phair, Jeffry Pilcher, Ron Pulicari, Danika Porter, Jeff Preston, Linda Pepe, Deirdre Pocase, Andrew Pelosi, Alan Rosenspan, Aaron Reid, Clare Robinson, Robin Riggs, John Sisson, Janet Sutherland, Elizabeth Stearns, Robert Solomon, Mary Stibal, Jay Schwedelson, Julie Sullivan, Tom Shapiro, Ruth Stevens, Marael Sorenson,

Richard Shaw, Joanie Swartz, Karla Tateosian, Leslie Tsui, Geoffrey Underwood, Brian Whipple, Tom Wilde, Scott Whittier, Tamsen Webster, Lianne Wade, Harry Wellott, Byron White, Jen Wiese, and Laura Walsh. Last but not least, my editors, Stephen Dunnell and Heather Wood, who guided me from start to finish.

Finally, to anyone I've inadvertently forgotten, please accept my apologies, know that I'll agonize over it, and chalk it up to my publisher's deadline.

ABOUT THE AUTHOR

Nancy helps marketers unlock automatic, hardwired "yes" answers from their customers and prospects. Her specialty is blending best-of-breed creative with behavioral science to prompt response. Perhaps that's why she's been named a Top 100 Creative Influencer, a Social Top 50 Email Marketing Leader, a Top 40 Digital Strategist, and one of the 10 Most Fascinating People in B2B Marketing.

A frequent speaker at marketing conferences, Nancy's shared her passion with audiences in London, Sydney, Moscow, Madrid, Stockholm, Sao Paulo, Berlin, and all over the US, including several return engagements at SXSW.

Prior to cofounding Massachusetts-based HBT Marketing, Nancy held senior creative management positions with agencies within the IPG and Publicis networks. In fact, she was the first home-grown Creative Director at the famed Bronner Slosberg Humphrey (now Digitas).

She and her teams have won over 200 awards for marketing effectiveness, for B2C, B2B, and nonprofit clients, with campaigns that have beaten benchmarks and controls by double and triple digits. She's worked with AT&T, Dell, H&R Block, Bank of America, Dish Network, *Boston Globe*, Seagram, HP, UnitedHealthcare, *New England Journal of Medicine*, AARP, Nationwide, GM Card, Sheraton, TripAdvisor, Principal Financial, University of Phoenix, Transamerica, and many other brands, both big and small.

Discover more at hbtmktg.com or follow her on twitter at @nharhut.

Introduction

Two kinds of people will pick up this book.

Some of you will be marketers who want scientifically proven ways to get people to do something—try, buy, buy again, recommend. Others will be marketers who want an effective way to *stop* people from doing something—say, ignore their targeted messages or switch to a competitor. Both seek ways to influence human behavior. And both will find what they're looking for here.

To influence behavior, first you must understand why people do what they do. If you've been in marketing for any length of time, you've probably been bewildered by the behavior of some customers and prospects. You may market exactly what they need—the ideal product at the ideal price—yet they fail to read and reply.

This is because people often don't *make* decisions so much as default to them. Science has proven that humans have hardwired responses—automatic, instinctive, reflexive reactions to the choices around them. In an innate effort to conserve mental energy, they frequently rely on these hardwired responses, rather than make well-thought-out, well-considered decisions. This can impact a spectrum of their behaviors, ranging from what they read, to whom they trust, to when they buy.

The advantage for marketers? These automatic behaviors are predictable—and they can be prompted or triggered

Yes, you read that right. There are proven approaches that you can take to influence your targets' decisions, to increase the likelihood they'll do exactly what you want them to. No, there is no magic bullet that will work for everyone, every time. But by skillfully applying the principles of human behavior to your marketing messages, you can gain a competitive advantage. One that will propel you further than depending on proven best practices alone.

The truth is, marketers can spend their careers trying to get people to behave a certain way, to take a particular action. Yet for the most part, marketers craft campaigns as if the people they're meant for actually stop to contemplate them—even though science tells a very different story. A story of fleeting attention and autopilot audiences.

However, in that story is your salvation. Because you can use what social scientists have found about human behavior in order to influence it. If you know that people are more likely to respond one way when they encounter a certain stimulus or prompt, why not build that stimulus or prompt into your marketing strategy and execution?

If you know people default to hardwired behaviors—giving them little to no thought—then let's make sure you construct your communications to trigger those hardwired behaviors. That is what this book will help you do. It's designed to be your go-to guide, jammed with behavior-influencing insights and real-world examples. And you can benefit from it immediately, with no need for additional investments in your marketing team, your martech stack, or your media.

Exactly what will you get from this book?

Throughout the next 17 chapters, you'll discover the details that will change the way you frame messages, structure offers, write copy, and essentially create your marketing campaigns. You'll learn the words to use and the mistakes to avoid. In short, you'll gain practical, easy-to-apply tactics that will increase your engagement and response rates.

How do I know that? Because I've tested most of these principles myself. But even more telling, other people have tested them. At conference after conference, people I don't know come up to me to say they'd previously heard me speak, took pages of notes, then went back to the office to try some of the ideas—and they worked.

So, if you want an incredibly effective way to increase your ROI, if you want to stack the deck in your favor when you test your marketing messages, or if you simply want to know the real reason some of your communications work while others bomb, you'll discover that in these pages. They will equip you to create more effective marketing messages, because they will reveal the tactics most apt to make your targets automatically pay attention and respond to you.

Among many other secrets, you'll find out:

- What one word gets people to agree with you—before they've even heard what you say next.
- How to convince someone who claims they're "not in the market" for your product or service—that they actually are.
- What you can do to prompt people to buy something now—when the benefit comes later, if at all.

These are tactics that are easy to apply and can improve your results, even if you've already done some market research... even if your previous tests haven't worked that well... and even if science isn't your favorite subject.

In fact, you'll find I go short on the scientific research and longer on the way to use it. So, you'll get just enough of the easy-to-follow reason why you should consider an approach for a particular goal—for instance speeding up sales, or convincing stubborn prospects to convert—and lots of examples of ways to put that approach into action to trigger your desired behavior.

Many verticals, many channels, and double- and triple-digit lifts over benchmarks and controls

Throughout this book, you'll find some eye-opening stories and case studies that show just how powerful using behavioral science in marketing can be. You'll see they cut across numerous B2C and B2B verticals, including financial services, insurance, telecom, high tech, automotive, publishing, education, healthcare, fundraising, credit cards, and quite a few others. In fact, you should be especially interested if what you market falls into the highly competitive, highly regulated, or hard-to-sell categories.

You'll discover how behavioral science has been used to help marketers sell everything from tequila to long-term care insurance, with results that beat benchmarks and controls by double- and triple-digit lifts. And you'll see how these tactics can be applied across channels—email, ads, direct mail, web copy, tv, print, social media, etc.

These are the same principles I share with clients, and at industry events all over the world. The same ones that prompt conference attendees to write comments like "Mind-blowing insights on how to persuade," "Wildly brilliant," and "It was amazing. Do you have a book?"

Today, I can answer that last one with a yes. After several years of testing and tracking creative executions, and collecting and curating studies, I have a book. It's a hands-on handbook that reveals exactly how to prompt automatic response by using behavioral science in marketing. And now, if you'd like, you can use the tactics in this book to radically improve your marketing. The choice is yours.

01

Emotional and rational elements in decision making

Behavioral scientists have found that in order to make a decision, people use both the rational and emotional parts of their brain. This means the most effective marketing messages will contain elements that appeal to each. Buying decisions of all types are often first made emotionally, and then later justified with rational reasons.

You know how people make decisions, right? At least you think you do. People decide based on a variety of factors—their needs, wants and goals, their past experiences, their preferences. Sometimes they make a list of pros and cons. Or they conduct a cost-benefit analysis. Other times they do some research, and then they sleep on it. Sometimes they talk things over with a spouse, a friend, or a colleague. Occasionally they choose the lesser of two evils.

You've likely seen examples of all these decision-making methods at one time or another. So yes, you know how people decide, right? They have a process, it's logical and deliberate, and as a result people know exactly what they're doing and why they're doing it.

All of this is true. Except when it isn't. And as it turns out, that's actually quite a lot of the time. If you're a little surprised to hear this, I understand. I was, too. The person who really opened my eyes to it was Dan Ariely. Among his many accomplishments, Dan is a world-renowned behavioral scientist, a *New York Times* best-selling author, and a Duke University professor.

One of the things Dan taught me, which you can find in his book *Predictably Irrational*, is that "We usually think of ourselves as sitting in the driver's seat, with ultimate control over the decisions we make; but alas, this perception has more to do with our desires—than with reality" (Ariely, 2008).

Essentially people think they're in charge. They think they make well-thought-out, well-considered decisions. But quite often, they're at the mercy of forces they are completely unaware of. And one of those is their emotions.

> Because of the way the human brain works, a marketer's messages need both rational and emotional components.

People decide based on emotional reasons—even really smart people, even in B2B

The truth is—and this is important—people actually make decisions for emotional reasons, and then later justify those decisions with rational reasons. They use those rational reasons to justify their decisions not only to the people they talk with, but also to themselves. They cite these rationales because in most instances they genuinely believe them. They're convinced they've made a decision for the right reasons. And they absolutely do not believe they were influenced by anything else. Or, for that matter, that they could possibly be making a choice that was not completely their own.

At this point you may be tempted to say, "Not me" or "not my customers." You may point to the fact that, unlike some other marketers, you target a highly educated, perhaps even highly professional audience. You figure they're too smart to make decisions emotionally. What's more, you may smile knowingly and think, "well that's interesting, but of course I work in the business-to-business space, so this just doesn't apply to what I do." But actually, it does.

How people make decisions has to do with how we are hardwired. Our brains process emotions faster than rational thought. Emotions also focus our attention and help us remember. From an evolutionary perspective, this is what helped humans survive. For example, our ancestors who responded appropriately to fear lived to see another day—and ultimately to pass their genes down to future generations. Those who chose to ponder the situation rather than immediately flee from an approaching animal outfitted with sharp teeth, claws, or tusks, did not.

Kevin Roberts, former Chief Executive Officer Worldwide of advertising agency Saatchi and Saatchi and author of *Lovemarks: The future beyond brands*, has stated that the buying decision is 80 percent emotional. Canadian neurologist Donald B. Calne puts a fine point on exactly why that's so important. He explains that "The essential difference between emotion and reason is that emotion leads to action, while reason leads to conclusions" (Roberts, 2005).

FIGURE 1.1 Emotion drives decision-making

The buying decision is 80% emotional, according to Lovemarks author Kevin Roberts.

The critical point for marketers to remember is that it's the emotional responses that drive the buying behaviors. And at this point I'm not talking about building brands, and influencing attitude and awareness, although emotion certainly plays a key role in those areas. Here we are talking about getting people to take action—the very thing marketers need to prompt their prospects and customers to do. If those prospects and customers come to the conclusion it'd be good to take action, but then they do not, marketers lose.

And that's why Antonio Damasio's research is so important. Antonio Damasio is a neuroscientist and author of the book *Descartes' Error*. He conducted research among people who'd sustained injury to the parts of the brain that generate and process emotions. What he found was these people were virtually incapable of making a decision—even a decision as simple as what they might like to eat for lunch that day. They would just spin round and round, considering all the options, but never coming to a decision. Humans need to access emotions in order to know what to do.

PEOPLE ARE PEOPLE, WHEREVER THEY ARE

When you're developing your marketing messages, and this includes when you are marketing to a business-to-business audience, you must factor in some emotion. Early in my career, when I was working on brands like IBM and Dell, I read a study that reported that even if a high-technology executive believed a marketer's product would be good for their company, they would not advocate for it if it seemed like it would be too hard to get the necessary buy-in to implement the solution.

Talk about a bucket of cold water in a marketer's face. Even if the prospect you were targeting was convinced your product was the right choice, they wouldn't try to buy it because the hassle at work wouldn't be worth it. While the study is now old, the lesson is evergreen.

People are people, whether they are at home or at the office. And people have emotions. They care about things like how they'll look to their boss, or the board, or their peers. And they care whether a product or service will help them finish work on time or keep them stuck at their desk. They also have professional reputations they worry about, egos that need to be fed, and a certain amount of self-interest that routinely creeps in.

All of these "human" factors get in the way of your business target making a completely objective, unbiased decision guided solely by what is best for the company. Do not make the mistake of assuming your target is somehow different. Your B2B targets won't respond to your marketing messages based only on price and features. They won't automatically choose you simply because you provide the best product or service to address their situation. Even if their own research points to you as the best solution, even if they are educated professionals, there will be other influences at play in their decision-making process—influences they may very well be unaware of.

But don't despair. This represents an opportunity for you. Inject some emotion into your marketing and let it work its magic.

Smart ways to inject emotion into your marketing message

- Prompt your prospect to imagine how good it will feel to save time and personal effort by using your product or service.
- Use pictures and colors to elicit an emotional response.
- Point out the painful situation your target can avoid by adopting your product (see Chapter 2 on loss aversion).
- Make your customer feel special or superior because they use your product (see Chapter 3 on scarcity).
- Proactively help your prospect before asking them to buy (see Chapter 4 on reciprocity).
- Emphasize that your prospect will be making a popular choice that no one will blame them for (see Chapter 5 on social proof).
- Tell the story of how someone became a workplace hero thanks to your product or service (see Chapter 6 on storytelling).
- Focus on the experience of owning or using your product, along with its features and benefits.

ADD EMOTION TO YOUR MARKETING STRATEGIES AND CREATIVE EXECUTIONS
An emotional component can easily be part of your creative execution. It can also help inform your strategy, as the following story shows.

When I was a young copywriter employed by Mullen Advertising, the agency was housed in a beautiful old mansion on Boston's North Shore. The building had once been the summer home of an heiress, and at another time a convent. At this point, it was an ad agency with all the various rooms repurposed to serve that use. One small room (possibly a sacristy in another life?) displayed framed prints of many of the advertisements the agency had won awards for.

Among them was also a *Wall Street Journal* ad featuring Paul Silverman, the agency's Chief Creative Officer at the time. Headlined "All of Paul," and with a dramatic black and white photo of him, it was part of the *Journal*'s famous Creative Leaders Series, which showcased interviews with prominent agency executives whose work had appeared in the paper. Each executive selected had a gloriously oversized newspaper page devoted entirely to themselves, in which they told their story, and answered questions about their creative philosophy or their approach to the business.

To this day, I remember walking by that ad on a regular basis and imagining what it felt like to be included in that campaign. And now I wonder how many creative directors might have, consciously or not, created ads for their clients specially designed to run in the *Wall Street Journal* with the hope of being chosen for the campaign. Why? Because even in business, personal emotions matter.

What's also worth mentioning about this series of ads is that the strategy behind it took advantage of the Commitment and Consistency Principle (see Chapter 8). The final question the featured ad exec was always asked involved their views on advertising in the *Wall Street Journal*.

So even after being featured in the Creative Leader Series campaign, there was an incentive to continue running advertisements in the paper, because the executive had gone on record saying what a smart, effective idea that was. Having made that public commitment, they were much more likely to remain consistent with it.

A CONTEMPORARY APPLICATION

With this classic *Wall Street Journal* campaign in mind, I read with interest an August 2021 *AdAge* article headlined "Spotify debuts songs honoring CMOs of CVS, Frito-Lay and more." The article described the music streaming company's B2B campaign as an album of songs created specifically for executives at major brands, with each song written to reflect the individual CMO's taste in music. The Spotify team reportedly worked with "both existing partners and those it was looking to engage with more deeply" (Diaz, 2021).

Co-CCO Michael Aimette of FCB New York, the agency that developed the campaign with Spotify, said it was designed to demonstrate to marketers "how fun and effective the platform can be" (Diaz, 2021). In the article, Sarah Kiefer, Spotify's global director of enterprise marketing, encouraged other CMOs to get in touch if they wished to be considered for a potential next album. Similar to the *Wall Street Journal* campaign, I suspect the allure and emotional appeal of having a song written about you may prove to be quite a powerful draw.

CASE STUDY
Adding emotion into a practical, B2B product's marketing campaign

While I was a creative director at a large US ad agency, my group was tasked with creating direct response print ads for a high-tech company that sold business intelligence software. First, we needed to understand exactly what the software did, which was to provide a unified look at data that resided in separate silos. Next, we had to understand the benefit to that, which was that business people would have a single view of all their data, in order to help them make better-informed decisions. Finally, we needed to know what the call to action would be, which was to visit the website.

Now it was time to get to work. The creative teams looked at various ways to serve up the message. Some took a problem–solution approach: because data sit in different places all around the company, business executives have a problem accessing the information they need. This product will solve that problem by essentially sitting on top of all the data silos like a sponge, and absorbing all the data into one place so the person can get at it. This explained what the product did and why it would be helpful. It was a solid attempt.

Another approach played off the butterfly effect—the idea that one small change can have large, subsequent impacts: If an executive missed a small but key piece of information because it did not show up in the data they pulled, and they made a decision without that bit of data, the impact of that decision with the omitted data could have significant, far-reaching consequences in the future. One thing impacts another, which then impacts another until there is a real issue. This put some context around the product and made more of a case for acquiring it.

But the winning campaign did something these other two did not. It injected serious, end-user emotion. It talked about the kinds of data-driven decisions that the target had to make every day, the kind that affected their employees' livelihoods and their company's profit margins. It acknowledged this might make the target feel a little panicked; that they might feel incredible pressure to get things right. It suggested this could lead to second-guessing and sleepless nights. And then it presented the product as the thing that would make the target feel confident and protected from making the wrong call.

With headlines like "The delete button for that voice in your head," the emotion in this campaign connected with the prospect. The prospects could see themselves in the ads. They felt that the marketer understood them and was talking directly to them.

All three ad approaches described the benefits of the business intelligence software. All included the rational reasons to learn more, citing what the product did, a stat about existing customers using it, and information about the company itself. But only this one made the emotional case, too. When the client tested it, this was the ad campaign that came out on top. And when it went into market, it increased brand favorability scores by 11 percent and, even more important, it increased purchase intent by 13 percent.

MISTAKE

Assuming that business products and practical products require completely rational marketing messages. Even these can benefit from injecting some emotion.

In both B2C and B2B, your goal is to create an emotional connection in your marketing

Naturally, because emotion drives decision making, it should also play a big role when marketing to consumers. That's perhaps easier to understand than when considering the B2B audience. However, it's worth discussing. Marketing messages to consumers or businesses that focus exclusively on price and features leave an important lever unpulled. As a marketer, you want to acknowledge how your product or service makes people feel.

As Kristina Radova reports in an *insideBE* article, an insurance company found that better prices alone were not enough to motivate drivers to use a repair shop on the company's list of qualified providers. In working with applied behavioral science consultancy Pragmatik, the company saw that only after addressing the emotional needs behind the decision to select a repair shop did the number of drivers who chose a provider from the list increase—by 30 percent (Radova, 2021).

The truth is, once you create an emotional connection with someone, you have that someone right where you want them from a marketing perspective, which is to say, in the perfect place to persuade them. If you can make your target audience feel something, you can connect with them. And once you connect with them, they are more open to responding to you.

Behavioral scientists refer to this as "emotional contagion." The term may not be all that attractive, but the end result can be. For example, if you can make someone feel excited about the prospect of using your product, or relieved at the idea of subscribing to your service, you've made emotional contagion work for you.

How can this be done? One way involves the language you use in the copy for your ads, emails, landing pages, letters, phone scripts, etc.—whether they are B2C or B2B. Paint a picture of what it's like to experience the product or service. Show the problem you're solving or the goal you're helping someone to achieve.

For example, you won't just install a burglar alarm, you'll help your customer feel confident their family is safe. You won't just provide public speaking instruction, you'll help someone crush their next presentation. Choose words that help people envision the outcome you offer. Set the scene, acknowledge your audience's fears, struggles, dreams or desires, and then bring your solution to life.

THE ROLE OF MIRROR NEURONS

In addition to choosing the right words (see Chapter 14 for more on this), another tactic you can use is Mirror Neurons. Mirror neurons were first discovered in Parma, Italy by neurophysiologist Giacomo Rizzolatti and his team of scientists. As the story goes, they were conducting experiments that involved having a monkey hooked up to electrodes to monitor its brain activity. During a break, one researcher went out to get an ice cream cone and returned to the lab eating it. When he was in the monkey's view, it became apparent that the neurons in the monkey's brain were firing as if the monkey itself were actually eating an ice cream cone.

Subsequent scientific research has shown that human brains behave the same way. When people see someone doing something, their brains respond as if they themselves were taking that action and experiencing that emotion. This is essentially why sports coaches will tell you to picture the perfect tennis serve or the ideal golf swing.

Obviously, this has huge implications for videos and tv commercials. But static pictures can also be used to trigger mirror neurons. Remember to include pictures of people happily using your product or service, whether it's in your email campaign, on your website or landing page, or in your social posts and ads.

How hot-state decision making may help you sell more

Do people ever know you're appealing to their emotions? As a good lawyer would answer, it depends. Often people won't, and as discussed earlier, will steadfastly cling to the idea that every decision they make is the result of careful consideration and forethought. Others may respond to your message, but not be completely aware of why.

Think of the times you've heard, or perhaps even said yourself, phrases such as "I just don't like it" or "I've got a gut feeling" or "I feel like this is the right choice." These are emotional responses to stimuli people may not be able to pinpoint. They are aware that something has prompted those feelings but won't necessarily realize they're responding to a specific part of your marketing message. If pressed for a reason why, they'll likely point to some rational benefit that is included in the message. Their brains will manufacture a rationale for their actions.

There are some instances, however, when people seem quite clear that a decision they're making is a more emotional one than a rational one. In fact, a good friend of mine once confessed that one summer she bought a white convertible because she thought it showed off her tan really well when she was driving it!

A behavioral scientist hearing that story might categorize the act as an example of "hot-state decision making." What scientists have found is that when people are in a "hot state", driven by some physical need like hunger or sexual desire or by a strong emotion such as anger or awe, they act in a way that addresses that immediate feeling and that feeling alone. They sometimes regret the actions they took once their cooler head returns. (Although not always. In my friend's case, she never expressed any buyer's remorse about that car.)

Hot-state decision making explains why people purchase more food if they go grocery shopping when they're hungry. Why a flash sale can prompt an impulse buy. And why donors can be moved to contribute to a charity after reading the evocative story of a particular victim (see Chapter 6).

Used properly, hot-state decision making can be another tactic a marketer can add to a campaign to increase the likelihood people will respond. The Snickers candy bar campaign that demonstrated "you're not yourself when you're hungry" is a good example of this. That messaging worked nicely combined with the ubiquitous placement of candy bars in supermarket check-out lines.

Fundraisers who mail their solicitations near Christmastime are also taking advantage of hot-state decision making. Christmas is traditionally considered a time of giving, and as a result, holiday emotions are heightened around that theme, so when better to ask for a donation?

HOW ONE COMPANY CREATED A HOT STATE FOR DECISION MAKING

One of the most interesting examples of hot-state decision making I've ever experienced occurred while I was working a summer job before heading off to Boston for college. The job involved selling coupon books over the phone. The coupon books were filled with discounts and offers for various local businesses, as a way to attract customers to patronize them.

As I explain this to you, you might conjure up visions of me calling area residents and explaining the many advantages of the coupon book. Perhaps you can almost hear me telling people how good they'd feel knowing they were paying less than the next customer for that haircut, or dinner out, or oil change. But that is not at all how we sold those books.

Each telemarketer was given a script to follow. When the person we called answered the phone, we were to begin with "Hello! Is this 555-0111?" in the most enthusiastic voice we could muster. Once the person who answered confirmed this was indeed their phone number, we quickly continued with "Great! This is Nancy from the WENM Strike It Rich Lucky Quiz Show." WENM was the radio station in town (although for the purposes of this story I've changed the real call letters).

I was then supposed to ask the "contestant" which of three available categories (sports, history, and politics) they would like their quiz question from. As soon as the person selected their category, I'd pose the question, which was incredibly, incredibly easy. In 2021, it would be tantamount to asking what reality television show host served as U.S. President? When the person correctly replied (as they invariably did), I was to excitedly congratulate them and tell them what they had won, which as you've no doubt guessed, was the aforementioned coupon book with all its local retailer discounts. But I didn't stop there. The script had us listing nearly every one of the discounts—a good couple of pages worth—building up the enormity of the prize as well as the person's tremendous good fortune.

At this point, the person on the other end of the phone may have thought they were on the air, and they knew they had just successfully answered their quiz question. Even better, they had won hundreds of dollars in savings.

They were decidedly in a hot state. Which is why, after listing off all the valuable discounts, we concluded with "all for just $9.99. Will you be home for the next half hour? We'll deliver your prize now!"

This last bit was especially important. Because a "now" delivery increased the chance of a sale. The longer it took before the delivery person could drive the coupon book to the house, the more likely the recipient would be to change their mind about accepting their prize, and decline to pay for it when it arrived. So, to incent the telemarketers to push for that immediate delivery, each time one of us got a "now" sale we were to rush to the front of the room, ring a small bell, and collect an extra 25 cents.

All those years ago, this was nothing more than a summer job for me. Of course, as I look back on it in 2021 through the lens of behavioral science, I see a lot more.

HERE ARE A FEW WAYS YOU CAN USE HOT-STATE DECISION MAKING TO SPUR SALES

- Send an email with a spin the wheel reward game offering the chance to win a deal on your product or service.
- Run a "scratch to reveal an instant discount" promotion, either in print or online.
- Issue an exclusive, time-limited code that customers must enter on your website to get a special gift or price.

The role of rational selling points in your marketing

Do people always respond emotionally and only consider the rational elements of a marketing message later, if they're looking to defend their decisions? No. There are certainly times when people put on their proverbial thinking caps and really sort through a decision. They may find themselves crunching numbers. Or they may set aside some time for deliberate pondering. This is most likely to happen when making a considered purchase, which, by definition, involves more rational thinking.

However, it's important for marketers to remember that people absorb both the emotional and rational reasons to buy as they consume your marketing communication. In many cases emotion drives the decision, but it is quickly bolstered by the rational reasons you present. And that is why you want to include both in your marketing.

Providing the reasons to buy is crucial if you hope to close the sale. For example, if you paint a picture of how wonderful owning your product will feel, but don't disclose the price, you can easily fail. Your prospective buyer may move on to a competitor whose product can also satisfy their emotional need, but who provides the necessary details to complete the purchase.

Similarly, your marketing copy can have someone swooning over the idea of owning your plush, luxurious new love seat, but if you do not provide its dimensions and the fact that it can fit in a studio apartment, you may lose the sale. If the information they want is not readily available, people may have no interest in trying to find it.

Keep in mind, also, that shoppers often compare their options. If you choose not to list a feature that your competitors do mention, that could be enough to cost you the sale, even if the feature didn't contribute to the emotional sell. And it's quite possible that a prospect may use the amount of copy you show as a proxy for the quality of the item. Even if all the copy is never read, its mere presence could be enough to suggest the product must be good.

TWO EXAMPLES OF BALANCING THE RATIONAL AND THE EMOTIONAL IN MARKETING

A B2C TV campaign

A marketing executive at a major property and casualty insurer was convinced that direct response television would sell auto insurance policies. However, prior to his arrival at that company, the DRTV approach had failed. After making his case, he finally got the okay to test the channel again, but knew that this time it must work. When he briefed us at the agency, he cautioned that the tv spot must do the heavy lifting of direct response to generate immediate calls, but that it could not hurt the company's brand metrics.

Our team created two commercials, both with benefit-driven art cards and a voiceover that covered all the main reasons to buy. Textbook DRTV. However, both also opened with identifiable fender bender scenarios designed to generate an empathetic response from viewers. Both also included some closeups of the drivers, showing the emotion on their faces.

After the campaign ran, the client was pleased to report that response was 126 percent over goal, and unaided brand awareness had increased 40 percent. The right combination of emotional and rational made this marketing message succeed.

A B2B print ad campaign

A major financial services firm needed to recruit more financial advisors to come work for them. They were already well-known in the industry as a successful company. And they offered a list of very smart, sensible reasons to join them, which included better income and better recurring revenue, as well as access to independent research and back-office support. Looking at things logically, why wouldn't a financial advisor want to sign on with them?

But as we know, people make decisions for emotional reasons. As a result, the visuals in the recruitment campaign were all about what these advisors looked like in their clients' eyes. An advisor would be shown in the ad with their clients. But also visible would be a reflection of that scene which appeared on the shiny conference room table or in the glass wall of the office. And in the reflection, the same clients would be interacting with the same financial advisor, but that financial advisor would now be attired as a boxing champion or a superhero.

This was meant to tap into an important finding about financial advisors, which was that they cared quite a lot about what their clients thought of them. The copy made all the rational points regarding why it made sense to join the firm. But the visuals and accompanying headlines carried the emotion. They weren't about the income potential or the practicalities of working at the firm. They were about how the advisors would be seen by their clients. And this added splash of emotion worked. The financial firm achieved an unprecedented 80 percent of their annual recruiting goal in the first four months that the campaign ran.

KEY TAKEAWAYS

1 Emotion drives action.

2 Include both emotional and rational reasons in your marketing messages. Your target needs both.

3 People will use the emotional reasons to decide and the rational ones to justify those decisions, to themselves and to others.

4 Your target's brain will process emotional messages faster. Those messages will also focus attention and aid memory.

5 Inject emotion into your marketing by using imagery, loss aversion, scarcity, reciprocity, social proof, and storytelling.

6 Emotion is needed even in B2B marketing, and even for highly educated audiences.

7 Forging an emotional connection, or triggering an emotional hot state, makes it easier for you to persuade people.

8 Don't just focus on the features and benefits of your product or service; help your target feel what it's like to experience them.

9 Show images of people enjoying or benefiting from what you sell to trigger mirror neurons.

10 Even considered purchases benefit from including emotional reasons to buy.

In conclusion

Include both rational and emotional elements in your marketing, whether your target audience is B2C or B2B. Omitting either can result in a lost sale. Provide the practical details that can cement the purchase, but lead with how people will feel when they experience your product.

And take note, as you'll see in the next chapter, that when injecting emotion into your marketing messages, not all of it needs to be positive.

References

Ariely, D (2008) *Predictably Irrational: The hidden forces that shape our decisions*, HarperCollins, New York

Diaz, A-C (2021) Shopify debuts songs honoring CMOs of CVS, Frito Lay and more, *AdAge.com*, 26 August, adage.com/article/marketing-news-strategy/spotify-makes-songs-cmos-cvs-frito-lay-indeed-intuit-kimberly-clark/2361101 (archived at https://perma.cc/5KLZ-SSWD)

Radova, K (2021) Case study: Insurance company used behavioral science to get 30% more customers to use certified repair shops, *insideBE.com*, https://insidebe.com/articles/behavioral-science-brought-more-customers/ (archived at https://perma.cc/G66Q-8M4P)

Roberts, K (2005) Love—The Highest Call—Style, 01 March, SaatchiKevin.com/interview/love-highest-call-style-pdf (archived at https://perma.cc/JS4R-MR6R)

02

Conveying customer benefits through loss aversion and the endowment effect

Even though marketers know that benefits sell, focusing exclusively on gains may not be the best move. Behavioral science makes the case for loss aversion, because the human drive to avoid the pain of loss is extremely motivating.

Benefits sell. As a marketer, you've likely had that idea drummed into your head since the beginning of your career. If you haven't heard those exact words, you've heard variations on the theme:

- You've been told to always remember "WIIFM"—the acronym for "what's in it for me?"—because that is what your customers and prospects will be thinking when they encounter your marketing message.

- You've been admonished to never just list features, but to always explain why that feature is something your target should care about. It's not enough to say the shirt is made from breathable cotton. You must immediately follow those words with a phrase such as "so you can feel cool during the humid days of summer."

- Perhaps you've even had the words of Mad Men-era advertising legend Howard Gossage quoted to you: "Nobody reads advertising. People read what interests them, and sometimes it's an ad" (Pulse Magazine, 2021). If you want your marketing message to appeal to your prospects, you have to interest them in it. You do that by pointing out why what you're selling would be good for them to buy.

Whichever way it was explained to you, you got the message. In your marketing communications, you should always emphasize the benefits.

You should always make sure you focus on what your customers and prospects want to hear.

As an aside, that last sentence, while simple, is also quite important. Because sometimes as marketers, we focus too much on what *we* want to say. It's an understandable misstep. We honestly believe in what we're promoting—be it a product, service, charity, membership, subscription, etc. As a result, we rush to tell people all the things we think are wonderful. We want them to have all the details—all the information that is important to us.

However, sometimes what our target market is looking for is not always what we insist on telling them. We need to focus on what they want to hear, not necessarily on all we want to say. For example, they may not be interested in how the company was founded. Or its history. Or that there are many other divisions with many other products. Or even that the company strives hard to try to keep customers happy. Even if these things seem important to the marketer or to the marketer's internal constituents, they may not be what's motivating to your prospects.

So, if the rule of thumb is to focus on benefits, the caution is to make sure those benefits are genuine customer benefits.

> Do not discount benefits. But remember to inject a little negativity into your marketing messages. Tell people what they're missing out on, or what they stand to lose if they don't do what you ask them to.

Is there anything better than benefits? Consider loss aversion

As a marketer, you likely bend over backwards to emphasize the benefits, the gains, the advantages, all the wonderful things that will happen if your prospects just say "yes" to you. If they just open your email, download your white paper, watch your video, try your product, subscribe to your service, recommend a friend... the list goes on.

And as we've discussed, there is nothing wrong with that. You know that benefits sell. You know that without them, your marketing messages are far less effective. But here's something you may not know. Behavioral scientists have found that people are approximately twice as motivated to avoid the pain of loss as they are to achieve the pleasure of gain (Kahneman, 2011). Yes, you read that correctly. Twice. They are roughly twice as motivated to avoid pain as they are to achieve gain.

So as a marketer, you have been doubling down on benefits. But now that may not sound like the best strategy. Since people are more motivated to avoid losses than to realize gains, you may wonder if your marketing messages should continue to be exclusively positive.

The answer I would offer is no—not every message, not every time. They shouldn't always be all about the benefits and all about the gains. In fact, it can actually benefit you to make your messaging a little "negative." You don't want to completely walk away from the benefits, of course. But you do want to get a little loss aversion working for you.

Nobel Memorial Prize Daniel Kahneman wrote the best-selling book *Thinking, Fast and Slow*, in which he discusses the idea of loss aversion. He explains, "When directly compared or weighted against each other, losses loom larger than gains." Kahneman also goes on to give a simple example. In a coin toss, you would win $150 dollars if the coin comes up heads. Nice, right? But if it comes up tails, you would lose $100. Suddenly not so nice. As Kahneman observes, "For most people, the fear of losing $100 is more intense than the hope of gaining $150."

As a marketer, you can use loss aversion to your advantage. It's not just about the wonderful things that will happen if someone becomes a customer. It's also about the terrible things that may happen to them if they fail to do so. Or, put differently, it's about the painful situations they can successfully avoid if they do become your customer.

You want to balance the benefits that you are offering with the losses that can be avoided. Inject a bit of loss aversion to your marketing communications to make them more effective, and more likely to prompt the response you are after. Remember that from the vantage point of your customer or prospect, providing them the ability to avoid a loss or to dodge a painful outcome is actually a benefit in and of itself. And from a behavioral science perspective, that particular benefit is even more compelling than a traditional, positive one.

Your temptation as a marketer might be to express everything in positive terms—to reframe anything that could be perceived as negative—but that inclination can cost you sales. A number of clients I've had the pleasure to work with have upon occasion asked me to rewrite something so it sounds more positive. For example, instead of saying "never," say "always." Or instead of saying "lose," say "gain." However, after they discovered the behavioral science behind loss aversion, they usually changed their minds.

Fear can be a powerful motivator

Make no mistake about it, fear sells. People do not want to lose out. Sales can go up when people fear they will miss a good deal, or when they fear a product may run out, or if they fear they will be less popular, pretty, sexy, or socially accepted if they don't own the trendy new item. And these are just a few of the ways fear has been used to fuel marketing.

People buy travel insurance because they are afraid they'll lose all their money if their trip gets derailed. They buy a backup pair of their favorite jeans because they are afraid they won't be able to replace them later if something should happen to them. They buy a spare key and hide it because they are afraid they'll lock themselves out.

And it doesn't stop there. Have you ever chosen a more expensive item instead of its entry-level alternative because you were afraid the less expensive one wouldn't be as good? Have you ever gone with the more costly brand name product because you were afraid the generic one would fail to perform? Fear doesn't just drive sales. It can drive more expensive sales (Zaltman, 2003).

The concept of fear, and of being averse to loss, is hardwired into humans. In Chapter 1 we talked about our long-ago ancestors responding to an approaching animal with sharp teeth, claws or tusks by fleeing. Behavioral scientists refer to this as the fight or flight response. Leidy Klotz, cofounder of the Convergent Behavioral Science Initiative at the University of Virginia and author of *Subtract: The untapped science of less*, also notes that people are biologically programmed to accumulate or add to what they have, not subtract from it. Humans do not like loss.

Even people who are aware of the concept of loss aversion can still be influenced by it, as the following story shows.

HOW FEAR OF MISSING OUT TRANSFORMED A CUSTOMER'S RESPONSE

I own a timeshare in Mexico. For a number of years, it worked out just fine. I wanted to escape Boston winters during school vacation week (my spouse is an educator, so that is when we can travel), and the timeshare allowed us to do just that. It is right on the beach. The weather is reliably sunny and warm. And the resort is quite beautiful. In fact, on a number of occasions we've remarked to each other that it is really more luxurious than we need.

With this particular timeshare, we had a window of time during which to book our vacation. We learned through experience that calling on the first day of that window was the smart thing to do, because it became apparent that we were not the only people looking to flee the winter weather when schools went on break.

As the years went by, we began to have a harder and harder time booking. While an arrival on Saturday with a departure the following Saturday was our preference, sometimes only a Friday arrival with a Friday departure would be available. And while we owned a two-bedroom unit, there were times we'd be told that a one-bedroom or a studio unit was our only option during that specific week.

After one particularly frustrating reservation experience, we decided to complain at the member services presentation when we got to the resort. Our representative acknowledged how we felt, and explained that because the resort was getting increasingly popular, our booking challenges were likely to continue. She suggested we upgrade to the next tier of accommodations, because with those we should have no difficulty securing our desired week given the more powerful booking value of this upgraded tier.

While we were more than happy with the level of amenities we currently had, we decided to spend the money to upgrade, thinking it would be worth it to be able to get the week and unit size we wanted going forward.

However, the next time we called to make reservations, we could not get into the upgraded tier building. Instead, we were offered accommodations in our former tier.

Now I was livid. We'd just spent a not insignificant sum to upgrade, only to find ourselves booked into a building we'd recently paid to upgrade out of. When we arrived and the member services group invited us to a presentation, we readily agreed, intending to give them a piece of our minds: we were not in the new building we'd just bought into. That new building was supposed to be the solution to our booking challenges. We felt taken advantage of, lied to. I imagine you can hear me ranting as you read this.

Our representative then explained that the timeshare company had decided not to add many buildings to the tier we'd purchased, and instead was concentrating on the tier above that. Buying into that new tier, she explained, would solve our problem. That made me even more livid.

I pointed out that this was the same "solution" I'd been sold last time. That it seemed this was all about squeezing more money out of the resort members. That every year the resort touted some new reason to move up a building tier. And finally, that I absolutely was not going to upgrade then, given we'd yet to even set foot into the previous accommodations we'd upgraded to.

Here is where things took a very different turn. The representative explained that there was only so much land on which the resort could expand. That this new upgrade could very well be the last. And that if we didn't take advantage of it now, we would not be asked to the following year.

Wait, I said. Every year you ask us to upgrade. Not only that, you're very persistent, and usually don't stop at the first or even the fifth "no." You're telling me this is our one chance to get into this new tier? Yes, she told us. This will give you the trading power to get your two-bedroom unit on that February week you want. But if you wait, thinking you'll do this sometime in the next few years, the opportunity will be gone. She explained the new tier buildings would sell out. And we'd be left with our current booking challenges, which would likely only get worse.

Loss aversion can trigger a very powerful decision-making shortcut. Despite all we'd experienced, despite how angry we were, despite our suspicion that this successful resort would always have something new to sell, we just didn't want to risk it. We upgraded again. The fear of losing out, and all the emotion that swirls around it, overtook our rational brains. Did I know loss aversion was at play during the conversation? Yes, I did recognize it. But that did not stop me from being influenced by it.

In truth, the new building has actually worked out quite well. And we have not experienced any of the previous booking challenges. But on our last vacation we did look with confirmed suspicion as the resort began to tear down some older buildings on the property in order to make way for their next, upgraded offering.

CASE STUDY
Using loss aversion to increase email open rates

How do you convince people to do something else with their money? That was the challenge that a major financial services company gave to the marketing agency where I was working. They asked us to create an email campaign that would motivate the employees of their customers to save more for retirement.

They believed that the bulk of the employees we'd be targeting for the campaign were either juggling several financial commitments, operating on tight budgets, or perhaps already feeling pretty good and self-sufficient about their money matters.

Each group presented its own challenges. While it's typically not easy to convince employees to contribute to work retirement plans, it can be even more difficult if the employee is pulled in several directions financially, or feels they have no money to spare, or believes they are currently on top of their financial situation.

The creative team decided to pursue a few different directions for the client to test. Knowing that people often didn't know how much they should be saving, one direction revolved around what other employees had done, so the recipient could follow suit (read more about social proof in Chapter 5). Another direction acknowledged the lack of information the targets felt by highlighting money-saving secrets (read more about scarcity in Chapter 3). And the final direction played off of loss aversion, by cautioning people not to make mistakes with this important decision.

Once the test results were in, both the client and the agency were pleased to find that all three of the concepts performed well. But the subject lines that consistently got employees of all three groups to open the emails were the ones informed by loss aversion—lines such as "Do you make this money mistake?" This held true when the client looked at the segments for both the under 50s and the over 50s.

Apparently, whether you were experiencing some financial concerns, or you were feeling you had a good handle on your money, the fear of making a misstep was a powerful motivator for prospects of all ages to engage with the marketing message.

Easy ways to use loss aversion in your marketing

- Indicate how many of an item are left in stock. You've probably seen hotels and airlines flag that there are only a few rooms or seats still available at the quoted price. Other online retailers will warn prospective customers when the quantity of a certain product is running low or let them know that it previously sold out.

- Tell people that an event may not be repeated, or that it won't be in the target's area again until the following year. Similarly, let people know that the event won't be recorded, so there is no other way to catch it.

- Or try the reverse. Encourage prospects to register for a webinar by telling them to sign up even if they are not sure they can attend, because you will send a link to the recording after the fact, so they won't miss out.

- Inform your customer or prospect that the offer you sent may not be sent to them again.

- Allow people to preserve their options by telling them they can decide now and cancel later. Rather than having to make a yes or no decision that is final, they can postpone that decision which means that, at least for the moment, they haven't lost anything. Often when people commit, they do not then go back and change their minds (see Chapter 8 on commitment and consistency).

- Replace language such as "Take advantage of" or "Get in on" with "Don't miss." Those two little words can be just enough to trigger loss aversion.

- Highlight deadlines and expiration dates. You can expect to see an increase in response close to them, as people rush to make sure they don't miss out.

- Offer a free trial. When something is free, it removes the fear of loss. As world-renowned behavioral economist Dan Ariely explains in his book *Predictably Irrational*, "there's no visible possibility of loss when we choose a FREE! item."

- Frame your message in terms of loss instead of gain (see more in Chapter 12). For example, your ad headline, email subject line, or direct mail teaser copy could pose questions such as: How many dieting mistakes do you make? Will your car fail its annual inspection? What did you forget to pack?

- Or you could use a declarative sentence that also leans toward loss. For example, your copy could state: Foods you should never eat before bedtime, this common error can cost you plenty, or you're about to lose your chance.

The important thing to remember is to follow through on the thought. Pay off the idea in the rest of your marketing message. Leading with loss aversion can be attention-getting and motivating, as long as you don't misuse the technique or resort to clickbait. If you say a deadline is approaching, make sure you reveal an upcoming deadline and hold to it. If you say an event won't be repeated this year, don't advertise it again a few months later. If you claim product inventory is running low, make sure you don't have an entire stockroom of it. And if you offer to point out common mistakes, be sure you show them. Always employ loss aversion ethically and responsibly, so that you give your customers and prospects the respect they deserve.

MISTAKE

Turning every negative message into a positive one. Instead, mention the negative situation your product or service can help people avoid.

Combine the endowment effect with loss aversion to trigger behavior

Imagine you are about to put the home you and your family have lived in for the last nine years on the market. You seek out a real estate professional with a good track record in your town. You give them a tour of your home, pointing out all the little things that make it so special, like the backyard where you've enjoyed countless family barbeques, and the fireplace in the living room, where you and your spouse often relaxed with a glass of celebratory wine after getting the little ones off to bed. Then you wait for your agent to return with the listing price.

The real estate professional does some research, looks at recent sales of comparable properties in your area—carefully noting the same lot size and amenities—and returns with a number. But you're disappointed. You feel that number should be higher. Why? Because of the endowment effect.

Coined by Richard Thaler, professor of behavioral science and economics at the University of Chicago and winner of the Nobel Memorial Prize in Economic Sciences, the endowment effect means people place more value on what they already own. Essentially "that people often demand much more to give up an object than they would be willing to pay to acquire it" (Kahneman et al, 1991).

As you can see, the endowment effect is closely related to loss aversion, in that the pain of giving up something we own drives up that price as compared to the price of acquiring it. Researchers have run numerous experiments that bear this out. One such experiment is recounted by Dan Ariely in his book *Predictably Irrational*. He describes a lottery situation in which some students obtained highly coveted tickets to a college basketball game. And of course, because it was a lottery, some did not. Ariely then interviewed students who'd won the tickets, asking how much they'd be willing to sell them for. And he interviewed other students who had not gotten tickets, asking how much they'd be willing to pay for one if it were to become available. The price difference was quite large.

Ariely found "the average selling price (about $2,400) was separated by a factor of about 14 from the average buyer's offer (about $175)." He explained it this way: "we fall in love with what we already have," "we focus more on what we may lose, rather than what we may gain," and "we assume other people will see the transaction from the same perspective we do."

FIGURE 2.1 Ownership leads to overvaluing

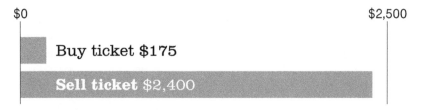

Students who won basketball tickets in a lottery overvalued them. On average, they required $2,400 to sell them. Buyers, on the other hand, were willing to pay an average of only $175 to acquire the tickets.

The endowment effect in action

Two of my favorite examples of the endowment effect come from experiences I've had. In both cases, I reacted first as a consumer, and only later as a behavioral science marketer.

AN ONLINE SERVICE

In the first case, I had subscribed to a service that, among other things, offered prompt shipping on items purchased through them online. This was largely motivated by me being behind on my holiday shopping and fearing I'd arrive at my parents' home for Christmas with no gifts in tow. Fortunately, the service delivered as promised. Things worked out well, everyone got their presents, and I felt good about my subscription.

However, as I got deeper into the new year, I realized I simply was not using the service at all. It had served its purpose. But it was no longer helpful to me. I decided to unsubscribe and get a refund for the remaining months of my term.

I went online, found the proper page, and indicated I wanted to cancel. Then two very interesting things happened from a behavioral science perspective. I was taken to a page that asked if I was certain I wanted to end "my membership." Notice the wording. They didn't ask if I wanted to cancel. They asked if I wanted to "end my membership," which underscored ownership and triggered the endowment effect.

Once they'd accomplished that, they offered me two options: I could "end now," immediately lose all my benefits, and get the appropriate refund. Or I could continue my benefits and choose to end on a specified date, which happened to be when the original term was up.

In both instances, I could do what I'd gone to the site to do, which was cancel. But one option kept me around longer, which kept more money in the company's accounts. Spurred on by the endowment effect, I reconsidered and didn't cancel at all.

A WINE MERCHANT

My second favorite example involves wine. I received an email from an online wine retailer telling me I had a credit for a certain amount of money in my account, and that the credit would expire the next day. Even though I'd never bought from them before, as a consumer my first thought was "I don't want to lose my money. I'd better hurry up and pick out a bottle of wine."

As a behavioral science marketer, however, my reaction was different. This was clearly an acquisition effort. And as such, the retailer could have said they were having a sale, and they were discounting all their wines by that specified amount of money until the next day. Or they could have invited me to try their service before the next day, and said they'd give me that specific amount of money off the bottle I purchased.

The difference was in the possession. The credit was in my account. They weren't giving me money off. They weren't taking money off. The money was positioned as already mine, not theirs. And that use of the endowment effect is what made the email so powerful.

Seven ways to inject the endowment effect into your marketing messages

- Tap into the IKEA Effect, a term Dan Ariely and Mike Norton use to describe the idea that "the more work you put into something, the more ownership you begin to feel for it," such as assembling furniture from the Swedish retailer (Ariely, 2008).

- Invite customers to become cocreators, offering them some ability to influence the end product they purchase, for example, by customizing the design or configuring the components from an available list. The more input they have, the more ownership they'll feel.

- Offer a free or discounted trial of your product or service. Once people begin to use it, they will start to think of it as theirs. This is even more true if in using it, they add data to it, such as playlists of music or contact details of friends.

- Inform people who've subscribed to your e-newsletter but have stopped opening it that you'll be removing them from your email list unless they begin to reengage. For some, perhaps those whose interests or responsibilities have changed, that may be fine. But others will react to keep what they think of as theirs.

- Notify customers who have earned membership in a specific recognition tier that if their level of business declines, they will drop down to a lower tier and lose the benefits they currently enjoy.

- When presenting options, lead with your most robust one. Once prospective customers read about everything included in it, they establish mental ownership. When they read about the next, less robust option, they will feel like they are losing benefits.

- In Chapter 1, we discussed getting people to imagine owning your product or service because that could help them feel positively toward it. It can also trigger the endowment effect, whereby simply imagining ownership begins to feel to people like they do in fact own the item. As a result, they are reluctant to give it up. Similarly, offering a return policy or guarantee can prompt people to give a product a try, intending to return it if it doesn't work out, but once they take possession, the endowment effect can kick in.

KEY TAKEAWAYS

1 Benefits sell. But relying on them exclusively can cost a marketer response.

2 Injecting some loss aversion into your messaging can be a powerful motivator.

3 People are approximately twice as motivated to avoid the pain of loss as they are to achieve the pleasure of gain.

4 Show people the pain your product or service can help people avoid, or the pain they may find themselves in if they do not purchase it.

5 Fear is a hardwired emotion. Even people who are familiar with loss aversion can still feel afraid to lose out and therefore respond to it.

6 Limited quantities and opportunities, deadlines and expiration dates, the ability to preserve options, and phrases such as "don't miss" and "free" are effective ways to use loss aversion.

7 Expressing things in the "negative," or using a loss frame, can be more impactful than positive framing.

8 When using loss aversion, be truthful and respect your audience. Pay off the concept in your messaging. And do not resort to clickbait.

9 People value something that they own more than something they've yet to possess, a concept known as the endowment effect.

10 The endowment effect is related to loss aversion because people want more money to give up or lose what they already have than they would be willing to pay to acquire that same thing.

> **11** Making people feel ownership by getting them to imagine possessing
> your product or service, inviting them to cocreate, offering trials or
> guarantees, and notifying them that they stand to lose something they
> currently have are all ways to use the endowment effect in your marketing.

In conclusion

People are about twice as motivated to avoid loss as to achieve gain. Marketers can use this human tendency by emphasizing the pain your product or service can help someone avoid, or by highlighting the pain people may find themselves in without it. Loss aversion works well coupled with the endowment effect, because people will react strongly to the threatened loss of something they already own.

Similarly, as the next chapter shows, people will respond more readily when items or opportunities are scarce.

References

Ariely, D (2008) *Predictably Irrational: The hidden forces that shape our decisions,* HarperCollins, New York

Kahneman, D (2011) *Thinking, Fast and Slow*, Farrar, Straus and Giroux, New York

Kahneman, D, Knetsch, J and Thaler, R (1991) Anomalies: The endowment effect, loss aversion, and status quo bias, *Journal of Economic Perspectives*, https://www.aeaweb.org/articles?id=10.1257/jep.5.1.193 (archived at https://perma.cc/244P-NVAA)

Klotz, L (2021) *Subtract: The untapped science of less,* Flatiron Books

Pulse Magazine (2021) Nobody Reads Advertising [Blog] 11 October, https://www.pulsemagazine.co.uk/blogs-articles/nobody-reads-advertising%E2%80%A6/ (archived at https://perma.cc/9X3U-H4FR)

Zaltman, G (2003) *How Customers Think: Essential insights into the mind of the market*, Harvard Business School Press, Boston

03

Creating urgency and exclusivity through the scarcity principle

Behavioral scientists have found that scarcity increases desirability. As a result, limited times, quantities, opportunities—and limited access to information—can all motivate your customers and prospects. So, too, can the feeling that they can obtain something that not everyone else can, simply because of who they are or the group they belong to.

You want what you can't have. I do, too. So do most people. You can find examples all around us. If you are religious, you might think of the biblical story of Eve and the apple. She could have anything she wanted in the garden of Eden, except an apple. So, what did she want? Or think of Mark Twain's tale of Tom Sawyer, getting his friends to do the fence painting because it wasn't something just anyone could do.

Or perhaps you had a friend in high school who managed to snag their dream date by first playing hard to get. Or maybe you have a friend like my friend Michael, who proudly points to his Playbill from the musical *Carrie*, proof that he saw the show whose Broadway run was over in an infamous five performances.

But when it comes to marketing, we sometimes think there are only two reasons people buy: they either have a practical need for the product or service, or they have a strong desire for the product or service. If it's something they need, people may decide they cannot make the item themselves, or that it's more convenient, faster, or cheaper to acquire one manufactured by someone else.

And if it's something they do not need? They can be driven by simply wanting to possess the item, regardless of a legitimate need. They may want it because of the way owning it makes them feel, or because it makes their lives easier, or more enjoyable.

As a result, marketers invest a good deal of time and effort pointing out the needs their products fill, or trying to create desire for them. Our marketing messages tout that what we're selling will solve the problems our prospects experience, or that our offerings are the ideal answer to the search they've undertaken. Alternatively, we focus on the emotional angle. We show people how wonderful they'll feel when they own our product or experience our service. Or—by injecting a bit of loss aversion (see Chapter 2)—how bad they may feel if they do not.

However, as a marketer, you have another option to make your products and services appeal to your target. It involves recognizing that often people want things that aren't easy to get.

Imagine this scenario. You sell a particular item that is readily available. People who want it, purchase it, as makes sense. People who do not want it, do not purchase it, again, as makes sense. But then some new information is introduced into the situation. Those people who were previously not interested are told that the item will only be around for a certain amount of time. Or that it will only be available to certain people, but not to everyone. Suddenly, that can change everything. It's like a switch flips in people, and they don't just want the item, they really, really want it.

You can think of this as the two halves of the scarcity principle. On one side you have urgency, the idea that the item in question is in limited supply, or will be available only for a limited time. On the other side you have exclusivity, the idea that the item can be obtained only by some people, but not by just anyone.

> People place more value on things that are harder to get, and on things that don't appear to be widely available.

Scarcity is a powerful driver of behavior

Robert Cialdini, author of *Influence: The psychology of persuasion*, lists scarcity as one of his six principles of influence. He explains that "opportunities seem more valuable to us when their availability is limited." He draws a reference to loss aversion by adding, "As opportunities become less available, we lose freedoms and we *hate* to lose the freedoms we already have." Finally, he states that "Not only do we want the same item more when it becomes scarce, we want it most when we are in competition for it." Urgency and exclusivity.

In the opening to his chapter on scarcity, Cialdini relates a personal story about deciding to tour a Mormon temple in his town. What prompted him to suddenly want to take the tour was that it would include access to a section that normally was off-limits to most people. And that this particular tour would only be offered for a few days.

After re-reading his account, I realized that something very similar had happened to me. In the middle of the seaside town where I spend a lot of my summer, there is a Masonic Lodge. I walk by it all the time. Never once had I tried to enter it, or even wondered if I could. But one day when passing by, I saw a sandwich board out front. The sign announced that due to a very special anniversary, the lodge, which normally restricted access to members only, was open to the public on that particular day. Immediately, I had to go inside. Why? Because I realized this was my only chance to see something that I otherwise would be forbidden to see. Adding fuel to that desire was the notion that the Masons have been described as a secret society.

People want items and experiences that are limited, and often enjoy them more. Researchers from the University of Virginia and the University of North Carolina conducted a classic experiment using chocolate chip cookies that showed just that (Worchel et al, 1975). The experiment used two glass jars. In one glass jar there were two chocolate chip cookies. And in the other glass jar there were 10 chocolate chip cookies.

During the experiment, the subjects evaluated cookies from one jar or the other. Researchers asked them to rate the cookies in terms of whether they wanted to eat more of them, how attractive a consumer item they thought they would be, and how expensive they imagined they were.

The researchers found that the cookies that appeared to be in scarce supply, the ones from the jar with only two, were consistently rated higher—even though it was the exact same kind of cookie in both jars! The researchers also found that when the cookies were made to previously appear abundant and then newly scarce, the subjects found them to be even more valuable.

Urgency prompts people to take quick action

As we've seen, when people think that quantities are limited, or that the time during which they can gain access to an item is restricted, they place more value on that item. As a result, they will be more likely to take action to acquire it. In the case of the chocolate chip cookie experiment, people were more apt to want additional cookies when they believed the supply to be scarce. For both Robert Cialdini and myself, we were each moved to take a tour of a place we'd not previously considered visiting, simply because we learned we had a limited window in which to do so, after which we could no longer just stroll in.

CASE STUDY
Compelling people to buy computer equipment

As a marketer, and as a consumer, I've seen how motivating the idea of urgency can be. When my creative team at a large US marketing agency was working on the account of a big high-technology client, we tested our way into what would become an unbeatable concept.

We were tasked with increasing hardware and equipment sales every month. And we were asked to find a less expensive way to do so than mailing more catalogs, which was the channel the client had been depending on. After trying a number of different concepts, some of which took a problem–solution approach, others of which focused on the many benefits of buying a specific desktop computer, color printer, etc., we landed on a winner.

We created a concept that was all about urgency. It mailed in a light-blue business-sized envelope with a yellow note stuck to the exterior. On that note were three product names, along with their original and new sale prices, and the limited time period those sale prices were in effect. Inside was a sheet of paper that functioned like a spec sheet.

Unlike the previous mailings we'd tested, these were not designed to look attractive or to romance the products. Rather, they appeared to be quickly printed and rushed into the mail—the sole purpose being to alert customers about the time-sensitive deals. And the concept worked. Sales took off, ROI shot up, and the campaign became virtually unbeatable.

Why? The copy and the design conveyed urgency. And the target market responded, not wanting to miss a great, last-minute deal. In fact, I'm willing to bet that, had the client decided to transfer the concept to email, it would have performed similarly well.

MISTAKE

Repeatedly advertising limited quantities when supply is plentiful. Misrepresentations like this can backfire on a marketer, eroding customer trust. However, genuinely informing prospects that their buying opportunity may disappear is helpful and can actually enhance your relationship.

Having just missed a deal may make prospects want it even more

Not wanting to miss a great deal is a big motivator. Discovering you may have already missed one can also be used to prompt behavior. I belong to a private online shopping club. This particular club takes brand name merchandise and offers it at a discount for a finite period. One day I got an email notifying me of a sale they were having on designer handbags. When I got to the site, there were several bags featured. But one of them had a notice indicating it was no longer available.

Of course, all of the bags were lovely. But not surprisingly, I found myself drawn to the one I couldn't have, the one that was no longer available to me. As I stared longingly at it, I saw the notice did suggest I check back in 12 minutes. Immediately, I began to hope. Perhaps one would become available after all. Maybe the site knew a certain number of the bags would be returned, or that some buyers would change their pending selections.

All of the handbags were on sale for only a limited time. That alone created urgency that was motivating. But the idea of possibly getting the deal I'd nearly missed proved even more so.

Easy ways to add urgency to your marketing messages

- Pop deadlines and expiration dates when you have them. Response will increase as the deadline nears.

- If you don't have a hard and fast deadline, imply one. For example, use phrases such as: Please respond this week, reply requested in five days, or for a limited time only.

- Show countdown clocks in your email, or on your landing pages and websites. Research from Worldata (2021) indicates a countdown clock in an email can increase your conversion rate by 22 percent.

- Use words that reference time, such as now, today, tonight, tomorrow, minutes, hours, this week only, soon, dated contents enclosed, time's running out, and right now. In fact, Worldata research (2020) shows that the words today, tomorrow, and days left used in an email subject line can lift opening rates by double-digit percentages.

- Choose words that suggest speed, such as hurry, rush, immediate, instantly, don't delay, don't be disappointed, flash sale, and open at once.

FIGURE 3.1 The scarcity principle in action

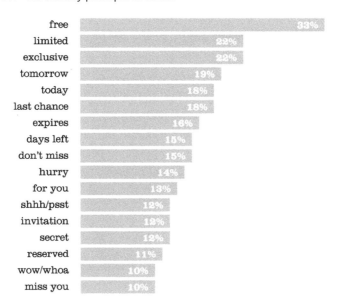

free	33%
limited	22%
exclusive	22%
tomorrow	19%
today	18%
last chance	18%
expires	16%
days left	15%
don't miss	15%
hurry	14%
for you	13%
shhh/psst	12%
invitation	12%
secret	12%
reserved	11%
wow/whoa	10%
miss you	10%

Urgency is a significant driver of subject line opens.
SOURCE Reproduced with kind permission of Worldata, 2021

- Write headlines, direct mail teaser copy, and subject lines with words that focus your reader, such as alert, attention, caution, and notice.

- Combine urgency with loss aversion (see Chapter 2), and include language in your messaging that warns the offer may not be repeated, or that this is the only chance to take advantage of it, or that the offer may be withdrawn at any time.

- Pop phrases such as last chance, final notice, reminder, and second attempt in key pieces of marcom real estate, such as email subject lines and direct mail Johnson boxes.

- Flag items that are newly back in stock or expected to sell out, and events that are filling up fast or have only a few seats left. Also highlight items that are only available seasonally. For example, NPD Group reports restaurants find that "Seasonal LTO (limited time offer) buyers typically visit more and are more valuable customers to the chain overall."

- Add a clock or hourglass emoji to your subject line. Worldata (2021) has reported lifts in opening rates of 24 and 22 percent respectively when these appear in subject lines.

- Use language that references availability, such as limited quantities and while supplies last.

- Indicate when other people are looking at the same item that has a finite quantity.

- Restrict the number of items any one person can purchase. For example, state there is a one per person limit, a purchase limit of X, or a limit of one visit per week. In fact, researchers ran an experiment using a soup sale at a grocery store. When there was no limit to the number of cans of soup people could purchase at the discounted price, the average number bought was 3.3. However, when a limit of 12 was posted, the average sale increased to 7 cans (Wansink et al, 1998).

Never underestimate the psychological appeal of exclusivity

Scarce quantities and limited timing can prompt people to respond to your marketing messages. So, too, can the news that your product or service is not widely available. People enjoy having access to information, perks, privileges, savings, experiences, and opportunities that other people do not. When I toured the Masonic Temple that day, it was both because I would probably never have the chance to do so again, and because I would gain access to sights and knowledge others wouldn't have.

People like to feel special. They like to feel singled out. They like to feel exclusive. When you make people feel that they are part of a select group, you are more likely to get them to take the action you want them to.

Three different ways marketers have used exclusivity to motivate consumer behavior

A *tax preparation firm* One of my clients is a tax preparation firm. They wanted to reach out to former customers with an attractive offer designed to get those customers to engage with the company again. The messaging opened by congratulating those clients because they were on the list of returning customers who were receiving an exclusive offer.

The offer actually was a very special one that included a free service. Additionally, the copy made the customer feel as if they were part of a select group. As a result, this campaign was one of the most successful this client could ever recall running.

The ability to make your target feel like they are members of an exclusive group is one way to leverage the exclusivity side of the scarcity principle. Another effective way is to position the opportunity you are offering them as one that is not widely available.

An automotive manufacturer   A car company I once worked with wanted to offer a $1,000 incentive to owners of mid-level vehicles to encourage them to upgrade to more expensive luxury models. They sent gorgeous pictures of the luxury vehicles, so the target could imagine themselves driving the car or envision it parked in front of their homes. But that was only part of the strategy. They presented the opportunity to acquire the new car as an exclusive one.

For example, in one part of the campaign, they suggested to the target that the only thing better than watching the wistful looks of their neighbors when they drove by in their new model would be the secret knowledge that they had paid less for that model than those neighbors would pay. The campaign oozed exclusivity. And it beat the control by 82 percent.

A marketer of long-term care insurance   Finally, marketers should be aware of the fact that when information is believed to be scarce, people will find it more persuasive (Cialdini, 1984). My creative team tapped into that finding when developing some messaging for a client that was selling long-term care insurance. One of the challenges with selling this type of insurance is that people have preconceived notions of it. And as you're probably aware, when your target thinks they already know what you're going to tell them, they usually don't bother to engage with your message.

To combat this assumption on the target's part, our headline took advantage of the scarcity principle. It said that the marketing materials contained three options that people would never expect to find when it came to long-term care insurance. We positioned the information as not widely available—as something they hadn't already heard from other sources. Of course, we delivered on the promise by addressing the misperceptions that people commonly held about this type of insurance, and showing it was more flexible than many imagined. The approach worked, approximately doubling the number of policies sold as compared to the control group.

> **EXCLUSIVITY CAN BE USED TO ENCOURAGE PEOPLE TO GET VACCINATED**
>
> In a June 4, 2021 *Washington Post* article, behavioral scientists Katy Milkman, Angela Duckworth and Mitesh Patel wrote about an experiment they conducted before the coronavirus pandemic hit. In it, they tested 19 different text messages designed to get people to accept a flu vaccine when they went to their upcoming doctor's appointment.
>
> They found that language stating a vaccine was "available for you" and that the vaccine had been "reserved for your appointment" increased the uptake in shots over the control group by 4.6 percentage points. The behavioral scientists speculated that the reason the copy was successful was that it "makes patients feel as if the vaccine belongs to them, and they may not want to miss out on 'their' dose" (Milkman et al, 2021).

Proven ways to add exclusivity to your marketing messages

- Provide prospects with a VIP code or a personalized identification number that is associated with their special offer, and tell them not to share it with anyone else.

- Offer them access to a phone number, landing page, or specific webpages that are reserved for certain members only.

- Give them special discounts, upgrades, complimentary services, or free gifts.

- Grant them early access, inside details, or a special preview for something that they care about or something you're about to launch. Similarly, let them know they are entitled to express processing, complimentary shipping, faster response, or a similar service because of who they are.

- Pepper your copy with words and phrases such as secret, a sneak peek, a behind the scenes look, the truth behind, the untold story, the real story, confessions of, what they don't want you to know, what they won't tell you, never before shared, not previously revealed, what very few people know, an insider account, and similar terms that suggest you have information they won't find in other places.

- Make your channel exclusive. In a webinar, Worldata (Worldata, 2020) reported that offers that are flagged as available only through email generate a 14 percent lift in open rates.

- Use language that makes people feel special, such as reserved for, only for, just for, especially for, private, select, not available to the general public, and not everyone, to underscore exclusivity. In fact, the subject line construction "Just for (fill in the blank)" drives a 17 percent increase in email open rates according to Worldata research.

- Similarly, when describing products, use phrases that highlight scarcity, such as sourced from the top 1 percent, found only in one part of the world, and made from the highest quality, to set your offerings apart. When describing services, use phrases such as white-glove, concierge, customized, and best in class.

- Additionally, inject exclusivity into your product or service descriptions by using language such as handcrafted, artisanal, craft, one-of-a-kind, collector's item, special edition, limited edition, rare, not often seen, small batch, one of the few, award-winning, unique, and singular.

- To emphasize that what you sell is better than the competition, choose phrases such as unlike other companies, uncommon in this category, unusual for, not typically available, and difficult to obtain.

- Make your customer or prospect feel special by pointing out they've been selected, chosen, pre-approved, or that the usual requirements have been waived for them. Remind them that although they qualify, not everyone does, that this is a member-only benefit, that they are one of only a certain number of people that are eligible, that they have already been accepted, or that they are invited.

- Choose empowering verbs that speak to exclusivity, such as you've earned, you've unlocked, you've achieved, you've been granted, and you've gained.

- When laying out your proposition, invite people to be one of the few or to be among the first, or to get the product or service before anyone else or before their friends.

- Create customer tiers, groups, and categories with desirable sounding labels, like silver, gold, and platinum, and congratulate your target on obtaining this advanced status. Similarly, offer charter memberships or membership in private groups.

- Send your target special recognition like membership cards, badges, and icons they can display.

- Personalize your messages by the recipient's name or their initials, or by their expressed interests or previous behaviors, so that your message feels exclusive to them.

Combining urgency and exclusivity

While this chapter breaks the scarcity principle into its two components—urgency and exclusivity—it is possible for marketers to use both halves in their messaging to create a one-two punch. For example, one subject line I've seen that did this especially well warned that it was my last chance to join a reward program before its public launch.

The first half of the subject line carried the urgency with the words "last chance." The second half added the exclusivity angle with the phrase "before the public launch." Being a person, I certainly qualified to join during a public launch! But what's the fun in that? The allure of exclusivity is that you can get access before all of those other people, before the hoi polloi. And that's what made this subject line so effective.

Another example can be found in the limited-edition Justin Bieber Crocs that went on sale in October of 2020. According to the *Daily Mail*, the clogs sold out in just 90 minutes and fans crashed the company's website (Stern, 2020).

Other examples of messaging that combine both halves of the scarcity principle include:

- New limited-edition SUV expected to sell out this week.
- Respond by <date> to be among the first to experience this advanced level of luxury.
- Last chance: Special preview reserved just for you.
- Member-only pricing expires in 24 hours.
- Gain early access with your VIP code this week only.
- You won't find this level of service anywhere else. But only two openings remain.
- Only five artist-signed limited edition prints available.

Remember, urgency and exclusivity will each prompt action, and serve to speed up the response you get to your marketing campaigns. So, you should always look for places to inject them into your messaging. Your goal is to make people feel time-pressed. Or special. Or both. Because the sooner people respond to your campaigns, the sooner you can monetize those campaigns. It's no longer enough to get a response. You want to get that response as quickly as possible. Pop any deadline you have or imply one. Emphasize the rare opportunity you've made available. Apply the scarcity principle to trigger action.

CASE STUDY
Using exclusivity to drive up class enrollments

A professional association approached the agency where I was working with an interesting challenge. They were about to launch an education series that would allow their members to obtain an advanced certification. The subject matter was specialized to the profession, and represented the newest thinking.

At this point, you might say—well, that sounds easy. The material is current, it's customized, and it's from a trusted source—the professional organization the members belong to. Those are some very solid support planks to make the sale. In fact, as long as the price is not exorbitant, things should go well.

But as the client provided more background, several reasons surfaced that made it clear the classes were not going to sell themselves:

- First, the subject matter was very new for the field, and revolved around an area that the members were not yet convinced was especially valuable or useful.

- Second, the client anticipated that this course would be confused with an earlier one they had offered on the topic.

- And third, if people who had taken the earlier course had not seen any meaningful impact on their careers because of it, they might not feel the need to take a more advanced one.

Our job was to convince members that this new class would be worth their time, effort and money. The client planned to offer it in 14 different locations across the country, and wanted us to drive enrollments for each of them.

As we thought about the best ways to achieve this, we considered a few different options. One was to focus on the content that would be covered in the new course. We could highlight what topics would be explored, show how they were applicable to the target's job, and list all the advanced information that members would master with the new certification. We could even include a quiz, to point out gaps in what members currently knew (see Chapter 9).

However, knowing that members were not yet convinced this topic was useful or valuable, focusing on the course materials and content did not seem like the most persuasive approach.

Another option was to message around the benefits of the new certification. We could position the course as laying the groundwork for the member's professional advancement—and the increased responsibilities, greater respect, promotions, and raises that could follow. We could even add in a little loss aversion (see Chapter 2), suggesting that employees who don't keep up with the industry may find themselves left behind their colleagues who do.

However, given that the client had no sense of whether members who took the original course experienced related career advancement or even greater job satisfaction, this seemed like a riskier move.

The third option we considered involved using the scarcity principle. We would target members who had already taken the original course, and offer them the first opportunity to sign up for the advanced certification. While doing so, we would also emphasize the time and space limitations.

On the exclusivity side of the equation, our emails used language that exhorted members to be one of the first to register, and to be among the first to achieve this new status. We also explained that because they already had the first certification, they were entitled to automatically advance to the one-day session for the advanced certification.

On the urgency side, we informed members that we anticipated the class would sell out, and that once it did, it would not return to their area again until the next season. Subsequent emails featured the dwindling number of seats that still remained.

Did the approach work? Yes, it did. The client happily reported that they had sold out every seat in all 14 locations. The campaign effectively used the scarcity principle, along with some help from the commitment and consistency principle, which you can read more about in Chapter 8.

KEY TAKEAWAYS

1 People want what they cannot have.

2 Things that are scarce are perceived to be more valuable and desirable.

3 The scarcity principle has two sides—urgency and exclusivity.

4 Urgency, expressed in the form of limited quantities and limited times, motivates people to take action.

5 Marketers can employ urgency in their communications by using deadlines, countdown clocks, and restricted quantities, as well as by using time-referencing words such as today, now, last, etc, speed-referencing words such as rush and immediate, and availability-referencing phrases such as limited quantities, back in stock, while supplies last, etc.

6 Exclusivity, which makes people or the opportunities presented to them, feel special either because of who they are, the group they belong to, or the way you value them, also motivates behavior.

THE SCARCITY PRINCIPLE   45

7 Marketers can employ exclusivity in their communications by using VIP codes, restricted phone numbers or webpages, special discounts and offers, advance or exclusive access, status-conveying groups and membership tiers, badges and cards that offer recognition, personalized messaging, and words and phrases such as secret, sneak peek, just for, reserved, sourced from the top 1 percent, white glove, handcrafted, unique, unlike other companies, you've achieved, you've unlocked, you've been selected, and you have been invited.

8 Urgency and exclusivity can be used separately or combined in an individual message or throughout an entire marketing campaign.

9 Use the scarcity principle to prompt people to respond faster.

10 Remember, make people feel special, or time-pressed, or both.

In conclusion

When your customers and prospects believe something is hard to obtain, or that they have access to an item or opportunity many people do not, they are more motivated to act. As a result, urgency and exclusivity can be powerful tactics for marketers.

However, limiting availability is just one way to prompt response. As you'll see in the next chapter, freely giving away items or information can also trigger a marketer's desired behavior.

References

Cialdini, R (1984) Influence, The psychology of persuasion, Quill William Morrow, New York

Milkman, K, Duckworth, D and Patel, M (2021) These are the text messages that get people to take vaccines, *Washington Post*, https://www.washingtonpost.com/outlook/2021/05/24/nudges-vaccination-psychology-messaging/ (archived at https://perma.cc/7SRM-PCSF)

Stern, C (2020) He's making Crocs cool again! Justin Bieber's limited-edition $60 yellow clogs with pizza and rainbow charms sell out in just 90 MINUTES—as frenzied fans crash the brand's website, *Daily Mail*, 14 October, https://www.dailymail.co.uk/femail/article-8840583/Justin-Biebers-limited-edition-Crocs-sell-just-90-minutes.html (archived at https://perma.cc/N62L-B96X)

Wansink, B, Kent, R and Hoch, S (1998) An anchoring and adjustment model of purchase quantity decisions, *Journal of Marketing Research,* 35 (1), pp 71–81

Worchel, S, Lee, J and Adewole, A (1975) Effects of supply and demand on ratings of object value, *Journal of Personality and Social Psychology,* https://psycnet. apa.org/record/1976-03817-001 (archived at https://perma.cc/XA44-QP7Z)

Worldata (2020) "Email only" offers when mentioned in subject lines generate a 14% higher overall opening rate, 4 June, https://www.instagram.com/worldata/ channel/?hl=en (archived at https://perma.cc/CVT2-T6H7)

Worldata, (2021) 22% higher click through rate for expiring offer emails including a countdown clock, 19 March, https://www.instagram.com/worldata/ channel/?hl=en (archived at https://perma.cc/CVT2-T6H7)

04

The reciprocity principle and the marketing value of give to get

People like to get things, particularly things for free. But behavioral scientists have found that once they receive them, they feel indebted to the giver and obliged to return the favor—even if they never asked for the gift in the first place. Marketers can tap into this hardwired desire to reciprocate, and use it to get more than they gave.

If you had to boil down the purpose of your marketing to a single, simple verb, what would that verb be?

From time to time, I've asked colleagues of mine this same question and have received what I consider to be some very practical, very perceptive answers. They have included words such as respond, reply, buy, enroll, activate, sell, consume, use, act, click, answer, convert, persuade, convince, motivate, influence, incent, communicate, try, choose, decide, commit, believe, perceive, want, need, desire, drive, compel, question, filter, focus, ignore, survive and unseat. The last several in this list seem to speak to a marketer's deeper need to remain in business by warding off the threat of competitors.

Did you see the word you were thinking of on this list? (If not, I'd love to know your answer. Feel free to share it with me by tweeting it to @nharhut with the hashtag #BeSciMktg.) After thinking about it for some time, the answer I've arrived at is the word "get."

When I find myself speaking with clients about their challenges and goals, or discussing industry award show entries with my fellow judges, or even simply describing a project I'm working on to my friends who aren't in the marketing world, the verb I tend to rely on is get. I'll say our goal is to get people to respond by a certain date, or to get them to try and buy and buy again, or to get them to switch from their current solution to the one we are offering.

Or I'll say a particular campaign is award-worthy because of the innovative way it gets people to think about the product differently, or its ability to get response rates that exceed industry benchmarks. Or I'll tell my friends I'm working on a marketing campaign designed to get customers to buy more than they ordinarily do, or a campaign to get companies to consider providing a new benefit to their employees.

At its heart, marketing means you try to get something. Yes, that something varies depending on factors like the vertical you're in, the part of the funnel your prospects occupy, and the mindset or beliefs of your target market. But in a word, you're going for the get. And if you're successful, your key performance indicators look good, your market share and/or your profitability grows, and you live to market another day.

Now after reading this, you may be convinced that as a marketer, your goal is only to get. And as a result, all of your marketing communications should concentrate on that purpose. You may think that your messaging needs to single-mindedly focus on those elements that will make it most likely you'll get the particular response you are looking for. So along with a strong and obvious call to action, including perhaps more than one way to reply, you'll want to make sure you list benefits, not just features, and that you include emotional as well as rational reasons to respond (see Chapter 1). You'll also want to look for places to inject loss aversion (see Chapter 2) and scarcity (see Chapter 3) into your messaging. In short, you'll want your campaigns to be tightly constructed communications whose sole purpose is to get people to do what you want them to.

And that would not be too far off. But there is something else you must consider. Something that doesn't negate all we've just covered, but that can work along with it in certain of your marketing communications. Something that also provides an emotional reason to respond, albeit not always an immediate one.

You want to consider the power of give to get.

> People don't like to owe other people. When you do something for someone, they'll want to find a way to pay you back.

Reciprocity is a hardwired human behavior

Human beings are hardwired to respond to other human beings in many ways, and one of the most powerful ones involves reciprocity. It's one of the behaviors that has helped ensure the continuity of the human race.

As Robert Cialdini describes in his book, *Influence: The psychology of persuasion*, the concept of reciprocity means "we should try to repay, in kind, what another person has provided us" (Cialdini, 1984). At first blush, you may describe that notion as being polite, or well-mannered, or even thoughtful.

When someone does something for us, we in turn want to do something for them. For example, I try to reach out with celebratory wishes on my friends' birthdays, but I especially try to remember to say happy birthday to people who remember my special day. If I'm out with my colleagues and one of them buys a round of drinks, my inclination is to pay for the next round. If that round doesn't happen, I make a mental note to pick up the tab the next time we're out imbibing.

Research shows things as small as candies and cards can trigger reciprocity

Based on an experiment conducted by sociologist Phillip Kunz, and recapped in a 2015 *Scientific American* post by Melanie Tannenbaum, I'm not the only person who feels the need to reciprocate. In the course of an experiment Kunz and his colleague Michael Woolcott were conducting, he mailed out holiday greetings to over 500 strangers, people whose names and addresses he pulled from a Chicago city directory. He found that 20 percent of these strangers sent back a Christmas card to him, even though they had no idea who he was. They got a card from him and felt the need to send him one in return.

While Kunz and Woolcott's research was not specifically designed to measure reciprocity, another experiment that Cialdini describes in his newer book *Yes! 50 scientifically proven ways to be persuasive*, coauthored by Noah J. Goldstein and Steve J. Martin, was. This experiment was conducted by behavioral scientist David Strohmetz and his colleagues, and involved the role of candy in restaurant tips.

In one condition, restaurant servers delivered the bill along with one piece of candy for each guest at the table. This got them a small increase in tips—3.3 percent—compared to presenting the bill with no candies. However, when the servers upped the number of candies to two per guest, their tips increased by 14.1 percent. The authors attribute this to the significance the diners attached to the extra candies. While receiving one candy apiece was not unexpected, receiving extra candies was. And as Cialdini et al note, "the more a person gives to us, the more we feel obligated to give in return."

The third part of the experiment is the part I find the most interesting. The servers delivered the check along with one piece of candy for each person at the table, and then turned to leave. But before they did, they turned back to the table, reached into a pocket, and withdrew additional candies, putting a second one on the table for each guest. The guests could have interpreted the move as one meant especially for them. This bit of personalization increased the servers' tips by a sizable 23 percent.

FIGURE 4.1 Reciprocity in restaurants

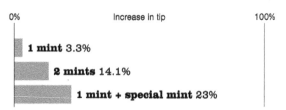

Researchers found that restaurant servers' tips increased when they delivered more candy with the bill—particularly if the additional candy seemed especially meant for the guest.

When people do something for us, even if we did not ask for it, we feel we should reciprocate. And the larger the gift we receive, the stronger that feeling is. Keep in mind, in the case of the tipping experiment, this was not simply about covering the cost of the candies. If it had been, the diners could have added a few cents to the gratuity. Or left the candies behind on the table. This was about going above and beyond. Because the servers had gone above and beyond what they typically do, the patrons went above and beyond in what they typically did.

While both the Christmas cards and the restaurant candies triggered relatively quick reciprocation, that is not always the case. In his book *Unleash Your Primal Brain: Demystifying how we think and why we act*, Tim Ash writes about "the power of future obligation." When the circumstances aren't right for immediate reciprocation, humans remember their obligations and are expected to honor them later. He goes on to say that "We are uncomfortable and even a bit anxious until we discharge or repay the debt." This in turn can lead to someone returning an even greater favor just to wipe the slate clean. As Cialdini notes, "We may be willing to agree to perform a larger favor than we received, merely to relieve ourselves of the psychological burden of debt."

The real reason I was invited to dinner?

I suspect I may have been on the receiving end of just such a transaction. For decades, I've thrown a large holiday party every December (only Covid-19 put a halt to it). The party is attended by friends, family, and, as the years went by, a growing number of people I've worked with. And although new people have been added to the invitation list, particularly when I changed jobs, the core group of guests remains very consistent from year to year.

A few years after the percentage of current and former colleagues attending began to outnumber the original family and friends, something happened that surprised me. On at least three separate occasions, colleagues who'd been coming to the party invited me and my spouse to their home for dinner. The reason this surprised me was that these were not people that I socialized with on a regular basis.

During the course of each dinner, they invariably brought up my holiday party and acknowledged in some fashion that they'd wanted to have us to dinner because they'd been to so many of those parties. As you might imagine, I'd felt there was no need to reciprocate in that way. After all, it was a large party. Had they happened to throw one, adding us to the guest list would have been welcome and appropriate. But cooking a special dinner for us alone seemed a disproportionate effort. After thinking about it through the lens of behavioral science, however, I understood what likely had transpired.

How savvy marketers employ the reciprocity principle

At this point you might be thinking, this seems very powerful, but what's the best way to use reciprocity if I'm not working at a restaurant or celebrating the holidays? The answer is simple. You want to give to get.

Rather than focusing all your marketing efforts on getting something, devote a portion of them to first giving to your customers and prospects. Provide them with something they'll value. Something they might not have asked for, but will appreciate either because it's useful, or it feels personal, or it's enjoyable.

Your upfront gift could be tangible or it could come in the form of a service. The key is to provide it first. When you do that, you pave the way for the reciprocity principle to work to your advantage. Because once someone accepts a gift or favor, whether or not it's one they asked for, they will feel obliged to the marketer who provided it to them. When you manage to surprise and delight people, those same people will feel they want to return the favor. They'll be more inclined to do business with you because they have already benefited from their relationship with you. More than wanting to be polite, they'll want to feel that they have evened the score.

CASE STUDY
Using the reciprocity principle to win back customers

How do you reengage someone who has stopped doing business with you? This was the challenge a large financial services company brought to my team at the agency where I was working. The company wanted to convince financial advisors who had stopped selling their funds and retirement products to once again start selling them. Their immediate goal was to secure a conversation between one of their wholesalers and their former customers, the lapsed advisors.

In the business-to-business arena, when a customer stops doing business with a company, it is extremely difficult to win them back. And this project carried one more challenge. The financial advisors had been gone for more than a year.

From that, we can make two suppositions: there was a reason they had decided to stop doing business with our client (as opposed to the advisor simply experiencing a temporary lull in their sales). And by this time, they had found a replacement they preferred (perhaps one that they found easier to sell). To make matters worse, financial advisors typically work with a set number of companies. If our client wanted to get back in, they would likely have to unseat one of their competitors.

As we thought about the marketing problem, we considered a few different approaches. We could remind the financial advisor about our clients' funds, reiterate the benefits of those funds, and emphasize the fact that other advisors were successfully selling them (a bit of social proof, which you can read more about in Chapter 5). But these advisors were already familiar with the funds and had experienced selling them themselves, so the idea that other advisors were selling them would not be particularly motivating.

We also thought about creating a loss aversion-fueled message (see Chapter 2), inviting the advisors to "see what you're missing." But because they had previously represented our client's products, that message would also be rendered ineffective. The target would think it unlikely that the advisors currently selling the funds knew something they didn't.

Reciprocity with a personal touch

But then the team hit on a brilliant solution that involved the reciprocity principle. The immediate goal of the campaign was to secure the phone call with the wholesaler. And of course, the ultimate goal was to win back the financial advisor. So, the creative team decided we needed to send these financial advisors something special, something that they would not only pay attention to, but that would speak to them.

In the financial services world, it's not uncommon for companies to send things to advisors. Coffee mugs and sleeves of golf balls are pretty standard gifts. For regulatory reasons, a gift can be valued at only so much, which does limit the options.

The team knew this gift had to be different. And that it couldn't exceed the value cap. They decided on a framed cartoon from a *New Yorker Magazine* artist. The cartoon caption was an amusing line about selling retirement products, and it included the financial advisor's name right in it, to really stroke their ego. This gift was different, it was relevant, and it was personal. Can't you just imagine the financial advisors clearing a spot on their office wall in order to display it?

Before shipping the packages, we sent the advisors an email, alerting them to watch their postal mail for a special gift that was picked out just for them. We also asked them to call the wholesaler when it arrived.

Then in a white box marked fragile, we sent the cartoon, which we framed along with some information about the artist to add to the feel of exclusivity (see Chapter 3). We also included a short letter highlighting how our client could provide the support and resources to do two things the financial advisors really cared about— look good to their clients, and increase their sales.

After that, we followed up with three brief emails that had links to information covering how to talk to clients about healthcare in retirement, a difficult-to-raise but important subject, and one that could set up the financial advisors to make a sale.

So, how did the campaign do? Did the unexpected gift of an elegantly packaged personalized cartoon drawn by an artist at the sophisticated *New Yorker Magazine* work? Did it catch the attention of the financial advisors? Did it pave the way for a conversation with a wholesaler? More important, did it help to reactivate those financial advisors? It most certainly did. The wholesalers got phone calls. They got emails. And, perhaps most telling, they got their financial advisors to return to selling the firm's products.

One wholesaler reported that an advisor he'd never previously met spoke with him because of the cartoon promotion. This advisor then went on to make a sale worth a substantial $2 million, a sale the wholesaler said would otherwise never have happened. Overall, sales increased significantly compared to previous winback campaigns, and the promotion was described by the client as a home run.

A campaign that set out to trigger the reciprocity principle helped to generate tens of millions of dollars in revenue. Not a bad return for taking a give to get approach.

> **MISTAKE**
>
> Attempting to trigger reciprocity by offering a gift in return for completing an action. While that can be effective, it is simply providing an incentive. To trigger reciprocity, make your gift unconditional.

Direct marketing is an ideal channel for reciprocity

Offline or online, the direct marketing channel offers an ideal opportunity to use the reciprocity principle. Marketers have ample opportunity to send something to their customers or prospects that they will appreciate, whether it's something useful or simply something fun or novel.

Good direct marketing is always well targeted, personalized, and relevant. That means that whatever gift you choose to include along with your message should also be. Examples include information, guides, and reports about your target's industry, hobby, or area of interest. These can be especially effective if they look like they were generated specifically for the target. For example, in a B2B mailing, you can include the name of the recipient's company on the report. In a B2C mailing, you can send an item such as a notebook or t-shirt, that is personalized with your target's name or initials. This more personal touch will increase the item's perceived value.

When selecting what to send, take care to make it relate back to the product or service you offer. If you sell hiking shoes, a map of trails in your target's geographic area would be a good tie-in—whether in a print or digital version. If you offer chiropractic services, a laminated card illustrating several beneficial stretches would make sense. If you sell social media consulting services to businesses, a downloadable guide detailing the specs for the most popular platforms could be a welcome gift.

Once you have decided to send a gift, make sure the recipient doesn't run the risk of missing it. Either mention the gift (or the presence of it) in the email subject line or outer envelope teaser copy, or send it in a box or padded envelope that suggests there must be something of value inside.

A dimensional mailer such as a box, tube, or padded envelope will typically get opened first among the day's mail, which is one advantage to sending them. They are attention-getting and memorable. And they provide a great reason to make a follow-up phone call. Because of the reciprocity principle, it's hard for the recipient to ignore a follow-up effort. If someone is enjoying the cool new gadget you sent, or has benefited from the customized guide they received, they'll feel bad if they don't at least take your call.

However, because dimensional mailings are more costly than sending a standard envelope, you'll want to pay close attention to your ROI numbers. Also make sure to choose an appropriately sized package. When people open a large box only to find a letter, brochure, or some other flat piece of paper inside, they can be disappointed because the contents didn't live up to their expectations. Additionally, they may feel you are being environmentally irresponsible because you used wasteful packaging. Either way, you don't want your target feeling negatively toward you as you're about to deliver your marketing message. It can negate all of the goodwill generated by the gift you sent.

If cost prohibits you from sending a dimensional mailing, don't fret. There are things you can mail in a flat, standard-sized envelope that will trigger the reciprocity principle. In addition to guides, maps, and reports, consider a doorhanger with a clever saying or a small, year-at-a-glance calendar for your B2B audience. Or a magnet, bookmark, or set of fun stickers for your B2C audience. Alternatively, send an email with a link that lets your target download the gift.

Fundraisers make good use of the reciprocity principle

If you have ever received a charity solicitation in the mail, you know that fundraisers have mastered the use of the reciprocity principle. You open an envelope you did not request, and inside you find a set of personalized address labels, or a notepad, or some stickers, or some greeting cards, or maybe all of those items. In one hand you hold the gift you did not ask for. And in the other hand you hold the letter, appealing to you to take pity on the plight of the charity's beneficiaries and make a donation.

What happens? It often works. That is why the fundraisers continue to use this tactic. I can recall speaking at a direct marketing conference and afterwards being approached by a woman who worked raising funds for cancer research. As we chatted, she confessed that although they had tried many different approaches, nothing could beat the personalized address labels they sent out.

And perhaps that's not surprising. The *Chicago Tribune* reported that "St. Jude switched from special-occasion to return-address labels in 2002, doubling its response rate. The Disabled American Veterans, on the other hand, has been sending return address labels since the early 1970s. The DAV sends 12 million packets a year, said Susan Loth, director of fundraising for the group" (Staples, 2006). If charities who measure every penny continue to send them, we can assume they continue to work.

Loyalty and retention programs are smart places to leverage the reciprocity principle

When trying to retain customers and earn their loyalty, incorporating the reciprocity principle into your marketing strategies and executions makes a lot of sense. Sending the occasional surprise gift can prompt a strong emotional reaction in your customers.

In fact, LeeAnn Renninger, co-author of the book *Surprise: Embrace the unpredictable and engineer the unexpected* (Luna and Renninger, 2015), explains that "research shows that surprise intensifies our emotions by about 400%, which explains why we love positive surprises and hate negative surprises." When people are surprised, it focuses their attention, and makes them remember what it is that surprised them (see Chapter 16). And those are two strong advantages for marketers.

Of course, you don't want to put yourself in a position where you are "buying" your customers' behavior, training them to respond only when you give them something first. But well-used, the occasional gift or perk can help cement a relationship and motivate the kind of loyalty marketers seek.

When determining your rewards, keep in mind that they can be tangible or virtual. Rewards that confer status, provide access (think exclusivity), and offer recognition can all be powerful choices. So, too, can gifts that are useful or helpful. The key is to ensure that they are relevant to your audience and appropriate for your brand.

Content marketers should think of reciprocity as a strategic tool

Just like direct marketers, content marketers can skillfully use the reciprocity principle in their campaigns. By offering information that is engaging, entertaining, or educational, marketers can give to get.

Marcus Sheridan is the author of the content marketing guidebook *They Ask, You Answer*, which he wrote after using content marketing to save his fiberglass pool installation company, which had suddenly found itself struggling. His story has been told numerous times and in numerous places, and I myself have had the pleasure of hearing him speak at a marketing conference or two.

When the economy took a turn for the worse, he and his partners saw their pool business drying up. People were canceling their installation orders and asking for their deposits back. In an effort to keep the business going, Sheridan started publishing content that answered people's questions about pools. He addressed prices, he wrote about the pros and cons of fiberglass pools, he even blogged about the best swimming pool builders in his area and named his competitors.

The result? Not only did his pool business survive, it thrived, becoming "one of the largest manufacturers and installers in the country," according to Sheridan. It's a terrific example of using content marketing to deliver on the idea of give to get.

Providing content that is genuinely helpful is what can set your organization apart from your competitors. Identify a need in your target market, and then be the company to fill it. One of my favorite examples on the business-to-business side is Subjectline.com from email company Worldata. So many different companies do email marketing, and one of the things they wonder about is the effectiveness of their subject lines. Will they get opened? Will they be flagged as spam? Subjectline.com offers a free tool that lets you enter a subject line and immediately get it evaluated. You'll not only receive a numerical score, you'll also see the reason for that score and, if applicable, some tips to improve it.

On the business-to-consumer side of marketing, I was impressed to hear about Mutual of Omaha's final expense estimator. One reason people buy life insurance is to leave money to their family, so that money can be used to help cover their funeral expenses once they pass. But who really knows how much their funeral will cost? This easy-to-use tool lets people select the items they anticipate having at their funeral (example: casket vs. urn, flowers or no flowers) and see the average cost for these items in their state.

In both cases, the email company and the insurer are providing free content that their target audience will find useful. And in doing that, they are paving the way for a reciprocal response when that person is ready to make a purchase.

More ways you can use the reciprocity principle in your marketing

- Email a series of weekly tips to your customers and prospects that will help them accomplish their business or personal goals.

- Send a regular e-newsletter that curates information that will appeal to your target, that will keep them current about a shared interest, or that includes content that you have created specifically for them.

- Consider not gating at least some of the resources on your website, so your prospects and customers can access tools and advice that they'll find valuable.

- Send reminders so that people don't miss important deadlines (example: a car company could remind people when their vehicle's inspection sticker needs to be renewed, or a travel company could remind people when their passports are nearing the expiration date).

- Offer free samples, free trials, complimentary assessments or evaluations, and other useful lead magnets.
- Reduce or remove friction in a process, which can make you the preferred provider choice among your competitors.
- Take the time and effort to be extra helpful to your customers; show you're interested in them.
- Surprise customers with a credit, discount, or secret sale.
- In B2B, recommend or refer other companies you work with, and put links to their content in the materials you publish.
- Recognize your customers' birthdays, anniversaries and other achievements with a small, unexpected gift or a warm acknowledgment.
- Provide content that delivers a short entertainment break in your target's day.
- Create a library of how-to videos that your customers and prospects can refer to.

KEY TAKEAWAYS

1 Humans are hardwired to return favors.

2 People feel obligated to you if you first do something for them, whether or not they asked for it.

3 The larger the gift that someone receives, the stronger their urge is to reciprocate.

4 To get out from under the obligation, people will sometimes reciprocate with an even bigger favor.

5 Marketers can use the give to get approach to prompt business.

6 Direct marketers and charity fundraisers have seen considerable success when they include gifts in their campaigns.

7 Surprising a customer with an unexpected gift can focus that customer's attention and make them more likely to remember you, leading to increased loyalty and retention.

8 Content marketers can leverage a give to get approach by providing information and assets that educate or entertain.

9 Marketers should offer content that is genuinely useful and not widely available.

10 E-newsletters, ungated content, timely reminders, complimentary assessments, unexpected gifts, and helpful resources can all trigger the reciprocity principle.

In conclusion

Give to get can be a smart strategy for marketers to use. People appreciate free help, information, and gifts, and often repay the favor by doing business with you. Using the reciprocity principle can ensure you are the company people think of when it's time to buy. As people prepare to make a purchase decision, they commonly default to the company that helped them. That way they don't feel guilty, and in fact, feel they're returning the favor.

Another way they commonly decide is to see what other people like them do, as you'll see in the next chapter.

References

Ash, T (2021) *Unleash Your Primal Brain: Demystifying how we think and why we act*, Morgan James, New York

Cialdini, R (1984) *Influence: The psychology of persuasion*, Quill William Morrow, New York

Goldstein, N, Martin, S and Cialdini, R (2008) *Yes! 50 scientifically proven ways to be persuasive*, Free Press, New York

Luna, T and Renninger, L (2015) *Surprise: Embrace the unpredictable and engineer the unexpected*, TarcherPerigee

Sheridan, M (2019) *They Ask, You Answer*, Wiley

Staples, G B (2006) Charity address labels present a sticky situation, *Chicago Tribune*, 24 September, https://www.chicagotribune.com/news/ct-xpm-2006-09-24-0609220424-story.html (archived at https://perma.cc/K4R4-BWDL)

Tannenbaum, M (2015) I'll show you my holiday card if you show me yours, *Scientific American*, 2 January, https://blogs.scientificamerican.com/psysociety/i-8217-ll-show-you-my-holiday-card-if-you-show-me-yours/# (archived at https://perma.cc/UV3Z-9TW5)

05

Social proof: harnessing the power of people like us, and the people we like

When your target is faced with a decision that they aren't sure how to make, they will look at what people similar to them have done, and do the same. Behavioral scientists have found that this decision-making shortcut conserves mental energy, and makes people feel more confident. As a marketer, you want to show your prospects that many other customers have already done what you're asking them to do.

Go ahead. Check almost any reference on good copywriting for marketers, and you're bound to find one of these three words: relevant, customized, and personalized.

In fact, you may find all three of them.

As marketers, we know that the more a message resonates with the target, the better the response we can expect. And to give a marketing message the best chance of hitting the mark, we should make it as relevant as we possibly can. That's why the old adage "the right message, to the right person, at the right time" is so often quoted.

If you do even a bit of research, you're likely to find numerous tests and case studies that attest to the wisdom of relevant, personalized communications. For instance, the Association of National Advertisers says that "companies that extensively personalize their messaging report greater than 20 times ROI, according to the Adobe Personalization Survey 2020" (Menon, 2021). And an Accenture Interactive study found that "91% of consumers are more likely to shop with brands who recognize, remember and provide relevant offers and communications" (Zoghby, 2018).

Certainly, this seems to make sense. Imagine this scenario. You're in the initial phases of speaking with a company about doing business with them. The representative there offers you a gift and says, "Here is a little something we've selected just for you." That feels nice. It feels personalized. It feels like that representative may have read Chapters 3 and 4 of this book, and put the power of exclusivity and reciprocity to work.

Now imagine a slightly different scenario. You're considering doing business with a company and the company's representative offers you a gift, saying, "Here, have one. We give these to everybody." How does that feel? Nice to get something for free perhaps. But not nearly as customized or special, right?

So, as we have learned, personalization, relevance and exclusivity can all influence behavior. They can work very well for marketers. However, there's a particular instance when they alone will not be enough. Or when they can potentially backfire, and cause a reaction that is the complete opposite of the desired one. And that time is when people don't know what they want. Because when people are not sure of what to do, there's something more important to them than feeling special. They want to feel safe.

As we learned in Chapter 2, loss aversion is a very powerful force. One way it manifests itself is that people do not want to make the wrong choice; they do not want to make a mistake. This desire to avoid the wrong move plays out in both B2B and B2C situations.

Think about it. Have you ever tried to decide between different products or different providers? If so, you know what can be at stake. Make the wrong choice, and you can be subject to the ridicule of your friends. Or your professional reputation can be damaged. No one wants to be made fun of. Or fired.

As a result, when your prospects or customers are on unfamiliar ground, when they aren't sure about the decision they need to make, what they want is to feel comfortable and confident. They will seek ways to avoid feeling buyer's remorse. They will look for ways to feel they are making a good choice, that they will fit in, and that no one, including themselves, can accuse them of picking the wrong product, service or company.

One way you as a marketer can provide that reassurance to your customers and prospects is to tap into social proof.

> When people are uncertain, they assume others know more than they do. As a result, it seems like a smart move to make the same choices those other people made. Since making the wrong choice could potentially be harmful, people will take a "safety in numbers" approach.

Relying on social proof is a very common decision-making shortcut

When people are not sure of what decision to make, they use a mental shortcut. They look to see what other people—especially other people like themselves—are doing, and then they follow their lead. Even though people love to feel special, even though they seek out customized experiences, and even though personalized communications perform exceedingly well in marketing, there are definitely times when, in the words of Meg Ryan in *When Harry Met Sally*, "I'll have what she's having" is the decision your customers will make.

Why? It will give them a sense of confidence that they are not making a wrong move. Richard H. Thaler and Cass R. Sunstein, in their book *Nudge: Improving decisions about health, wealth, and happiness*, explain it this way: "If many people do something or think something, their actions and their thoughts convey information about what might be best for you to do or think."

Adam Alter, in his book *Drunk Tank Pink: And other unexpected forces that shape how we think, feel and behave*, recounts the story of a power company that successfully used behavioral science to reduce electricity consumption. The company sent reports to their customers showing them how their power consumption compared to that of their efficient neighbors.

Once the company started doing this, they saw a reduction in kilowatt hours consumed. Before receiving the report, a customer would probably not have any idea that they were using "too much" electricity. But once they were shown how they compared to their efficient neighbors, they used this information as a way to decide to consume less.

This same principle of social proof, applied in a slightly different way, motivated hotel guests to reuse their bath towels instead of having them replaced each day. The experiment, recounted in *Yes! 50 Scientifically proven ways to be persuasive* by Noah J. Goldstein, Steve J. Martin, and Robert B. Cialdini, involved people seeing one of three different signs in their hotel bathroom.

One "was designed to reflect the type of basic environmental-protection message adopted by much of the hotel industry." The second sign told guests that "the majority of guests at the hotel recycled their towels at least once during the course of their stay." And the third communicated to guests that "the majority of people who had previously stayed in their particular room participated in the towel reuse program at some point during their stay" (Goldstein, et al., 2008). The authors report that while the second approach was more successful than the first, this last approach was the most effective.

When people are trying to decide what to do, especially when faced with a choice they never had to think about before, they use what other people similar to them did as a guide for how they should behave. That similarity can have a fairly broad definition, ranging from people in your neighborhood to people who chose the same hotel as you and ended up in the same room you did. One study even showed that the similarity could be as simple as having previously dined in the restaurant where a person is now eating.

Social proof can make popular choices become more popular

An experiment conducted by researchers from Duke University and Peking University showed just that (Todd, 2009). In a Chinese restaurant chain, researchers randomly placed one of two placards on the tables. One half "named the top-five most popular dishes from the previous week; the other half listed five sample dishes that were not identified as being popular."

Researchers found that the demand for the top five most popular dishes "increased by an average of about 13 to 20 percent." The sample dishes, however, did not see increased demand. When a dish was described as popular, it actually became more popular.

People rely on the decision-making shortcut of social proof even in matters more important than what to order from a dinner menu. For example, in a global study reported in the August 2021 *British Journal of Psychology*, researchers found that people follow pandemic guidelines most when their social circle does (Tunçgenç et al., 2021). The study's authors went on to state that "Such social influence mattered more than people thinking distancing was the right thing to do."

In other words, what someone's family and close friends were doing was more likely to affect their behavior than whether or not they themselves believed social distancing was important. You read that right. It overrode even their personal convictions on the topic.

Social proof isn't always about following the crowd. Sometimes people think that others actually know more than they do

We've established that when people aren't sure of what to do, they follow the lead of other people. You may also have heard the terms bandwagon effect or herd mentality to describe similar behavior. People can instinctively feel safer when following the crowd. But there's another reason social proof can be so powerful for marketers.

As Robert Cialdini states in *Influence: The psychology of persuasion,* people apparently "assume that if a lot of people are doing the same thing, they must know something we don't."

Imagine how convenient that is for marketers. When your prospective but uncertain customers see another customer buying from you, they don't think that person is equally in the dark or does not know about any alternatives. On the contrary, they think that person knows something they don't.

A classic piece of behavioral science research, as well as a classic television show, both provide a window into this effect. The classic research was conducted by social psychologist Solomon Asch in 1951 (Mcleod, 2018). In the experiment, participants believed they were taking part in a vision study, and were asked to evaluate line lengths. What they did not know, however, was that the seven other subjects in the study were actually plants, who had earlier agreed to give the wrong answer to the question at prearranged times.

FIGURE 5.1 Which lines match?

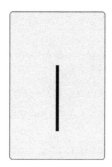 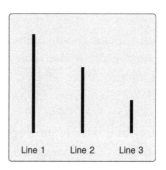

Line 1   Line 2   Line 3

In a famous experiment, a majority of subjects followed the others in the room and chose the obviously incorrect answer when asked which of three lines matched the line they had been shown.

The participants were shown a line, and then a set of three lines. They were asked to choose which of the three lines most closely matched the first they had been shown. While the answer was obvious, the seven plants, all of whom answered before the real participant did, provided the wrong answer in 12 of the 18 trials. What Asch found was that "about one third (32%) of the participants who were placed in this situation went along and conformed with the clearly incorrect majority" during those times.

Over the course of the 12 trials, "about 75% of participants conformed at least once." However, in the control group, which had no planted participants to deliberately provide the incorrect response, "less than 1% of participants gave the wrong answer." So, were the 75% caving in to social pressure? Or, like contestants on the tv game show *Who Wants to Be a Millionaire*, were they relying on the wisdom of the crowd, assuming other people knew something that they did not?

While Asch's experiment took place in a lab, where only so many people could witness it, this next example played itself out before an entire television audience. The classic hidden camera show *Candid Camera* ran its own version of the Asch experiment, using people riding in an elevator.

The episode, titled "Face the Rear," featured a man wearing a trench coat who got into an empty elevator. Every passenger who entered after him faced the back of the elevator, instead of turning to face the doors, which is the custom. As this happened, the first man looked very confused, before gradually starting to turn himself. The show's host Allen Funt narrated the episode. He said "You'll see how this man in the trench coat tries to maintain his individuality. And little by little… He looks at his watch, but he's really making an excuse for turning just a little bit more toward the wall."

Later in the episode, another unsuspecting passenger finds himself in an elevator car with people who periodically turn to the back, to the sides, and to the front. To make things more interesting, on cue the male passengers removed their hats and then put them back on again. Each time the elevator door opens, the television audience sees that the unsuspecting passenger has done the same thing as all the other passengers, who were of course *Candid Camera* personnel.

Interestingly, in 2011 a research team from Bethany Lutheran College ran their own version of the elevator experiment. They found that "People turned around to match other passengers without question, while others confusedly asked if there was a second door that opened."

A counterintuitive application of social proof

Social proof is very powerful. It's a hardwired human behavior. And one that marketers can make good use of. In fact, one of my favorite applications is actually one that may seem a little counterintuitive to a marketer. It was devised by a very successful direct response copywriter named Colleen Szot, and described in *Yes! 50 Scientifically proven ways to be persuasive* by Noah J. Goldstein, Steve J. Martin, and Robert B. Cialdini.

Szot was writing an infomercial for a client, and actually added some friction—as well as some social proof—to one of her scripts. She replaced the stock call-to-action line "Operators are waiting. Please call now" with "If operators are busy, please call again."

As a marketer, you may say that sounds crazy. Informercials try really, really hard to convince people to call. That is their primary purpose. So why, after selling its heart out, would this company suggest to prospective customers that when they call they might have an unpleasant experience? That in fact, they might need to hang up and redial? It can be hard enough to convince someone to call once, let alone multiple times. Why would the marketer deliberately introduce the prospect of friction into the pitch?

The answer, as you might have guessed, is social proof. When viewers hear that the phone line might be busy, it communicates to them that many other people—people like them who are watching this same television show at this same time, and perhaps thinking they might need a little less tv and a little more exercise in their lives—are calling. While a viewer couldn't know that for sure, it certainly seemed to be the case. As a result, those three changed words in Szot's infomercial script "caused a huge increase in the number of people who purchased her product."

Definitely an interesting twist to the idea of using social proof in advertising.

How the author was almost misled by social proof

When visiting Spain, I had an experience with social proof that also resulted in an unanticipated ending. I had been invited to present a keynote at DES2019, a large international conference focused on digital transformation. The conference was in Madrid, and my spouse and I decided to take a few days to explore both that city and Barcelona while we were there, because this would be our first trip to that part of the world.

One of the things I love to do is eat, so upon arriving in Spain, I began filling my social media posts with accounts of all the wonderful meals I was having. As luck would have it, when I posted about a restaurant in Barcelona, a business acquaintance replied that the post had her dreaming about the incredible tapas she used to enjoy at a particular restaurant in that city. When I looked up the restaurant she mentioned, I was delighted to find that it was in walking distance of our hotel. Perfect, we thought. That is where we'll head for dinner this evening.

As we were leaving the hotel, the concierge stopped me to ask how I was enjoying my stay, and could she be of any assistance. I eagerly explained I was on my way to try the tapas at a restaurant I'd heard was very good. When I gave her the name, she replied that it was right next door to another tapas restaurant.

That seemed like an odd response to me. And it made me wonder if she was trying to suggest that I should dine there instead. So, I asked her which restaurant was better. Being very diplomatic, a skill I suspect is necessary in that line of work, she replied that they were both good, and that the restaurant she'd brought up was known for some very inventive dishes that people raved about.

Now I was faced with something of a dilemma. Should I rely on social proof, a recommendation from another American who belonged to the same professional association that I did, and who also appreciated good food? Or should I default to the authority principle, and take the suggestion of the concierge, who worked in Barcelona and whose profession it was to know the best places in town (read more about the authority principle in Chapter 10).

Since the two restaurants were literally side by side, I decided a reasonable approach would be to walk over and make my choice after checking them out.

THE PHYSICAL SIGN OF SOCIAL PROOF

When we arrived, there was a lengthy line in front of the restaurant my business associate had recommended. The restaurant itself was full of people eating and enjoying themselves. And a hostess out front was managing the ever-growing wait list with the precision of an air traffic controller.

Next door was a quiet restaurant with no line and only one table inside that appeared to have any diners at all seated at it.

In that moment, I knew I would be adding my name to the wait list of the first restaurant. All those people were yet another demonstration of social proof. I even found myself entertaining the less-than-charitable thought that the hotel's concierge might have suggested the other restaurant because she would get some kind of kickback from them.

When we were escorted to seats at the bar, which happened in fairly short order thanks to the skills of the hostess, we had a phenomenal meal. Like my business acquaintance, I now dream of those delicious tapas.

However, when I was sitting at that bar, I also thought about what would happen when I returned to the hotel. If the same concierge were still on duty, she would undoubtedly inquire about my evening. She had been nice enough to offer a restaurant suggestion even though I'd not asked for one. And I knew I'd feel a little guilty admitting I did not take it (remember Chapter 4 on reciprocity!). So, I decided I would stop in next door for a small dessert.

And here is where the surprise ending comes in. When we paid our bill and stepped outside the restaurant, the previously quiet spot next door was jammed with diners. The hostess there had a phone that seemed stuck to her ear as she waved waiting guests to their tables and waved good night to others who were departing with large smiles on their faces.

Newly intrigued, I managed to wriggle my way in through the crowded doorway and up to the hostess stand, just as the hostess was finishing a call. I asked about the possibility of a table for two, *por favor*. She smiled and said they were completly booked, but the last caller had just cancelled so it must have been "meant to be." She led us to the only available seats in the restaurant and placed menus in front of us. It looked phenomenal! I immediately revised my plan to have a small dessert, and proceeded to order several tapas—plus a dessert.

In the end, we dined at two wonderful restaurants. It turned out that the social proof indicators for both of them just came at different times. When it was high for the first one, it looked low for the second. By the time it was high for the second, we'd already eaten. But thanks to the concierge at my hotel, we got to experience a small taste of that restaurant, too!

CASE STUDY
How social proof sold hard-to-sell insurance

People rely on social proof to make all kinds of decisions. One day, a client reached out to me at the agency where I was working to ask for assistance developing a multichannel campaign. The client sold voluntary workplace benefits, which are various kinds of insurance that people could purchase where they work, but pay for on their own. Some examples would include disability insurance, accident insurance, and critical illness insurance.

The challenges with selling these types of insurance are that people are not sure whether or not they need them, they don't want to consider the possibility that they may become disabled/have an accident/fall ill, and that getting a policy means less take-home pay because the cost is typically deducted from the employee's paycheck.

The client had already decided that one approach they wanted to take was to use social proof in their marketing. The question for us was how to best leverage it. We could have pursued a couple of avenues:

- One would be to tout the number of these kinds of policies the company had sold. The sheer volume of them would suggest that they are a popular choice. We could have even made the marketing more personal by making a reference to something that people in that area would be familiar with. For example, if the employees worked for a company in New York, we could say the number of current policyholders would fill Yankee stadium ten times.

- Another avenue would be to say that most people who purchased policies like these did so after receiving an email like the one the target just read. This could prompt the target to infer that many people similar to them had made a buying decision, and since email was primarily how the coverage was marketed, the claim would be factually correct.

Where the creative team landed was actually an avenue that felt even more personal. They customized the headline by using the target's name, age, and the field in which they worked. The line delivered the information that people like them who were in their age range and occupation had purchased these policies. The campaign, which also included other elements of behavioral science, was a big success. It exceeded all the client's benchmarks. Most notably, it delivered double-digit increases in enrollments and in premiums per employee.

Four more effective applications of social proof in marketing

Many other of my clients have benefited from the successful addition of behavioral science to their marketing campaigns:

- A telecom company that was introducing itself to people in a new geographic area launched messaging around the idea that "Finally, the wait is over." This suggested pent-up demand for their services, which is another indicator of social proof.

- A software client's acquisition campaign noted that six top competitors in the target's industry already used them.

- A financial literacy company with a product for students targeted college decision makers by asking them what their colleagues at a named, nearby university knew that they did not. (The named, nearby university had already signed on to work with the financial literacy company, which is why we could say this.)

- And finally, a financial firm attracted new employees by showcasing the long list of employees who had joined them in the last several months. It wasn't that the company expected the prospective new hires to recognize the names; it was the large number of names that delivered the social proof. If that many people were leaving their existing employer to join this one, it must be a good choice!

A few words of caution when applying social proof in marketing

One mistake that marketers must avoid when adding social proof to their marketing messages is writing them in a way that delivers the wrong takeaway.

The book *Yes! 50 scientifically proven ways to be persuasive,* mentioned earlier in this chapter, includes the details of an experiment run at the Petrified Forest National Park. The park wanted to discourage visitors from stealing pieces of petrified wood.

Some people saw a sign that spoke to the fact that the thefts were compromising the forest. It said, "Many past visitors have removed the petrified wood from the park, changing the natural state of the Petrified Forest." Others saw a sign that said, "Please don't remove the petrified wood from the park, in order to preserve the natural state of the Petrified Forest."

The authors report the first version actually prompted more people to steal, almost tripling the number of thefts versus the control condition, which had no sign. It was almost as if the sign planted the seed to steal where it might not have been. The second version of the sign, with no element of social proof, managed to deliver a modest reduction in theft.

When trying to influence behavior, don't spotlight the number of people who aren't yet doing what you want them to do. The message it will send is that lots of people aren't taking action. As a result, your target likely won't either.

Instead, focus on those who are doing what you hope they will. For example, I've been known to tell my fundraising clients to hold off showing those thermometers that depict the volume of donations still needed until the goal is more than halfway achieved.

MISTAKE

Indicating many people still do the thing you don't want them to do. Rather than prompting people to take different action, this will reinforce their current behavior.

Your customers will imitate people like themselves, and also people whom they like

Social proof can work very well when your prospective customers can compare themselves to other people who are similar to them. However, there's another way for marketers to use it. That way highlights people who aren't similar to your target, but rather who are people your target likes and admires.

This is the reason celebrity endorsements can be so effective. Your target may not be a sports star, movie star, entertainer, or influencer, but they may feel a connection to those people because they are fans.

A very popular singer in the US endorses a facial cleaning regimen. She is neither a cosmetologist nor a chemist. She is a singer. But her face looks great in videos and on concert screens. And people, especially young girls, like her. As a result, they are more likely to trust her when she endorses the product.

There's also a US actor who stars in a long-running television show where he plays the chief of police. His character is known for making good decisions, and for doing the right thing. He also appears in ads selling reverse mortgages. When the target market sees him in those ads, they may well be reminded of the qualities of his tv character and as a result, be more likely to trust what he says about the mortgage company.

Of course, as a marketer, you need to be careful when choosing celebrities to represent your product, lest the chosen celebrity become embroiled in a scandal and experience a fall from grace, taking your product down along with them. There's also the cost of hiring a celebrity, which can be pricey.

A bank in India found a very inventive way to tap into social proof and skirt the high cost of hiring famous people. Union Bank ran a campaign that featured the relatives of celebrities in their ads. In a way, it taps both angles of social proof. It reminds the target of people they like (the celebrities), and it actually shows the target people who are arguably more like them (non-celebrities). If a famous person's family has chosen that bank, doesn't it seem like a good bank to consider?

Smart ways to use social proof in marketing

- Feature a customer testimonial, and make sure the testimonial giver is similar to the testimonial reader (example: they live in the same general area or work in the same industry). For the testimonial to be most effective, choose one in which the customer admits some earlier hesitation or skepticism before revealing your product was a great choice. While "Acme products are really wonderful" is a good testimonial, an even better one is "I thought all of these products were pretty much the same, but then I switched to Acme. Their products are really wonderful." When a prospective customer reads a testimonial like this, their reaction is, "That's exactly what I was thinking—aren't all of these products basically the same? But I guess they're not. I should go with Acme."

- Provide case studies and a list of satisfied customers.
- Highlight the number of users, subscribers, retweets, views, likes, followers, downloads, etc. you have.
- Use descriptions such as: popular choice, fastest-growing, most requested, best-selling, previously sold out, expected to sell out, and back in stock (these last three can also trigger urgency or loss aversion, as noted in Chapters 2 and 3).
- In B2B, show client logos and logos of professional associations you're associated with, as well as a list of industries and customer titles you serve.
- When appropriate, mention the number of years you've been in business or how much your company has expanded since starting.
- Use language such as: most people, many people, people like you, people in Massachusetts, other professionals in accounting, and people who also like golf.
- Highlight positive ratings, and keep in mind that a Northwestern University study (Collinger and Malthouse, 2015) found that "A shopper is more likely to purchase a product with an average star rating between 4.2 and 4.5 than one with a 5-star rating." The thinking is the less than perfect rating is more believable.
- Tell people that customers like them also purchased certain other items.
- Tap into brand ambassadors and social media influencers.
- Flag the number of a product sold, the number of people currently looking at it online, or the percentage sold out.
- Choose reassuring modifiers such as often, typically, usually, generally, and common.
- Market to affinity groups.
- Encourage referrals from your customers.

KEY TAKEAWAYS

1 When people are not sure of what to do, they'd rather feel confident than special.

2 People who are uncertain will follow the lead of others who are similar to them.

3 Social proof helps reassure customers they are making a good decision.

4   Social proof also helps cue people about how they should behave.

5   When a person sees other people doing something, that person often assumes those other people know something they don't.

6   Marketing can trigger social proof by pointing out that a large number of people already do something, or that people who are similar to your target do.

7   When using social proof, take care not to inadvertently leave people with the opposite message (that more people are doing something you don't want your target to do).

8   In addition to following the lead of people like themselves, people will also follow the lead of people they like.

9   When using celebrities, be aware of the associated costs and the fact that if the celebrity experiences a sudden scandal, it can hurt your brand.

10   Testimonials, case studies, customer lists, ratings, referrals, labels such as popular and back in stock, and words and phrases such as often and people like you and often can all trigger social proof.

In conclusion

People do what people like them—and people they like—do. Sometimes your target will feel pressure to conform, or feel they're missing out. Other times your target will be looking for help to make a choice. What they see others doing can be very influential.

In fact, your prospect may tell themselves that these other people know something they don't. And that's just one way that the story someone hears, or tells themselves, impacts their behavior, as you'll see in the following chapter.

References

Alter, A (2013) *Drunk Tank Pink: And other unexpected forces that shape how we think, feel, and behave*, Penguin Books, New York

Cialdini, R (1984) *Influence: The psychology of persuasion*, Quill William Morrow, New York

Collinger, T and Malthouse, E (2015) From Reviews to Revenue, Volume 1: How star ratings and review content influence purchase, *Northwestern University Power Reviews*, https://www.powerreviews.com/wp-content/uploads/2019/02/From-Reviews-to-Revenue-Northwestern-Report-Volume-1.pdf (archived at https://perma.cc/GP6N-VYR5)

Goldstein, N, Martin, S and Cialdini, R (2008) *Yes! 50 scientifically proven ways to be persuasive*, Free Press, New York

McLeod, S (2018) Solomon Asch—Conformity Experiment, *Simply Psychology*, 28 December

Menon, S (2021) How marketers sharpen their personalization playbook, *ANA*, 20 July, https://www.ana.net/magazines/show/id/forward-2021-07-adobe-personalization-playbook (archived at https://perma.cc/62H5-JFBS)

Thaler, R and Sunstein, C (2008) *Nudge: Improving decisions about health, wealth, and happiness*, Penguin Books, New York

Todd, J (2009) 'Most popular' status affects what people eat, study finds, *Duke Today*, 2 June, https://today.duke.edu/2009/06/dining_study.html (archived at https://perma.cc/WX5P-RYJT)

Tunçgenç, B, Zein, M, Sulik, J, Newson, M, Zhao, Y, Dezecache, G and Deroy, O (2021) Social influence matters: We follow pandemic guidelines most when our close circle does, *British Journal of Psychology*, 20 January, https://bpspsychub.onlinelibrary.wiley.com/doi/10.1111/bjop.12491 (archived at https://perma.cc/P2PU-WLWM)

Zoghby, J (2018) Making It Personal: Pulse Check 2018, *Accenture Interactive*, https://www.accenture.com/_acnmedia/PDF-77/Accenture-Pulse-Survey.pdf (archived at https://perma.cc/B7FV-3XP4)

06

Storytelling: increasing consumer involvement and engagement

Stories are not only engaging and involving, they are processed in the brain differently than facts and figures are. Behavioral scientists have shown that people better understand and remember information when it's delivered in a story. This means that a properly constructed story can be an ideal vehicle for a marketer to deliver their message.

Everybody has "that" summer job story. For me, it involved a statue of the Virgin Mary and a potentially sacrilegious act. But perhaps I should start at the beginning.

The summer between my freshmen and sophomore years in college, I went home to Meriden, CT. Like the rest of my friends, I needed to earn some money, so I answered a help wanted ad for a sales associate at The Glassworks. After a short interview, which included the question "Do you like to dust?", I was offered the job.

The Glassworks was a factory story in downtown Meriden. It sold what today would be called call mid-century modern glassware. There were shelves and shelves of colorful items made of glass—vases, paperweights in the shape of small animals, figurines, candlesticks, bowls molded to look like pineapples, goblets, candy dishes with ornate swans on the lids, and other assorted knickknacks.

As it turns out, these are actually considered collector's items today. But at the time I worked in the store, let's just say foot traffic was on the light side and there was ample time to dust. One day a customer did walk into the store and really wanted to make a purchase. Naturally, I really wanted to help her. But there was a problem. The woman had come in to buy a glass statue of the Virgin Mary, the Madonna.

We were well-stocked in Madonna statues. The problem was, it wasn't just the Madonna she wanted. It was supposed to come in a set that included a glass base to sit the statue on, and a small votive candle that the customer could put on that base behind the statue, to let the candlelight illuminate the Virgin Mary from behind. We had the statue. We had the votive candle. But for some reason I never understood, we could not seem to find the base.

The woman was growing distressed. She really had wanted to buy this set. In her mind, the statue and the candle alone were not enough. She needed a base to display them on. Seeing her disappointment, I said "Wait a minute, let me check something. I may have a solution." I dashed to the stockroom in the back. I quickly scanned the shelves. And I found what I was looking for.

To the mild horror of the store manager, I returned with a glass ashtray that was monogrammed with a large letter "M" on the bottom. I told the customer M could stand for "Mary" or "Madonna."

"Mother of God," she added helpfully.

"Yes," I emphatically agreed.

The ashtray was about the size of a small dinner plate. I flipped it over and explained that the M shape could work perfectly. On the overturned ashtray, she could tuck the votive candle into the V space that forms in the middle of the M. And then she could center the statue right at the bottom of the M. It was like a customized base for the Blessed Virgin statue.

The customer was delighted. She was able to get what she wanted. She bought the statue, the votive candle holder, and the ashtray to display them on—and went home a happy woman. I, on the other hand, probably should have gone to confession.

In 2021, I read Tamsen Webster's new book, *Find Your Red Thread: Make your big ideas irresistible*, which provides excellent advice for creating your marketing story. In it, she advises, "If you want to drive action, you need to build the story people will tell themselves about your idea." While my Madonna and ashtray example may not be exactly what she had in mind, I think it may prove the point. The customer wanted a base for her statue. My rather unconventional idea was to use a monogrammed ashtray. I pointed out that M was the letter Madonna and Mary began with. I showed her how the letter shape seemed tailor-made to accommodate both the statue and the votive candle. And she bought into my story. It became the one she would tell herself and others.

FIGURE 6.1 M is for Mary

With the right story, a monogrammed ashtray became a pedestal for a religious statue.

Stories stoke emotion. And emotion drives decisions. For this reason, stories can quite literally move people.

Stories can be magically persuasive for marketers—and science shows us why

Storytelling has become a bit of a buzzword in marketing. All of a sudden, lots of gurus started to recommend the approach. Blogposts, conference keynotes, and workshops were devoted to the art of storytelling. Once reserved for movies and books, storytelling became a marketing tool. Marketers were advised that instead of getting to the point right away, instead of leading with the most important information, they should tell a story.

While there are times it still makes sense to get to the point quickly and to lead with the big news, there are other times when starting with—or incorporating—a story is a smart strategic move. After all, stories are engaging. Stories are involving. Stories are how information was passed from generation to generation before the written word. Clearly, they wield power.

Neuroeconomist Paul Zak puts it this way: "When you want to motivate, persuade, or be remembered, start with a story of human struggle and eventual triumph. It will capture people's hearts—by first attracting their brains" (Zak, 2014).

The human brain is hardwired for stories. Science has found that stories help people make sense of the world. They make important lessons easier to remember. And they let people come to their own conclusions, which is especially important to marketers who need people to make decisions. As Joe Vitale notes in *Hypnotic Writing: How to seduce and persuade customers with only your words*, while a person may argue with what someone else, such as a marketer, tells them, they "rarely argue with their own conclusions." This can make storytelling especially effective if you're dealing with skeptical or difficult-to-convince prospects.

A fine example of leading a prospect to draw their own conclusion is the classic *Wall Street Journal* subscription letter, written by Martin Conroy. It remained an unbeaten control for 28 years, and generated an estimated $2 billion in subscriptions for the paper. The letter, referred to as "A Tale of Two Men," told the story of two college graduates who were very similar, and who ended up working for the same Midwestern manufacturing company.

When the two men attend their 20-year college reunion, the reader finds out that one is now the president of that company and the other is just a middle manager. As the story unfolds, readers discover that the man who is president is also the one who subscribes to the *Wall Street Journal*. While the letter never explicitly says that is why he became president, readers come to the conclusion that this played an important role in his success.

Brain differences between stories and factual statements

When your prospect or customer hears or reads your story, it engages their brain differently than if you were just feeding them facts and figures. Scientists have found that Broca's area and Wernicke's area are the two parts of the brain responsible for processing language. But when a person gets involved in a story, more parts of their brain are engaged.

For example, if the story involves smell, the olfactory cortex will get activated. If it involves motion, their motor cortex will get activated. The end result is that the more parts of a person's brain that are activated, the better they will understand the information and the longer they will retain it. And the powerful impact doesn't stop there. Kendall Haven, author of *Story Proof* and *Story Smart*, reports that "Research confirms that well-designed stories are the most effective vehicle for exerting influence." In other words, stories are not just for building your brand. They can be used to prompt action too.

As a marketer, you can use storytelling to land your message and motivate your desired behavior. Rather than try to bombard your target with all the pertinent information, or argue them into buying, you can draw them in and make them part of your tale.

Tim Ash, author of *Unleash Your Primal Brain: Demystifying how we think and why we act*, notes the powerful effect stories have on humans. He says, "Consuming stories influences our beliefs, teaches us facts, *alters our future behaviors*, and changes our personalities.... They [stories] effortlessly bypass logical and conscious defenses, and shape our closely guarded core beliefs" (emphasis mine).

In fact, through storytelling, not only can you make your target part of your tale, you can also make your tale part of your target. You can put your ideas into their heads. Neuroscientist Uri Hasson has studied the effects of stories on humans. In his words, "A story is the only way to activate parts in the brain so that a listener turns the story into their own idea and experience" (Widrich, 2012).

His research has shown that when one person listens to another person tell a story, their brains actually synchronize. The neurons in the listener's brain fire in the same way as the ones in the storyteller's brain. Behavioral scientists refer to the activity of these mirror neurons (see Chapter 1) as neural coupling. Stories can literally put you and your customers on the same wavelength.

Additionally, stories have the ability to create empathy and emotional connections. As your customers get more involved in your story, they undergo a process called narrative transportation. They are transported into the world of the story's characters, and they experience what those characters are feeling. For example, they can feel stress, fear, frustration, anger, dread or any of the emotions someone may feel when encountering the problem your product can solve. Similarly, they can also feel pride, relief, happiness, confidence, delight or any of the emotions that come with solving a problem using your product. Since emotions drive decisions, and marketers seek decisions, creating communications that prompt people to experience emotion is very important (see Chapter 1). The stories you tell can make people feel what you need them to in order to make a purchase.

As your customers and prospects are caught up in the emotions of your story, their brains respond by releasing certain hormones. These hormones include dopamine, which is linked to the brain's reward system, cortisol, which focuses attention, and oxytocin, which promotes trust. If you set out to create a chemical cocktail for marketing, this would be a pretty good mix. The dopamine fuels the seeking of rewards (your product or service and what it allows someone to accomplish). The cortisol makes people attentive and alert (to your messaging). And the oxytocin engenders trust (when people trust you, they're more likely to buy from you).

Research shows stories also add value to your product

A group of journalists became researchers and conducted a very interesting experiment, called the Significant Objects Project (significantobjects.com). They began by going to yard sales, garage sales, thrift stores and the like, and buying items people were trying to get rid of. This would ultimately include a Utah snow globe, a duck vase, and a set of Bar Mitzvah bookends, among many other things.

Then they wrote a story about each of the objects they'd bought, and listed the object along with the story on eBay. The stories weren't meant to be factual, they were just meant to be stories. And that was made clear in the eBay listings.

In the first phase of the experiment, they spent $128.74 on the objects (roughly $1.25 apiece) and sold them for $3,612.51, which was quite a handsome return on their investment. In the second phase, they spent $134.89 on objects, and sold them for $3,992.93, which was donated to charity.

Their goal had not been to make money *per se*, but rather to demonstrate that stories can add value to an item. Or, as the Significant Objects Project authors put it, "that the effect of narrative on any given object's subjective value can be measured objectively." By way of example, the Utah snow globe, which they'd purchased for 99 cents, sold for $59. If stories can make trinkets and yard sale junk this valuable, imagine what they can do for your product or service.

Stories have another scientific advantage that works for marketers

Stories, by definition, have a beginning, a middle, and an end. It turns out that humans are hardwired to want to get to that end. Social scientists have identified a principle they refer to as the Zeigarnik Effect, which is the human tendency to remember things that are incomplete, and to want to complete them (read more about this in Chapter 8).

A well-told story can trigger the Zeigarnik Effect. Once people get pulled in, they want to know what happens next and how things end. As a result, they will keep reading, watching, or listening.

Perhaps that's why Jonah Berger, author of *Contagious: Why things catch on*, says "You can deliver any message inside, if the Trojan Horse—or vehicle of the message—is a story" (Weldon, 2014). The stories you use in your marketing can prompt people to invite you in, without even realizing that you come bearing a sales message.

Additionally, that message will be more memorable. Cognitive psychologist Jerome Bruner claims that "a fact, wrapped in a story is 22-times more memorable" (Harris, 2012). And Paul Zak offers a possible explanation as to why. He states, "Stories that are personal and emotionally compelling engage more of the brain, and thus are better remembered, than simply stating a set of facts" (Zak, 2013).

While not one of Zak's studies, the following example supports his finding.

Traveling by trimaran in Tortola

The story starts in Tortola. No, actually, it starts way before Tortola. For quite some time, I had wanted to take a sailing vacation. I live in Massachusetts and grew up in Connecticut, both along the eastern seaboard, but I've never really sailed. Sure, there'd been a handful of one-hour harbor tours and tranquil sunset sails, but those hardly counted. I wanted to spend a week on a sailboat, with the wind in my hair and a rum drink in my hand.

So, I talked it up with friends. For years. I described island hopping about the Caribbean. Snorkeling over shipwrecks. Sipping PainKillers at the famous Soggy Dollar beach bar. I was relentless in my enthusiasm. About five years in, they finally acquiesced, and agreed that our next group vacation could be on a trimaran in Tortola, complete with a four-person crew who would sail, cook, and be our guides. I was ecstatic.

I was also concerned about motion sickness. Any air travel I did was always on Dramamine®. And the one time my friend Ken took me fishing in his brother's motorboat, I turned green as soon as we dropped anchor. I knew seasickness could pose a problem. So, I had my doctor write me a prescription for a Scopolamine patch, and I bought some Dramamine® as backup. But I had reservations. Apparently, you were supposed to avoid alcohol with the Scope patch, and I had no plans to see Tortola as a teetotaler. Plus, Dramamine always made me fall asleep, and while this was my dream vacation, I wanted to be awake for it.

After doing more research, I discovered a battery-operated device called a Reliefband, which purported to stop nausea from motion sickness or chemotherapy by blocking the nerve signals that tell your brain you feel sick. No drugs, and no side effects. It looked like a sports watch and sounded like a miracle. I bought one and added it to my motion sickness arsenal.

Finally, it came time to fly to Tortola and, the next day, board our boat. The first mate greeted us at the dock in a rigid-bottom inflatable dinghy and motored us out to the trimaran, which was anchored in the bay. As the seven of us stepped onboard, the captain invited us to store our bags and sit down to enjoy the beautiful lunch she had laid out for us.

With the trimaran gently rocking, I eyed the shrimp and salad on the plate in front of me and knew that was where they would stay. The waves in the bay were ripples compared to the waves of nausea that were washing over me. All I could think of was that six of my best friends were on that boat because of me, because I'd sold them on this idea of a great vacation, and I was going to ruin it because I felt sick before we'd even set sail. I froze my lips into a smile and then, through gritted teeth, urged my cabinmate to Go. Get. The. Wristband.

And then, within minutes of putting it on, I felt fine. The nausea completely disappeared. Unlike a motion sickness pill, which needs to be taken hours in advance of the anticipated distress, this stopped the queasiness in its tracks. My vacation was saved. The Tortola trimaran trip remains an all-time favorite. And I have told this tale to anyone who mentions motion sickness. It would not surprise me to learn that a number of product sales can be traced back to me. Because rather than just telling people there is a battery-operated wristband you can buy that stops seasickness, I told them my story.

MISTAKE

Missing the opportunity to associate your product or service with a story. When you choose the story, you control the narrative—influencing how people think of your brand.

CASE STUDY
A spicy story

From the Caribbean, let's head to Mexico, home of tequila. When a US-based spirits company was launching a premium spiced tequila, they needed the agency where I was working to create some direct marketing for it. The proprietary blend of herbs and spices was meant to enhance the flavor, and to make the spirit smooth. Our job was to create a direct mail package that generated some buzz around the new tequila and offered a rebate to purchasers.

The creative team explored several options. To call attention to the spiced taste, one involved sending a partially shredded letter, that appeared about to reveal the secret blend of spices right where the shredding began.

Another emphasized the smoothness of the premium beverage, with copy inviting people to experience the tequila "naked"—without the salt and lime that traditionally accompany shots of the liquor, and that can mask an inferior product.

But the winning concept told a story. It started with the package exterior, a mysterious, lumpy, brown padded bag. The mailer, which was designed by art director Carla Baratta, carried no teaser copy and no return address, just a Mexican Customs mark and a faux postal cancelation stamp from Tequila, Mexico. That stamp was positioned next to the US canceled stamp. It looked so believable that when a sample was mailed to the production manager's house, his wife was convinced he'd been on a press check in Mexico and had sent her some turquoise jewelry.

Inside was a letter, a wanted poster, a rebate form, and a cork and a label from the bottle. The letter told a story about how the secret recipe for the new premium tequila was believed to have been smuggled over the border from Mexico into the United States. It said there was reason to believe some of the spirit was going to surface in the recipients' area, and requested their help in tracking it down.

The wanted poster showed the front and side shots of the bottle, and listed the identifying characteristics. The cork and label were offered as ways to help confirm a sighting. Recipients were instructed to locate and buy a bottle, and send proof of capture on the rebate form to collect their reward.

Like many good stories, this one relied on a willing suspension of disbelief. But it was engaging, imaginative, and successful. The key facts were woven into the story. And the package pulled a double-digit response rate, claiming Best of Show honors at the Target Marketing Awards.

What makes a good story?

In order for a marketer to tell a good story, you need to move beyond facts, features, benefits, and statistics. Instead, you want to paint a mental picture for your customers and prospects, involve their emotions, and make them care. In order to do that, follow these guidelines:

- Start strong—make sure you grab the attention of your audience.
- Choose a subject that they will find interesting and compelling. Hint: it's not about what you're selling, it's about what the product you're selling can do for the person who buys it.
- Remember that good stories are relatable and forge connections. As Rohit Bhargava writes in his *Nonobvious Guide to Marketing & Branding Without a Big Budget*, "People trust stories they can relate to."
- Choose specific nouns and powerful verbs that help readers envision the action. My high school writing teacher used to say there was a big difference between "Sam True smoked" and "Sam True ate cigars." He was right.
- Write in an active versus passive voice.
- You can structure your story to follow the dramatic arc: exposition, rising action, climax, falling action, and resolution.

As Tim Ash explains in *Unleash Your Primal Brain*:

> All stories, despite the variety of superficial differences, share a basic structure. In a story, we want something and need to overcome obstacles to achieve it. The story reliably proceeds from complication, through crisis, and finally to resolution. In its own way, big or small, each story has a hero confronting some sort of trouble and struggling to overcome it.

A SPECIAL NOTE FOR FUNDRAISERS

When used properly, storytelling can be a very effective approach to fundraising. The key is to resist the urge the talk about all the people your organization helps, and instead tell the story of just one person.

Social scientists call this the Identifiable Victim Effect. What they've found is that people are more likely to feel empathy, and as a result to help, when they hear about the plight of one person versus that of a bigger, vaguer group of people. In fact, research shows focusing on a single victim can double the donations that a charity solicitation receives (Small et al., 2005).

While it's wonderful that a large number of people benefit from your charity, tell the story of just one of them in your marketing messages. Use your statistics as support points. Some fundraising organizations do this particularly well. The Wounded Warrior Project, which assists veterans and active service personnel, sent me an email under the banner "I am living proof," with a subject line that stated, "Here's my story." The message featured one warrior's personal story. As Mother Teresa is quoted as saying, "If I look at the mass I will never act. If I look at the one, I will" (Slovic, 2007).

I've also seen some impressive examples of storytelling in political fundraising. An email from US presidential candidate Hillary Clinton began with a story that was studded with specific details, and made the author relatable:

> When I started my freshman year at Wellesley, I didn't hit my stride right away. I thought I might study to be a doctor or scientist—until I enrolled in some math and geology courses! I tried my hand at foreign languages, and my French professor said, "Mademoiselle, your talents lie elsewhere."

Similarly, when Michelle Obama was fundraising for Organizing for Action (OFA), a nonprofit spearheaded by former US President Barack Obama, she sent an email that began:

> Every year on Valentine's Day I can't help but think back to my first date with Barack. I had been reluctant to go out with him, but he was persistent, and I eventually said yes.

Starting the email with this story grabs the readers' attention, and makes them feel like they know Michelle a little better.

9 proven ways for marketers to use storytelling

Your story can appear in a number of formats—written in an email or social post, featured on your website, captured on video, recounted in a tv commercial, radio spot, print ad or direct mail piece. Similarly, your story can serve a variety of needs. For example:

- You can use a story in order to broach a difficult or delicate topic. Poo-Pourri is a product that people spray in the toilet bowl before using the bathroom in order to prevent odors. Not necessarily a topic that is comfortable to talk about. They created a humorous video story about a girl having dinner with her boyfriend's family to demonstrate the need for, and use of, the product. It received over 14 million views on YouTube.

- You can tell the story of how your company came to be. Life is Good is an apparel company, best known for their fun t-shirts. Their founder's story is featured on their website, with the headline "One van. Two brothers. Three simple words." It tells the story of the two Jacobs brothers, who were selling t-shirts they designed out of a secondhand van, and how when they started printing shirts with optimistic sayings, their business took off.

- There are also disruptor stories—stories of companies, products, or services that changed the way we do business. Think about Tesla, Amazon, Uber, Netflix, Lemonade, and others, and the stories they tell about why they exist.

- Birth of a product stories can also make excellent marketing content. Post-it® Notes from 3M are a good example. A scientist is trying to invent stronger adhesives and instead invents one that's weaker. He shares his discovery with his colleagues and keeps trying to find a use for it. One day, a colleague is frustrated that the scraps of paper he uses to mark pages in his church choir hymnal keep falling out, and the rest is history.

- Some brands use stories to promote their corporate social responsibility. For example, the shoe company Toms invests one-third of its profits for grassroots good. Hearing that story likely sways some people to shop with them over their competitors.

- Product usage stories can be very powerful, whether they introduce a new product, feature different ways to use an existing product, or highlight customers telling a story about their use of a product, similar to my story about the Reliefband.

- You can also tell "customer as hero" stories, accounts of how your customer succeeded with the help of your product. For example, imagine you sell employee health plans to companies. You can, as one company I know did, tell the story of a human resources executive who, after choosing your insurance, commented it was the only time in her career that employees didn't complain about having a new plan. Telling a story like this is more impactful and memorable than a marketer simply stating that their product is highly rated by customers.

- If you're in a commodity or competitive marketplace, tell your single differentiator story. Find the one story you can talk about that sets you apart, even if it is only ancillary to what you sell. For example, the Magic Castle Hotel in Los Angeles has a red popsicle hotline phone by their modest swimming pool. When guests pick it up, a gloved server arrives with a tray bearing a free ice pop. This story of what makes them different also makes them popular.

- Finally, stories that define a company's standard of customer service can be very powerful and very effective. Years ago, I heard the story of a young guest who left a teddy bear behind at a Grand Hyatt in Hawaii. Not only did the hotel find the bear and ship it back, they sent pictures of it enjoying its "extended stay" at the resort. That effort to go above and beyond communicates so much, and makes the story both emotional and memorable.

KEY TAKEAWAYS

1   Stories are engaging, entertaining, and the way information was passed from person to person before the written word.

2   The human brain is hardwired for stories. It uses them to make sense of the world.

3   Stories are more memorable than facts.

4   Stories allow people to come to their own conclusions. While people may argue with what others tell them, they usually don't argue with themselves. This makes storytelling a smart strategy when dealing with skeptical prospects you'd like to win over.

5   The brain processes stories differently than data and statistics. More parts of the brain get activated when hearing or reading a story. As a result, people understand the information better and remember it longer.

6   Stories impact people's beliefs and their behaviors, making them useful for building brands and for motivating response.

7   According to neuroscientist Uri Hasson, "A story is the only way to activate parts in the brain so that a listener turns the story into their own idea and experience." As a marketer, you can plant your ideas into the minds of your target using a story.

8   Listening to a story can prompt neural coupling, when the brain waves of the storyteller and the listener sync up.

9   Stories also cause narrative transportation, pulling readers in so that they feel what the characters are feeling. They generate empathy and create emotional connections.

10   When engaged in a story, a person's brain releases the hormones dopamine, oxytocin, and cortisol, which can aid the buying decision.

11   Research proves stories can add value to an item.

12   Stories take advantage of the Zeigarnik Effect, the human tendency to remember incomplete things and want to finish them.

13   Good stories grab attention, are compelling and relatable, include specific details and powerful verbs, and often follow the dramatic arc structure.

14   You can tell various stories, including a founder's story, a birth of a product story, a customer as hero story, your single differentiator story, and a customer service story.

In conclusion

Stories are powerful. They engage more parts of the human brain than facts do. As a result, they are more memorable and more persuasive. By telling your customers a story, you can plant ideas in their heads, influence the emotions they feel, and increase their inclination to trust you.

In a not insignificant way, people are under your control when they are under the spell of your story. And that puts you in a very desirable position. Because as you'll see in the next chapter, humans don't yield control easily.

References

Ash, T (2021) *Unleash Your Primal Brain: Demystifying how we think and why we act*, Morgan James, New York

Bhargava, R (2021) *Nonobvious Guide to Marketing & Branding Without a Big Budget*, Ideapress Publishing, Virginia

Harris, M (2012) Neuroscience proves stories trump facts, *Insight Demand*, 01 November, https://insightdemand.com/neuroscience-stories-trump-facts/#_edn1 (archived at https://perma.cc/BEQ6-BEJW)

Haven, K (2007a) *Story Proof*, Libraries Unlimited

Haven, K (2007b) *Story Smart*, Libraries Unlimited

Significant Objects and How They Got That Way, https://significantobjects.com/about/ (archived at https://perma.cc/WCZ5-RLM7)

Slovic, P (2007) "If I look at the mass I will never act": Psychic numbing and genocide, *Judgement and Decision Making*, 19 April, http://journal.sjdm.org/7303a/jdm7303a.htm (archived at https://perma.cc/G94V-HJ34)

Small, DA, Loewenstein, G and Slovic, P (2005) Can insight breed callousness? The impact of learning about the identifiable victim effect on sympathy, Unpublished manuscript. https://scholar.google.com/scholar?q=identifiable+victim+effect+Small,+Loewenstein,+Slovic,+2005&hl=en&as_sdt=0&as_vis=1&oi=scholart (archived at https://perma.cc/D9MQ-D7L9)

Vitale, J (2007) *Hypnotic Writing: How to seduce and persuade customers with only your words*, John Wiley & Sons, Inc., New Jersey

Webster, T (2021) *Find Your Red Thread: Make your big ideas irresistible*, Page Two Books, Vancouver

Weldon, M (2014) Your brain on story: Why narratives win our hearts and minds, *Northwestern Now*, 24 April, https://news.northwestern.edu/stories/2014/04/opinion-pacstandard-weldon-narrative/ (archived at https://perma.cc/HZA7-6C7L)

Widrich, L (2012) The science of storytelling: Why telling a story is the most powerful way to activate our brains, *Lifehacker*, 05 December, https://lifehacker.com/the-science-of-storytelling-why-telling-a-story-is-the-5965703 (archived at https://perma.cc/NE58-JCUZ)

Zak, P (2013) How stories change the brain, *Greater Good*, 17 December, https://greatergood.berkeley.edu/article/item/how_stories_change_brain (archived at https://perma.cc/8VJR-HNJL)

Zak, P (2014) Why your brain loves good storytelling, *Harvard Business Review*, 28 October, https://hbr.org/2014/10/why-your-brain-loves-good-storytelling (archived at https://perma.cc/VM54-VXJ4)

07

Autonomy bias: harnessing the human need for control

Humans have an innate desire to be in control of themselves and their surroundings. Marketers who can give their customers some sense of control, including the opportunity to co-create or to make choices, will appeal to those customers. However, providing too much choice, or providing choices that are not easily distinguishable from one another, can put off customers and produce a negative effect on response.

While writing this chapter I developed an earworm. You know what I mean, one of those songs that gets stuck in your head and just stays on repeat, as if it were playing on a vintage '80s record player with the arm set in the perpetual replay position.

The song in question is the classic "My Way." It's being performed by the legendary Frank Sinatra. In particular, it's the refrain that is stuck in my head. His rendition of the "I did it my way" part of the lyrics.

I keep hearing it over and over in my head. To me it sounds as if Mr Sinatra is broadcasting a message meant just for marketers, as if he were using a special version of one of those high-frequency dog whistles that only canines can hear, but this one works by being tuned in to the frequency for marketing.

As marketers, we do lean toward doing things our way. We are laser focused on our key performance indicators, continually monitoring a variety of open rates, click rates, response rates, and more. Some of you may have spent a good deal of effort developing customer personas and plotting out customer journeys, in a comprehensive effort to understand the mindsets and typical actions of your targets. Others of you may boil things down to their essence, and concentrate primarily on beating controls, benchmarks, and projections by continually testing offers, creative, and lists.

Either way, you know exactly what you want your customers and prospects to do. And you have a careful plan to get them there. You have engineered a path, be it simple or sophisticated, that leads to the desired result. Whether you intend for them to take a series of prescribed actions that culminate in a sale, or you just want them to go for that immediate purchase, your focus is on making things happen. You have figured out what people should do and how they should do it... which, in a phrase, is your way.

However, there's a problem with that. Because as fervently as you want your customers and prospects to do things your way, as convinced as you are that it represents the ideal and perhaps even well-researched way, your target audience may feel differently. In fact, they likely do. The reason? They, too, are channeling their inner Frank Sinatra. At the end of the day, they want to know they did things their way.

Think about it. Who wants to be told what to do? Virtually no one. Unless someone is really lost and looking for direction, they rarely want to be dictated to. Add to that the fact that people often have their own methods of doing things, the approach that works for them or suits their situation, and you have found even more reasons for your target to do things their way. This means that your plan for the way you want your target to behave has to factor in their need for autonomy.

> People are driven by a strong need to exert some control over themselves and their environment.

Autonomy bias is one of the most powerful drivers of human behavior

Humans innately desire agency—the ability to make their own decisions and to act with a certain level of independence. When people have it, they feel happier, less stressed, and more satisfied. Studies show people who can exercise a level of autonomy are often healthier and more productive, too.

Researchers observed an interesting example of autonomy bias as they watched people at crosswalks in New York City. The city had converted the crossing signs to an automatic system that alternately displayed either the walk or do not walk signals. However, because it was costly to remove the buttons that people had formerly pushed to produce a walk signal, the city left them in place. Researchers saw that when people pushed the button, they would be more likely to wait to cross the street, even though pushing the button did not affect how quickly the walk sign appeared. However, the mere fact that people thought they had some control influenced their behavior.

In another study, researchers found that when people who were encouraged to exercise could choose their own exercise regimen, they stated they were more satisfied with the program than those people who had randomly been assigned specific exercises to do. Being able to exert some control over the exercise program versus having it imposed on people made a difference in their perception of it.

And in a third study, perhaps the most eye-opening, residents of a facility for the aged were divided into two groups. The test group was allowed to make a couple of simple choices. They could choose which plant they wanted to grow in their room, and which movies they wished to watch. The control group could not.

At the end of 18 months, researchers noted there were twice as many deaths in the control group. Research such as this has led some scientists to believe the human need for autonomy has a biological basis. In other words, people don't acquire their desire to exert control over themselves and their environments, they are born with it.

In all three of these studies, the role of choice is key. As Dan Russell notes in his 2020 Vivid Labs article "Autonomy Bias," "The existence of a choice means a person has autonomy, and the existence of autonomy gives a person confidence that they are in control." When people have choices, they feel in control. And feeling a sense of control answers the deep-seated human need for autonomy.

Even with the walk signal buttons that were no longer functional, people still felt they were in control—that they were taking an action that would help shape their situation. Researcher Ellen Langer puts it this way: "Taking some action leads people to feel a sense of control over a situation, and that feels good, rather than just being a passive bystander" (Prisco, 2018).

MISTAKE

Providing only one option. When possible, offer two or three. This will prompt people to choose between them, instead of focusing on whether or not they want to respond at all.

Marketers can use single choice aversion to increase sales

Marketers looking to trigger autonomy bias can certainly do so by offering their customers and prospects a choice. When you put one option in front of your target, for example one product, one proposal, or one service level, that person has nothing to compare it to, and no immediate context in which to evaluate it.

As a result, people often delay their decisions. They tell themselves they'll do some research, they'll think it over, or maybe they'll discuss it with a spouse, friend or business associate. But what happens? They typically don't get around to doing that. Life intervenes, and the buying decision gets delayed or in some cases never happens.

Researcher Daniel Mochon of Tulane University studied single option aversion. He ran an experiment in which people could purchase a DVD player (Mochon, 2013). In some cases, they were shown a Sony product. In other cases, they were shown the Sony product along with a Philips product. Mochon found that when the Sony DVD player was the sole option, only 9 percent of study participants said they would buy it. But when the two options were presented, 32 percent of participants indicated they would buy the Sony product, nearly quadrupling purchase intent. Additional research showed that when there is only one option presented, people might even refuse to purchase a product that they ordinarily would have chosen.

Being offered only one option is also known as a "Hobson's Choice." When presented with it, people focus on whether or not they want that individual item. However, when two or three options are presented to them, the decision shifts from "do I or do I not want this?" to "which of these would I like?" While the option to not buy at all still remains, it can drop out of the consideration set as people's mental energies are focused on comparing and contrasting the two or three choices they've been offered.

Similarly, simply reminding people that they have a choice can also prompt them to make the decision you hope they will. Rather than just focus your entire sales message on your product or service, you might try including what *Neuromarketing* blog author Roger Dooley describes as the "Four words that double persuasion." He's referring to using the BYAF technique, where the letters stand for the phrase "but you are free" (Dooley, nd).

Once you deliver your marketing argument and strong call for action, conclude with those words, which remind customers that they are in control. Christopher Carpenter of Western Illinois University reviewed 42 studies that involved 22,000 participants, and found that the BYAF technique can double your success rate (Dooley, nd).

What's more, you don't have to use those exact words. Other phrases, such as "the choice is yours," or "it's up to you" can also be effective. The key is to point out that it's the customer who is in control. They're the ones with the power. And if they agree to your request, it's because they are choosing to do so.

AUTONOMY BIAS AND THE PANDEMIC

As I write this chapter in the summer of 2021, it is apparent that Covid-19 is still a threat. The pandemic has provided behavioral scientists with plenty of opportunity to both observe human behavior and to test ways to influence it.

Loss aversion (Chapter 2) and social proof (Chapter 5) are two obvious behavioral science principles that are relevant to the situation. The desire to protect against the loss of life, income, routine, and so many other things threatened by the pandemic has certainly triggered the feeling of loss aversion. And the sense of uncertainty brought on by this new coronavirus has made many people feel they're not sure how to behave, and as a result they're following the lead of others, on everything from stockpiling toilet paper to wearing a mask. Autonomy bias is another behavioral science principle that definitely comes into play.

Here in the United States as well as around the world, groups of people protested forced lockdowns and mandated mask wearing. While the reasons they cited were varied, it can't be denied that these covid restrictions impacted their autonomy. People did not feel the same sense of control that they had pre-pandemic. In fact, for many, events felt wildly out of their control. Additionally, people found their choices being restricted in numerous ways, from the large, sweeping ones to smaller ones such as what products were and were not available on their store shelves.

The impact of the pandemic will likely be felt for some time. Even once things begin to approach a new normal, your customers and prospects will still be feeling the effects of what they've been through.

As a marketer, you'll want to factor that into your plans. Consider how autonomy bias, and choice and control, should influence the messages you send. While offering people options is generally a smart marketing move, it may become increasingly more so. Additionally, you may wish to find new ways to let your customers and prospects experience a feeling of control, both in the decisions they'll make and in the way they're asked to make them. This can have implications for your user experience, customer service, and message clarity, among other aspects of your marketing.

Keep in mind, too, that some customer expectations and behaviors may never revert back to those of pre-pandemic times. An October 2020 McKinsey survey found that "responses to Covid-19 have speeded the adoption of digital technologies by several years." A key response for companies was "interacting with customers in digital channels" (LaBerge et al., 2020).

Customers who have enjoyed any increased control will in all probability want to retain it. Innovations such as curbside pickup and contactless delivery are two that come to mind. Marketers will not only want to maintain the level of control the pandemic may have forced them to offer to their customers, they'll want to be aware of the fact that they'll be judged against other companies who may have offered more.

It will be important for your marketing messages to highlight any relevant aspects of autonomy, because this will help them resonate with your target.

CASE STUDY
Appealing to people's desire for control

In a vintage *Saturday Night Live* skit, comedian Lily Tomlin played a telephone operator and delivered the line "We don't care. We don't have to. We're the phone company." At the time the skit aired on the comedy show, the United States was served by a single phone company, AT&T. But in 1984, a court judgment presided over by Judge Harold H. Greene broke up the AT&T monopoly and, among other ramifications, really opened the door to competition in the long-distance market (Hershey, 2020).

At the time, I was a newly minted copywriter working for a marketing agency that was tasked with retaining AT&T's long-distance customers. While you might think that inertia and the human bias toward the status quo (see Chapter 11) would be all that the telephone company needed, there were several factors that could offset this. For one, consumers and businesses now had a choice of which telecom they could use. Choice and novelty (see Chapter 9) are both powerful draws.

Additionally, these new long-distance competitors were underpricing AT&T's long-distance service, advertising attractive savings to prospective customers. As we know, people do not like to lose out on savings (see Chapter 2).

And, perhaps most important, inertia alone would not be enough. Because people who did wish to remain with AT&T still needed to make that desire known. They were required to actively designate a long-distance company, even if the company they were picking was the one they'd historically used.

Naturally, the agency created campaign after campaign to convince customers to stay with AT&T. But as the deadline for businesses to designate their long-distance carrier loomed, Frank Parrish, my creative director at the agency, was laboring over the messaging for a final attempt letter to get them to pick AT&T. Because the company's mailing list was (surprisingly) not segmented at the time, he knew the message "would have to appeal universally to all business owners—from the pizza shop owner to the owner of a mega-million dollar-enterprise."

One morning he came into the agency, and I remember him saying he'd finally found a way into the letter that he thought would work. His first sentence read, "You're facing an important decision and if you don't act quickly someone else will decide for you."

He was triggering autonomy bias. As we know, people are hardwired to want control over themselves and their environments. What business owner wouldn't pay attention to a letter with that lead? No one wants someone else taking away their power to make a decision that could impact their livelihood. And the phrase "act quickly" added just the right amount of urgency (see Chapter 3) to the copy.

The message hit home. The mailing delivered a 38.6 percent response rate, retaining significant business for AT&T, and demonstrating the power of a well-wielded behavioral science principle.

Reading that letter lead in the context of this chapter, you may see it as an easy application of the trigger. And now, with all you've learned, you may see other instances where tapping autonomy bias is the readily apparent solution to a marketing challenge. But for this assignment, Frank recalls that while he wrote the bulk of the lengthy letter in a day, it took him two weeks to write the lead. It is my hope that reading this chapter just saved you some time and effort!

Find ways to provide choice and control to motivate response

In the AT&T example, the strong autonomy message was "don't take control from me." However, there are other ways marketers can employ autonomy bias in their messaging.

Let's flash-forward a few decades, to a different client at a different agency where I was now a creative director. My creative team used autonomy bias in another way to create an extremely successful campaign for a satellite television company.

The company was trying to grow its customer base in a cord-cutting environment, in which many viewers were canceling their subscriptions in favor of streaming services. Research revealed that one of the biggest reasons people canceled was that they felt they were paying for too many channels they didn't watch, or that they couldn't find programing they liked. Our client was introducing some new programming bundles that offered fewer base channels at a lower rate—with the opportunity for customers to customize their television lineup by adding theme-based channel packs.

The creative team saw this as a great opportunity to leverage autonomy bias. People could take control and choose the channel packs they actually wanted, so they'd no longer be stuck paying for channels they never watched. In addition, viewers could choose to add or change packs whenever they felt like it.

The package delivered a 52 percent lift in sales over their long-standing control, the largest increase they'd seen from creative in many, many years. Key to its success was the use of an autonomy bias message that, by providing choices, put control into the hands of the customers.

While the idea of choice was central to the messaging for the satellite television company, there are times when the idea of choice can play a supporting role in your marketing campaigns. For example, some work I did for a tax preparation company focused mainly on the benefits of using that particular company—their considerable expertise, as well as the peace of mind a customer would feel when working with them.

However, we also emphasized that customers could choose how they wanted to get their taxes done. They could meet with a tax preparer. They could drop off their documents. Or they could send in their paperwork electronically. While not the main message of the communication, these several choices provided yet another reason to do business with the firm.

Making the most of choice

Another way you can employ autonomy bias is by emphasizing that it is your target—and not you—who is in charge. The children's cleft palate charity Smile Train did this brilliantly with one of their fundraising solicitations.

If you have ever donated to a charity, you know that it seems as if one donation opens the valve on a hydrant and suddenly, you're flooded with additional requests. As a result, some people may prefer not to donate in the first place. Smile Train overcame this barrier by sending a fundraising package with an envelope teaser that read: "Make one gift now and we'll never ask for another donation again."

The charity's CEO suggested the message mirrored the charity's work. Because the charity provides surgery that makes a permanent change in a child's life, the fundraising appeal would also allow a donor to make a permanent change with a single donation.

In the pilot program, the new messaging beat the control by 72 percent. Equally as important, only 39 percent of the donors indicated that they did not wish to be contacted again. The remaining 61 percent were open to some communications or to regular updates from the charity. These results allowed Smile Train to successfully roll out this approach to their entire list, knowing they could increase donations and still be able to resolicit the majority of their donors. The power of the appeal, I believe, lies in putting the donor in control.

Some companies sell products and services that by definition put their customers in the driver's seat. For example, I've done some marketing work for a couple of online colleges and universities.

One of the benefits I recommended emphasizing was that the students had more control. They could choose when and where to study. They could fit their classwork in around existing jobs or parenting responsibilities. They were in charge, unlike at a traditional university that would require their physical presence at set times.

This appeal to the human need for autonomy can be very motivating, and can help make the sale. What's important to note is that while other online universities might also offer this flexibility and control, if they don't emphasize it, they miss the opportunity to trigger autonomy bias and reap the resulting rewards.

Using choice as a competitive advantage

Some marketers are in the fortunate position to use choice as a competitive advantage. Because of the way they do business, or the way their business is structured, customer choice is an integral part of what they offer, and it sets them apart from competitors in their vertical.

One such company is Zillion Group, which is a health technology company that "empowers companies and individuals to make better health choices." They offer The Restore Suite of health and wellness programs, often through an employer, that help people manage or even prevent chronic medical conditions. Some of the conditions they commonly target include diabetes and high blood pressure. One of their core recommendations in combating these conditions is that people make healthy food choices and that they achieve a healthy weight, two behaviors that are not always easy to master.

What struck me when working with the company was the way they approached behavior change. For example, to encourage weight loss, you might think they would require people to count calories or to monitor meal portions. Or that they would have a hard and fast list of dos and don'ts, foods to eat and foods to avoid, and that some foods would be immediately forbidden. In other words, like some companies in that space, they would have a rather rigid system that needed to be adhered to in order to produce results.

But that is not what Zillion does. Baked into their program is a large element of customer choice. Customers are invited to work with their Zillion coaches to prioritize what they'll focus on, and choose what goals they plan to reach.

As a result, instead of being told to eliminate dessert from their diet, for instance, a member might choose to start skipping dessert every other night as they create their personalized pathway to weight loss. Similarly, someone who needed to drop some pounds might choose to first focus on consistently getting a good night's sleep, and only after achieving that goal decide to tackle changing the foods they eat.

As Zillion CEO and President Cheryl Morrison Deutsch says, the company is "focused on supporting individual choice and preference in order to nudge users toward long-lasting healthy habits." She points to the company's combination of "emphasizing individual lifestyle choices and engaging digital and human interaction" as the way to improve people's well-being and motivate real behavior change.

When she told me this, one of my first recommendations for how Zillion could use behavioral science in their marketing was to leverage autonomy bias. I suggested that they really play up the choice and control the customer would have, knowing this would appeal to an innate human desire. Additionally, it would help set them apart from other companies whose approach would appear more formulaic. Just as their program benefited from behavioral science, their marketing could, too.

Zillion was not my only client that offered a product with choice built in as a competitive advantage. If you are a US resident over the age of 65, you are probably familiar with Medicare, the federal health insurance program. And you may know that Medicare covers only about 80 percent of a person's healthcare costs, leaving them responsible for the remaining expenses.

FIGURE 7.1 Appealing to autonomy

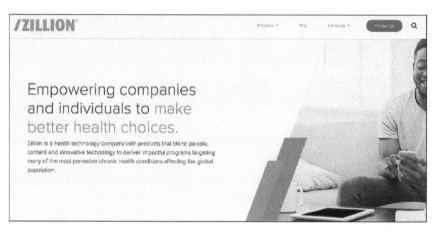

The homepage of Zillion.com highlights choices, which feed the human desire for autonomy.
Reproduced with kind permission of Zillion Group, 2021

Because of this, most people purchase either a Medicare supplement insurance plan or a Medicare Advantage plan to help cover the other costs. One of the big differences between the two options is that with a Medicare supplement plan, a person can choose to see any doctor that accepts Medicare. With a Medicare Advantage plan, people are generally restricted to a network of doctors.

I've helped clients market both Medicare supplement insurance and Medicare Advantage plans. With the former, I always come down hard on the ability to choose your own doctors, something the other option denies you. Along with price, it's one of the biggest factors in a decision like this. People want control. And when it comes to their healthcare, I suspect that desire is especially strong.

Autonomy bias can be used to prompt people to spend more

In the Medicare insurance example, the supplemental plans that let you choose to see any doctor you wish typically cost more than the Medicare Advantage plans that restrict you to doctors within a network. And that is not the only example of people being willing to pay more to feel in control. For instance, people will:

- Pay more to choose their own seat on an airplane. Tickets that do not allow them to pick where they'll sit can cost less.

- Pay more for the ability to change hotel reservations. The nightly price of a room can be higher if you want the ability to cancel and get your money back.
- Pay more for 100-calorie packs of certain snack items, so they can control how many calories they consume in one sitting. Buying a larger package of cookies or candy would be more economical, but require more attention and self-restraint.
- Pay more to stream music with no ads to interrupt what they choose to listen to.
- Pay more for a beach chair that has three position choices versus just one.
- Pay more for a fixed-rate home mortgage with a "float down" option that allows them to change their interest rate after it's been locked in.

BEWARE OF CHOICE OVERLOAD

While some choice is good, too many choices can actually backfire on marketers. People initially like all their options, but then struggle to make a decision. Some won't. Others, if they finally do, can experience buyer's remorse, wondering whether there was a better choice they didn't take.

In a famous experiment, psychologists Sheena Iyengar and Mark Lepper set up a table where people could sample jams in a supermarket (Geerts, 2017). On some days the table would have 24 different jam jars on it. On other days, it would have only six.

While more people stopped to taste when the table had 24 jams on it, fewer of those people actually bought any jam. In fact, people were about 10 times more likely to make a purchase if they visited the table when it displayed fewer jams.

As a marketer, make sure you provide enough choices to prompt a decision, but not so many that you overwhelm your customers.

More smart ways for marketers to use autonomy bias

- Use empowering language such as "Take control," "Puts you in control," and "Regain control."
- Invite customers to choose what they want—their free gift, level of service, type of rewards, or degree of product functionality.

- Consider a slogan that highlights control (example: Burger King's famous "Have it your way").

- Let customers customize certain aspects of their purchase, like the color or design. This act of co-creation can activate autonomy bias as well as the endowment effect (See Chapter 2).

- Offer two or three product or service level options instead of just one.

- Make sure the choices you provide represent clear, easily distinguishable options. If people cannot easily differentiate between choices, that can prevent them from making a decision.

- Use color, position, and size to nudge people to make your desired decision when you offer options.

- Chunk similar items into groups or categories to reduce choice overload.

- Highlight your most important features or choices and provide drop-down menus or links for others.

- Employ the illusion of choice, where you offer two options that both result in a positive sales outcome (example: Would you like to buy the blue or the green coat? Would you like to take delivery on Thursday or Friday?).

- Where applicable, display progress bars to remove uncertainty about how much time something will take or how much more information a person needs to complete, because this knowledge will give them a sense of control.

- Avoid undue friction and dark patterns (example: making it deliberately difficult to cancel a subscription), which can make people feel they have no control.

- Give customers control through back buttons, undo buttons, and confirm before purchase buttons.

- Provide easy-to-access assistance and guidance (example: phone, text, email, FAQs, assessment tools, usage examples representing different personas) to make customers feel in control as they make buying decisions.

KEY TAKEAWAYS

1 People have an innate need to feel in control and make decisions about things that affect them.

2 Giving customers choices makes them feel in control.

3 Presenting a single option can delay or even prevent a purchase decision.

4   Research shows having a second option increases the likelihood someone will purchase at that time.

5   Asking for action, and then reminding people they are free to do what they want (the BYAF technique), can increase the likelihood people will do what you've asked.

6   As the world emerges from the restrictions of the pandemic, triggering autonomy bias may be an even more important tactic for marketers.

7   You can trigger autonomy bias by making customers and prospects feel in control, by informing them they are about to lose the ability to make a decision themselves, by offering people choices, and by highlighting aspects of your product or service that naturally hand control to customers, especially if your competitors can't make the same claims.

8   Marketers can charge more for products and services that give people more control.

9   While choice can prompt decisions, too many choices (choice overload) can prompt indecision.

10 Marketers tap into autonomy bias when they use empowering language such as "regain control" and "choose," offer several options instead of one, allow customers to make customization decisions, and remove friction to make it easy for people to accomplish a task.

In conclusion

People crave autonomy. Your customers and prospects want to be in control, or at least feel as if they are. To foster that feeling, present them with clear options, and provide them with opportunities to offer input into or customize the products and services you sell.

This latter tactic can have the added benefit of triggering the Commitment and Consistency Principle, as you'll see in the next chapter.

References

Dooley, R (nd) Four words that double persuasion, *Neuromarketing by Roger Dooley* [Blog] https://www.neurosciencemarketing.com/blog/articles/byaf.htm (archived at https://perma.cc/D4FX-Z5X8)

Geerts, F (2017) The Jam Experiment: How choice overloads makes consumers buy less [Blog] *Medium.com*, 17 August, https://medium.com/@FlorentGeerts/the-jam-experiment-how-choice-overloads-makes-consumers-buy-less-d610f8c37b9b (archived at https://perma.cc/2KT7-H3GZ)

Hershey, R (2020) Harold H. Greene, judge who oversaw the breakup of the AT&T colossus, dies at 76, *New York Times*, 30 January, https://www.nytimes.com/2000/01/30/nyregion/harold-h-greene-judge-who-oversaw-the-breakup-of-the-at-t-colossus-dies-at-76.html (archived at https://perma.cc/6K2K-UUB5)

LaBerge, L, O'Toole, C, Schneider, J and Smaje, K (2020) How Covid-19 has pushed companies over the technology tipping point—and transformed business forever, McKinsey & Company, 5 October, https://www.mckinsey.com/business-functions/strategy-and-corporate-finance/our-insights/how-covid-19-has-pushed-companies-over-the-technology-tipping-point-and-transformed-business-forever (archived at https://perma.cc/SU3L-5NDA)

Mochon, D (2013) Single-option aversion, *Journal of Consumer Research*, http://web.missouri.edu/~segerti/capstone/SingleOptionAversion.pdf (archived at https://perma.cc/7RXL-7F3Y)

Prisco, J (2018) Illusion of control: Why the world is full of buttons that don't work, *CNN*, https://www.cnn.com/style/article/placebo-buttons-design/index.html (archived at https://perma.cc/KQY6-2Z2A)

Russell, D (2020) Autonomy Bias [Blog] *Vivid Labs*, 29 April, https://teamvivid.com/neurotactics/autonomy-bias/ (archived at https://perma.cc/EB5F-2JMG)

08

Encouraging sales and loyalty through the consistency principle and the Zeigarnik effect

Once people make a decision, they typically remain consistent with it as a way to conserve mental energy. That means if marketers can get one "yes," they are more likely to get subsequent ones. This is particularly true if your initial request is somewhat small. Marketers can tap the Commitment and Consistency principle to ladder up to their ultimate ask, making it much easier to get an affirmative answer.

When you're a marketer, you are expected to know things.

Not only the customary things, like what makes your product a good choice, who your ideal customer is, and how to calculate the return on your marketing investment. No. You're expected to possess other, more nuanced information, such as when a prospect will be ready to buy, which of your customers will be most likely to buy again, and how to increase the amount a customer will spend.

In a way, you're asked to be something of a mind reader. And it's not easy. Which is perhaps what prompted legendary department store founder John Wanamaker to purportedly say, "Half the money I spend on advertising is wasted; the trouble is I don't know which half."

Predicting buyer behavior is not an exact science. To be sure, marketers have more help at their disposal today than in Mr. Wanamaker's day. For example, your market research department may have instituted a voice of the customer program, or perhaps they conduct regular focus groups to try to get a bead on consumer preferences. Your CRM system may track every interaction a customer has with your post-sale support team, so you're on top of common questions, complaints, and compliments. Or you may tap into social media listening and sentiment analysis, looking for clues about how your target market is feeling or what they're doing.

Additionally, your predictive analytics or data science group may have developed sophisticated models and algorithms to keep you informed about your customers and their forecasted behaviors. You may be monitoring everything from your customers' net promoter scores to their digital footprints. You may even be benefiting from continuous advances in artificial intelligence (AI) and machine learning, so you're regularly supplied with faster and more accurate ways to get the right message to the right person at the right time.

But there is something else you should be aware of.

Whether you use some, none, or all of the above techniques, there is a simple behavioral science principle that you'll want to know about. It will help you predict when someone may buy, or buy again, or buy more. In fact, you can use it to predispose your customers toward each of those actions. Social scientists refer to this principle as the commitment and consistency bias. You'll see it can be quite powerful and telling.

> Social scientists have found that once people take an action or take a stand, they like to remain consistent with it.

Commitment and consistency bias strongly influences a person's behavior

Remaining consistent with earlier actions is a common decision-making shortcut that helps conserve mental energy. Robert Cialdini, author of *Influence: The science of persuasion*, lists commitment and consistency among his seven principles of influence. He says, "Once we have made up our minds about an issue, stubborn consistency allows us a very appealing luxury: We really don't have to think hard about the issue anymore."

Maintaining this consistency is easy. It doesn't require any subsequent thought time or further analysis. It also feels right. There's a certain comfort in doing something again or in the same way. And it doesn't subject us to the personal or professional embarrassment of being accused of flip-flopping. People like to be thought of as following through on what they say they will do, and of being a person of their word.

Two classic behavioral science experiments prove just how powerful the concept of commitment and consistency can be. One was conducted by psychologists Jonathan Freedman and Scott Fraser, and took place in a California neighborhood (MacNaught, 2014). In the experiment, a researcher went door to door posing as a member of a community group that advocated for traffic safety. The researcher asked the homeowners if, as part of a public service campaign, they would display a billboard on their front lawn that encouraged people to drive carefully. When they made the request, they showed the person a photo of an attractive house with a large, poorly lettered sign in front of it. In the picture, the sign took up much of the lawn and completely concealed the doorway of the home.

As you might imagine, the great majority of people said no. Perhaps they thought it would obscure their views, decrease their property value, or anger their neighbors during the week or two that the sign was supposed to remain up. Or perhaps they just thought it was a crazy request. Whatever the reason, only 17 percent of the people who were asked agreed to display the billboard.

However, there's more to the story. There was a group of homeowners who were very agreeable to the billboard. In fact, over three-quarters of the members of this group agreed to have the sign erected in their front yard. What was the difference?

The people in this group had been contacted by a researcher about two weeks earlier, and had agreed to a request to display, either in their window or in their car, a small three-inch square sign that encouraged safe driving. When a researcher returned with the new billboard request, 76 percent of these people agreed to it. Why? Consistency.

It was consistent with their previous behavior. It was consistent with the stand they had taken. It was consistent with how they now viewed themselves, as people who took action on matters such as this. In short, these people relied on a decision-making shortcut. They made things easy on themselves. Unlike the other homeowners, they didn't spend a lot of time thinking about their answer, objectively weighing the pros and cons of having a billboard supporting a good cause planted in their front lawns. Rather, they simply defaulted to a decision—one that felt reassuringly similar to their previous one.

As you can see, when triggering the commitment and consistency principle, getting people to agree to a smaller request first can lay the groundwork for their agreement to a larger one. In this next experiment, researchers found that when people agreed to what they *thought* would be a small request, they kept their commitment even when the request actually turned out to be much larger.

People stand by their words. And their plans

This experiment, led by Thomas Moriarty, was conducted on a beach in New York (Dutton, 2015). A researcher posing as a beachgoer set up a blanket about five feet away from a subject on another blanket. The researcher then proceeded to pull out a radio and listen to a rock station at a high volume.

A couple of minutes later, the researcher walked over to their neighbor's blanket and asked one of two things: In the control group, the researcher said, "Excuse me... I'm here alone and have no matches. Do you have a light?" In the experiment group, the researcher said, "Excuse me, I'm going up to the boardwalk for a few minutes...would you watch my things?" to which the neighbors agreed.

After this brief exchange, the researcher headed off toward the boardwalk, leaving their radio playing loudly where they'd left it on their blanket. A few minutes later, another researcher, this one playing the role of thief, walked over to the blanket, picked up the radio, and quickly walked off in a direction different than the one the "radio owner" had taken.

What do you think happened? And what, if anything, do you think you would have done? The researchers found that in the control group, where no commitment to watch things had been requested, only four out of 20 times did the beach blanket neighbors intervene in the theft, either calling out to attempt to stop the thief or actually chasing after them. However, in the experiment group, where people had been asked to keep an eye on the things of their neighbor who was heading to the boardwalk, 19 out of 20 people responded. These were the people who had made a commitment to their radio-listening neighbor.

Of course, at the time they made that commitment, they probably had no idea they would be put in a position to try to stop a thief. At most, they may have thought they'd need to shoo away some seagulls. But as the experiment showed, once people make a commitment, they feel the need to live up to it.

In fact, research has shown this is particularly true if someone not only says they will do something, but also articulates how they'll do it. According to an article by Supriya Syal and Dan Ariely that appeared in *Scientific American*, behavioral scientists David Nickerson and Todd Rogers found that "voter turnout could be increased by helping people make a concrete plan to implement their intentions" (Syal and Ariely, 2016).

Better than simply asking people if they intended to vote, the scientists proved that when people had a plan that included "*when, where*, and *how* they would accomplish their goal of voting*," more of those people actually showed up at the polls. According to the authors, "Voter records showed that making a plan was more than twice as effective as simply asking people about their intentions."

The authors also note that scientific research indicates "making concrete plans can help people translate goals into actions across a number of domains." So, if you want your customers and prospects to do something, encourage them to make a plan to do it. Have them describe their commitment to do so in a detailed way.

How a seemingly unrelated commitment can spur action

Sometimes marketers can predispose people to take an action by getting them to commit to something that doesn't seem related to their request at all.

In 2017, I was in Austin, Texas, invited to present at the prestigious SXSW conference for the second time. The weather was warm, sunny, and felt like early spring. The conference atmosphere was pulsating with energy and innovation. And my presentation had gone well, attracting a room packed with attentive attendees. I was feeling great.

As I walked down Trinity Street, I could see a young person wearing a Greenpeace t-shirt and carrying a clipboard heading in my direction. My first reaction was, "Oh no, she's going to try to get me to sign a petition."

It's not that I have anything against Greenpeace or the work they do. I just wanted to get to my next conference session quickly and without interruption. However, the idea of crossing the street to avoid the young woman seemed rude. So, I resigned myself to the fact that I'd be approached, and resolved not to get drawn into a lengthy discussion.

As she got close to me, she smiled.

"Beautiful day, isn't it?" she said.

"Yes, it is," I agreed.

Nodding to the SXSW badge around my neck, she asked "Is the conference going well for you?"

"Yes, it's great," I replied.

"Do you have a minute to sign a petition to help the plight of the sea turtles?" she continued. At that point, I felt I couldn't say no.

"Okay...," I said. And while she handed me the clipboard, she proceeded to tell me about the horrors of plastic garbage in the ocean, pointing to heartbreaking photos of entangled sea creatures to drive the story home.

"Would you like to make a $10 monthly donation to help?" she finished. "You can use a credit card." Naturally, I said yes.

So, you may wonder, what happened to that resolve I'd had a few moments earlier? How did I go from wanting to rush across the street to avoid the fundraiser to handing over my credit card for a monthly donation that I still make to this day?

Behavioral scientists will tell you it all started with those first questions. The young woman got me to agree that it was a beautiful day. She then got me to state that I was feeling great. While neither of those answers had anything to do with the plight of sea turtles, they set me up to agree to what she really wanted to ask me.

As Cialdini explains it, "The theory behind this tactic is that people who have just asserted that they are doing/feeling fine—even as a routine part of a social exchange—will consequently find it awkward to appear stingy in the context of their own admitted favored circumstances." He goes on to cite research that found this technique actually doubled response when tested in market.

To put things a different way, the fundraiser elicited a series of yes answers (public commitments) from me, which made it more likely I would continue to answer in the affirmative.

Of course, in addition to commitment and consistency, there were other factors at play. First, it was a gorgeous day, and the Borgen Project reports that people are more likely to donate when the weather is good. Second, I could donate using a credit card, which lessens the pain of paying. And third, because it was my credit card, I was free to cancel whenever I chose (see Chapter 7). Of course, it was also a good cause. Had I not believed in it, these other factors most likely would not have made the difference they did.

CASE STUDY
Commitment, consistency and car insurance

How do you convince people to switch to your product when they've historically shown no interest? A property and casualty insurance company approached the agency where I was working with this interesting challenge. They marketed auto insurance with a special discount to members of affinity groups (alumni associations, professional associations, etc.).

Despite their considerable success with other groups, they could not manage to make the relationship pay off with one particular group, although they'd tried really hard. It was a group that supported the rights of lesbian, gay, bisexual, and transgender (LGBT) individuals.

Apparently, no matter what the insurer's messages said, not enough people in this one group would purchase the coverage. As a result, our new client was on the brink of canceling this organization's participation in the program, which they were understandably reluctant to do. They came to us hoping we might have the answer that would turn things around. Of course, we were more than happy to try.

As we dug into the assignment, we explored—and rejected—several approaches. We considered leading with the savings, because we knew people hate to pay more for the same thing than others do (see Chapter 2). The affinity discount meant they'd actually pay less. However, the client cautioned us that their discount was not very large, and if drivers were looking for low-cost insurance, there were other companies that were less expensive.

Not to be deterred, we played with packaging the affinity discount with a superior customer service promise. This insurer had really high customer satisfaction ratings, and we thought the combination of discounted price and satisfied customers could be an especially compelling proposition.

But the problem with that was, unless a driver had experienced an accident and submitted a claim with their existing insurer, they wouldn't know if their service was lacking. Or if what our client promised sounded any better. After all, they were likely told their insurer's service was good when they signed up, and without any experience to the contrary, it's easy to prefer the status quo (see Chapter 11).

The next logical area to explore was the affinity relationship. While it entitled group members to an exclusive discount (see Chapter 3), we'd already learned it wasn't a large one, so it wouldn't feel particularly special. But certainly, we thought, there was something in the idea of partnering with the group, and the support that implied, right? Sadly, we were told that other insurers advertised more to the LGBT community, and as a result had more traction there.

At this point, we could see why our client might be having so much trouble selling to this particular affinity group.

Then we found an approach we thought would be quite powerful, based on commitment and consistency. The message began by saying that if the target were like most people who were reading it, they believed it was important to support companies that supported LGBT rights. This set the stage for consistency. People who were reading the message had received it precisely because they belonged to an affinity group that supported the rights of LGBT people. (Privacy concerns prevented our client from specifically mentioning the name of the affinity group in their marketing.)

The copy then suggested that some companies might target the LGBT community simply because they think it's good for marketing. This was intended to unseat our client's competition. We wanted to plant the seed that buying insurance from some other company might actually be inconsistent with our target's values, intentions, and previous actions.

Next, we established our client's exemplary record supporting LGBT causes, including the community recognition they'd received, to show that their values aligned with those of the target. After that, we detailed the advantages of obtaining auto insurance from them.

And the approach worked. The client now had a winning message. They saw a significant 56 percent lift over their previous efforts. Not only did they keep this affinity group in their program, they increased their budget for campaigns to target it. The commitment and consistency message had made a connection.

Three other companies that drove behavior with the commitment and consistency principle

Our auto insurance client used the commitment and consistency principle to point out the parallel between the targets' actions in other parts of their lives and their choice of insurance provider. We positioned choosing insurance from our client as the move that was consistent with their values and beliefs.

There are other ways marketers can trigger the bias toward commitment and consistency. Three more of my clients successfully used it to influence customers and prospects in different phases of the purchase continuum.

DISABILITY INSURANCE FOR DOCTORS

A company that sold disability insurance directly to medical professionals found that there was a segment of the population they targeted that never purchased the coverage, despite repeated attempts. Rather than write off this segment as unmarketable, we decided to inject some commitment and consistency into our communications to them, replacing the usual request to buy with a smaller request to reply.

We sent the doctors a questionnaire, telling them they'd been selected to represent their peers in a short survey about insurance decision making in their field. The survey consisted of a series of questions designed to get the doctors focused on the importance of disability insurance.

For example, one question asked if they knew any doctor who'd had to stop practicing, either temporarily or permanently, because of neck or back pain, which were common in their specialty. Another question asked how long they could keep their practice open without financial hardship in the event they suffered a disability.

Just under 10 percent of the doctors responded to the survey, representing the first time these professionals had ever replied to our client. After answering the survey, they continued to receive the insurer's regular solicitations. Our thinking was that once they'd answered survey questions that made the case for having disability insurance, it would be inconsistent to refuse to buy it.

At the end of the year, the client had exceeded their annual sales goal by 25 percent, driven in part by some new business from these professionals who'd historically never responded.

COMMUNITY BANK CHECKING ACCOUNTS

A small community bank client wanted to increase the business they were getting from a certain segment of their customers. However, they faced considerable competition from larger banks with more locations and bigger advertising budgets.

The bank suspected that for the segment of customers they were targeting, the bank had been a local, convenient choice for a specific need, such as a loan or certificate of deposit. These customers, they surmised, might not think of the bank for their other financial needs. The client's goal was to get them to expand their business with the bank by opening a checking account.

The message we sent to these customers started out by triggering the commitment and consistency principle. It reminded people they were already customers of the bank. This was designed to prompt a mental energy-saving shortcut, so people could simply default to a decision without a lot of thought. We then listed three attractive benefits of expanding their relationship with the bank by opening a checking account. The campaign turned out to be one of the most successful ones the bank had run.

ONLINE NEWS SERVICE SUBSCRIPTION

A publishing client was having difficulty converting the free trial subscribers of their e-news service to paid subscribers. One part of the challenge was that people were not used to paying for news online. Another part was that if people did not subscribe, they could still find other free sources that kept them up to date.

Working with the client, we created an email campaign with an offer and a message that would trigger commitment and consistency. One headline read: "Because you accepted our free trial offer, you're now entitled to an exclusive 25% discount." The idea was to get to the next "yes." People had agreed to a free trial. Now we wanted them to agree to a discounted subscription. After that, we could push for full price. The campaign's copy also encouraged readers to keep reading their favorite columnists and sportswriters, and to continue their access to the award-winning coverage they had come to rely on.

The approach delivered a double-digit response rate, by systematically increasing the ask. It convinced an impressive percentage of free trial readers to take the next step and become paid customers.

MISTAKE

Always asking for the sale right away. In some cases, you're better off securing small commitments or "yeses" before making the ultimate ask.

More ways marketers can trigger commitment and consistency bias

Marketers can choose very simple or more sophisticated ways to trigger commitment and consistency. You can do so in a single communication or over a series of them. And you can aim for immediate agreement, a cascade of yeses, or a commitment that will pay off in the future.

When I made my first visit to the Toms website, an online retailer committed to corporate social responsibility, I was greeted with a pop-up box that said "I love companies that give back," followed by two buttons. One said "I agree." The other said "I disagree." After clicking "I agree," the next screen succinctly summarized their mission, and encouraged me to become a customer. Since I had just indicated I love companies that give back, it would now feel inconsistent to leave and shop elsewhere.

Around the holidays, I use the Harry & David company to send my clients gifts. Each year, the company sends me a list of who I sent gifts to the previous year, and what those gifts were. It makes things very convenient for me. It also makes it more likely I will use Harry & David again that year.

And that I will send the same people gifts, even if a few of those people were no longer as top of mind.

One fall, Amtrak emailed me to announce a double points promotion they would soon be running. The email asked me to preregister so I would be able to earn double points for any train trips I took during the promo period. That was their first small ask. I didn't have to buy a ticket or even plan a trip. I just had to say I wanted to be eligible for the extra points when the time came.

When the double point promo began, they sent me another email saying that double days were here, and since I'd already registered, all I had to do was travel. They positioned it as the logical next step. Because I had already signed up, it made it much more likely I'd take a trip.

On a hot summer night in a suburb of Boston, I was having dinner with my friend Kim Borman. Kim is the executive director of the Boston Women's Workforce Council, an innovative public-private partnership dedicated to eliminating the city's gender/racial wage gap. It's an important cause, and one that won't be remedied all at once.

In the course of our conversation, she mentioned the 100% Talent Compact they ask greater Boston employers to sign. Having a C-level executive sign the pledge makes the company's long-term commitment to work toward gender and wage equality stronger, she explained, adding, "We really like to get that commitment in writing, to get it on record." Once an employer signs the Compact, they can display the Compact seal, which both recognizes and reinforces their commitment, as well as serving as an indicator of social proof (see Chapter 5).

FIGURE 8.1 Reminders trigger consistent behavior

When employers sign the Boston Women's Workforce Council pledge, they can display a seal, which recognizes and reinforces their commitment to pay equity.

THE POWER OF COGNITIVE DISSONANCE

People like what they say and do to be in sync, especially if what they have said was public. When those two things do not match, people can experience cognitive dissonance. And that is an unpleasant feeling. Not only psychologically unpleasant, but physically unpleasant, too. As a result, people will often change their behavior to match what they have gone on record as saying.

Or, as Robert Cialdini says, "Something special happens when people personally put their commitments on paper. They live up to what they have written down."

Marketers can harness the human distaste for cognitive dissonance. For example, a wine organization ran a Twitter contest. They asked people to tweet about their favorite wine and food pairings for a chance to win a swag bag. Imagine someone tweeted that whenever they eat bruschetta, they always have a glass of the company's red wine. Maybe the person wins a swag bag. Maybe they don't. But the next time they order bruschetta, they'll find themselves thinking they should also have a glass of that red wine, because it's what they said they do.

Similarly, a software company ran a contest asking business people to review their products for a chance to win a suite of software for their office. Hoping to be chosen, maybe a person would write that they always recommend that company's software when colleagues inquire. Whether or not they win the contest, they have now gone on record as saying they recommend the company. And the next time a colleague raises the topic, whose software do you think they'll suggest?

Zeigarnik effect: how marketers can harness the need for completion

Behavioral scientists have found that people remember unfinished tasks better than finished ones. Those tasks can nag at people until they are completed. This principle is called the Zeigarnik Effect, after Bluma Zeigarnik, the psychologist who first noticed it when observing that waiters were able to remember their patrons' orders until they served them. But once they checked them off their lists, they'd forgotten who had ordered what.

The Zeigarnik Effect is also at play when people watch a television series that goes on hiatus with a cliffhanger. They keep wondering how things will get resolved (see Chapter 6). The Zeigarnik Effect can work hand in hand with the Ovsiankina Effect, which is people's innate desire to finish what they started, and to not leave things incomplete. In fact, researchers at USC and Wharton found that people are more likely to complete the purchases on a loyalty punch card when it has 10 squares with two of them prechecked than when it has eight empty squares, even though the number of required purchases is the same (Nunes and Dreze, 2006).

In addition to loyalty punch cards and stories, marketers can trigger the Zeigarnik Effect in other ways. For example, I went to the Vistaprint website and designed a business card. But I did not purchase it. A few days later I received an email with a picture of the business card I'd designed and a message reminding me to buy a box of them.

Alan Rosenspan, in his book *Confessions of a Control Freak: How to get the results you want from your next direct marketing program*, recounts an award-winning business-to-business direct mail campaign that CIT Group sent out. Over the course of two mailings, they sent a baseball autographed by Willie Mays, a baseball autographed by Mickey Mantle, and a stand that had a space for *three* baseballs, with an identifying label under each spot.

In order to get the third ball, autographed by Hank Aaron, recipients needed to schedule a meeting with the CIT Group. Assuming the mailing list was well-targeted, this was a powerful way to trigger the need for completion as a way to secure a sales call.

Other powerful ways for marketers to use commitment, consistency, and the Zeigarnik and Ovsiankina effects

- Invite people to take a poll or survey prior to asking them to purchase.
- Encourage follows, likes, retweets, and views, which are easy ways to say yes.
- Ask for other low-commitment first steps—such as download a white paper or guide, watch a short video, or sign up for an e-newsletter.
- Encourage potential customers to pre-register their interest before your product comes out or before your event registration is open.
- Offer trial memberships, starter kits of your products, and free limited functionality versions of your service. This will not only activate the

endowment effect (see Chapter 2), it can also trigger the commitment and consistency principle, paving the way for your next ask.

- Let people "test drive" or try before they buy.
- Offer a satisfaction guarantee or return policy that will encourage people to make a purchase.
- Remind people they previously said yes to you or made a smart decision by buying from you. Once they've made the commitment, they're more apt to keep it.
- Point out how a prospect's values are in sync with yours or how your product supports what they care about.
- Get your target to sign a petition, or to publicly register their interest or support.
- Send abandoned cart emails, return to finish messages, or alerts that something your prospect viewed is now on sale/running low in stock/just added a new feature, color, or size.
- Market add-on products that complement a recent purchase, and upgrades to services you offer.
- Retarget prospects who spent time on your website but left without purchasing.
- Use softer language that doesn't sound final and decisive (which can scare people off), such as try vs. subscribe, or get started vs. buy, or take the next step vs. enroll.

KEY TAKEAWAYS

1 Once your customers make a decision or take a stand, they like to remain consistent with it.

2 Defaulting to consistent decisions saves mental energy and avoids the appearance of being a flip-flopper.

3 A small commitment from your customers can pave the way for larger ones.

4 Having someone make a plan for how they'll do something increases the chances that they'll follow through.

5 Prompt someone to first say they're feeling good before delivering a fundraising request.

6 Point out where your customers' values align with those of your company to foster commitment and consistency.

7 Start with a smaller, low-commitment request from your customers. Get that first small yes and then escalate your asks.

8 Use language that reminds people that they've already said yes to you in the past.

9 Ask your customer to answer a question or sign a pledge to gain an initial commitment.

10 Once people publicly state something, they'll adjust their behavior to match it in order to avoid cognitive dissonance. People like what they say and do to sync up.

11 Use the power of the Zeigarnik effect by reminding customers of incomplete purchases, abandoned shopping carts, and additional steps they still need to take to finish something they've started.

12 Letting customers try your product or service will make them more likely to purchase it. Once they purchase, offer add-ons and upgrades.

In conclusion

People are surprisingly consistent. Once they make a decision, they don't care to revisit it. Marketers can benefit from this by encouraging people to say yes to a small request, because those people will be more likely to say yes again when faced with larger requests—without really thinking about them.

Additionally, once people start something, they feel a strong urge to complete it. This desire to not leave things unfinished is similar to the desire to not leave things unknown, as you'll see in the next chapter. Both can be powerful drivers of behavior.

References

Cialdini, R (1984) *Influence: The Psychology of Persuasion*, Quill William Morrow, New York

Dutton, V (2015) How experts influence—commitment and consistency [Blog] *Positive Change Guru*, 10 October, https://positivechangeguru.com/how-experts-influence-commitment-and-consistency/ (archived at https://perma.cc/DM8T-AD8D)

MacNaught, S (2014) Freedman and Fraser: Compliance without pressure (The Billboard Experiment) [Blog] https://www.staceymacnaught.co.uk/freedman-and-fraser-compliance-without-pressure/ (archived at https://perma.cc/C3PG-LQG9)

Nunes, J and Dreze, X (2006) The endowed progress effect: How artificial advancement increases effort, *Journal of Consumer Research*, https://www.jstor.org/stable/10.1086/500480 (archived at https://perma.cc/QW3D-NPBB)

Rosenspan, A (2002) *Confessions of a Control Freak: How to get the results you want from your next direct marketing program*, CyberClassics, Inc., Anaheim, CA

Syal, S and Ariely, D (2016) How science can help get out the vote, *Scientific American*, 01 September, https://www.scientificamerican.com/article/how-science-can-help-get-out-the-vote/ (archived at https://perma.cc/2BPY-BHZL)

09

Information gap theory: prompting consumers to take action through curiosity and the need to know

People's need to find out what they want to know can be extremely motivating. Behavioral scientists have found that if there's a gap between what people already know and what they still want to know, they will take action to close that gap. Marketers can use their target's hardwired urge to find answers as a powerful tool to prompt engagement.

What one word gets people to agree with you... before they've even heard what you say next? How do you convince someone who initially claims they're "not in the market" for your product... that they in fact are? What can you do to prompt people to buy something now—when the benefit comes later, if at all?

If you want to know the answers to these questions, you're likely a curious marketer. That can be a very beneficial trait to have in this industry. Of course, it also means that now may not be the best time to remind you of the old adage "curiosity killed the cat." Although maybe at this point, that wouldn't deter you.

Speaking of which, do you know there is more to that cat saying? Have you ever heard anyone tack a second sentence on at the end of it? One that can dramatically alter the meaning of the saying?

If you haven't, I'll tell you the rest of the proverb soon. Not only that, you will also learn the answers to the first three questions.

Did those two statements give you the motivation to read on? Were they enough to get you to continue down the page, hopscotching over these next few words, intent on finding the answers that will satisfy your curiosity?

If so, you have just experienced the pull of information-gap theory. And if you are like many people, you've found that pull to be quite strong. Coined by neuroeconomist George Loewenstein, the term information gap theory refers to the fact that if there is a gap between what people already know and what they still want to know, they will take action to close that gap.

That last phrase, take action to close that gap, is an important one. Because as a marketer, you want people to take action. You want them to open or click or buy or buy again. Anything that can help you motivate that action becomes a powerful tool to have at your command.

Information gap theory is one such tool. I used it as I opened this chapter, with questions that would deliberately intrigue a marketer. Then I added a pinch more to the dose, with the mention of a well-known quote about curiosity that has a lesser-known sentence which completes it. My intention was to raise some subjects you'd want to know more about, point out a gap in your current knowledge, and prompt you to continue reading to pursue the missing answers.

Joanna Wiebe, founder of Copyhackers, explains the approach in her blogpost, "Should You Use a Curiosity Gap to Persuade Your Visitors to Click?" She says, "Your job, as a copywriter or marketer, is to delay the filling of the gap for as long as you can—without introducing too much discomfort—in order to keep your visitors engaged... To keep them hanging on, really" (Weibe, 2014).

If you've been hanging on for the answers that will satisfy your curiosity, it's time for me to reward your persistence. Because while curiosity killed the cat, it's been said that "satisfaction brought it back."

So, if you want to know the one word that gets people to agree with you before you've finished your sentence, see Chapter 13. If you want to know how to convince people who claim they're not in the market that they actually may be, see Chapter 15. And if you want to prompt people to purchase a product that they don't see an immediate benefit to, head to Chapter 17.

But don't go too quickly. Because this chapter is about to reveal several effective, scientifically proven ways to use information gap theory to increase your leads and sales. Aren't you curious to know what they are?

> People feel good when they satisfy their curiosity. It actually activates the brain's reward center.

Information gap theory is a natural driver of behavior

"Curiosity can exert a powerful motivational force," according to Loewenstein (1994). When people want to know something, it can nag at them until they find out. If your target is curious about information you have, chances are they will feel driven to pursue it. And that can ultimately lead them right where you want them, which is standing in front of your cash register.

As Loewenstein explains, "If curiosity is like a hunger for knowledge, then a small "priming dose" of information increases the hunger, and the decrease in curiosity from knowing a lot is like being satiated by information. In the information-gap theory, the object of curiosity is an unconditioned rewarding stimulus: unknown information that is anticipated to be rewarding. Humans (and other species, such as cats and monkeys) will expend resources to find out information they are curious about, much as rats will work for a food reward."

In other words, people will make the effort to satisfy their curiosity. The more curious they are, the more likely they are to act. Once they obtain the information, it feels rewarding.

In a 2008 experiment led by Min Jeong Kang, that Loewenstein was also involved in, research subjects were shown trivia questions while inside of an fMRI machine (Kang et al., 2008). They were asked to silently guess their answers, and indicate how confident they were in those answers, as well as how curious they were to find out if they were correct. Researchers found that curiosity is fueled by uncertainty (when people know a bit but not too much about a topic), and linked with activity in the brain's reward region.

A 2021 study involving toddlers and reported in *The British Psychological Society Research Digest* found similar results. It showed "that children are motivated to learn more about a topic when there is a gap in their knowledge that they want to fill. The results suggest that for young children there is a sweet spot for learning, when they already know enough to find a topic interesting, but not so much that it becomes boring" (Reynolds, 2021).

Clearly, this desire to find out what we don't know is a hardwired human behavior. The key for marketers is to use it to properly pique their customers' curiosity, highlighting a topic their audience is somewhat familiar with and interested in, but doesn't yet have deep knowledge of.

If you can pose a question that they are not certain they can answer, or offer information that promises to supplement their current understanding of an intriguing topic, you can motivate them—not just to take action, but to do so quickly. Similar to stories, which people feel compelled to finish (see Chapter 6), information-gap theory can motivate a prompt response from a target. Once you make people aware of the gap in what they know, they will want to fill that gap quickly.

On an interesting related note, researchers who conducted an experiment involving macaque monkeys and water rewards discovered a similar finding. The scientists "found that monkeys expressed a strong behavioral preference, preferring information to its absence and preferring to receive the information as soon as possible" (Bromberg-Martin and Hikosaka, 2009). Researchers stressed that having the information did not impact the size of the reward the monkey ultimately received, and they concluded that the "monkeys treated information about rewards as if it was a reward in itself." Apparently, it's not just people who feel compelled to find out things. Primates seem to share the same drive. It feels good to be certain.

A well-crafted question is a smart way to trigger the effect of information-gap theory

In December of 2008, on the morning after the agency holiday party, I fell victim to the downturn in the US economy. The advertising agency that employed me needed to reduce expenses, and I turned out to be one of them.

Sparing a few minutes to mourn a job I loved and lost, I began looking for my next position that afternoon. But given the recession, there were not a lot of prospects. After a few months passed, I was excited to hear from Lianne, a former colleague of mine from my early days in marketing. She wanted to know if I'd be interested in interviewing for a part-time, contract-based creative director position at the agency where she was working. They, too, had taken a hit from the economy, and no longer had a creative director on staff.

Since there were no agencies rushing to my inbox with the offer of full-time employment, I was very interested to interview. And I was both happy and grateful to accept the position when Neal, the agency's president, called to offer it to me.

A few weeks into the job, I received a phone call from one of the sales executives who worked for the agency's parent company, which was a printing business. He wanted to schedule a meeting with me to discuss "how can we make you full-time." This was the kind of calendar-clearing, lean way in question that immediately grabbed my attention. It was a topic that interested me, and a query I did not have the answer to. In short, it was a fine example of deploying information-gap theory.

When we met, it turned out his idea was that I provide him an introduction to some of my clients from my previous agency, who he would then try to call on. His reasoning was that if he sold more, the company would do better, and there would be more money available for the agency to hire a full-time creative director. While there was a certain amount of logic to that thinking, it wasn't the conversation I had anticipated.

To be fair, had he called me and said he wanted to meet so he could ask for a list of my former clients, I would not have had the same calendar-clearing reaction. He was definitely a savvy salesman. And whether he knew it or not, he'd demonstrated an insightful understanding of how information-gap theory worked. At least up to a point. I suspect what he hadn't considered was that I might not share the same enthusiasm for his plan, and that I might actually walk out of the meeting feeling it was not the same one I had walked into.

This brings us to a word of caution about a marketer's use of curiosity, and the attendant teeing up of information gaps. Make sure you pay off what you promise. While it may be tempting, do not be misleading. Do not resort to clickbait. Do not risk angering or disappointing your customers and prospects.

Because if you do, the approach will backfire. And once it does, you will have rendered the information-gap approach useless for future marketing efforts to that audience. Additionally, you will have eroded the trust between you and your target, and that may be impossible to regain.

CASE STUDY
Asking the money question

Not everyone feels comfortable making personal financial decisions. In fact, money can be an intimidating topic for many. So, when a client came to the agency where I was working with an assignment to help them market fixed index annuities, we knew it would take some serious strategizing.

A fixed index annuity is an insurance product that provides customers with a regular stream of income, typically for their retirement. Its rate of return is tied to a market index, such as the S&P 500 Composite. The amount of money a customer puts into the annuity cannot be lost, but the amount of interest they may earn is capped. The call to action for the campaign was to contact an agent.

The creative team explored several concepts as they looked for the ideal message, one that would not be difficult to understand and that would offer a compelling reason to respond. One option was to make the message revolve around "how fixed index annuities provide automatic cash in retirement." It offered a relevant, attractive benefit. However, we worried that the target, who was likely unfamiliar with the term fixed index annuities, might not think the message was meant for them.

Another approach keyed off the theme "Did you overlook this time-tested option for your retirement savings?" It had a nice nod to loss aversion (see Chapter 2), and a solid amount of intrigue. Given that the audience profiled as being less financially experienced, however, we feared they'd assume they probably had indeed overlooked a number of financial opportunities. But because they weren't "big money people," they would have already made their peace with that.

Finally, we found the information-gap theory question we believed would do the job. We created a campaign that revolved around "Could you earn better returns than a CD and still protect your retirement cash?" This referenced a bank product, a certificate of deposit, that our target would be familiar with. It flagged two goals they likely had—making and protecting money for their retirement. And it highlighted a meaningful gap in the target's knowledge. What's more, it worked, with the client reporting an 85x return on their marketing investment.

MISTAKE

Posing questions your prospect already knows the answer to. Instead, intrigue them with a question about a topic they have some knowledge of, but are neither experts in nor utterly unfamiliar with.

Two more examples of information-gap theory in action

HOW A TRADE SHOW EXHIBITOR USED CURIOSITY TO ATTRACT ATTENDEES

Imagine you have a booth at a trade show for dentists. You're surrounded by other exhibitors, who sell the latest tools and equipment, as well as dental practice building services. You, on the other hand, sell life and disability insurance, an admittedly low-interest product. How would you attract dentists to your booth?

You could resort to an awesome giveaway. That would generate traffic, but probably result in the "grab and go" kind. Or you could employ an information-gap theory tactic, which is what we did for this client.

Rather than focus on the benefits of having insurance, the agency's creative team looked for an interesting bit of product information they could use. Something that would spark the dentists' curiosity. They found it in the rule of thumb that said people should have enough life insurance to replace five to seven years' worth of their current income.

That data point led to the "Find your 5 to 7" theme, which was clearly more intriguing than "Find out about insurance." Headlines told dentists that while everyone had a 5 to 7, dentists typically had a higher one than that of the general public. Dentists were encouraged to take an "IQ" challenge that revealed their current 5 to 7, where the IQ stood for insurance quotient.

The intrigue worked. Dentists came to the booth, because they wanted to know what a 5 to 7 was, why their profession had a higher one, and what their individual number was. The best part? When all those dentists were at the booth, satisfying their curiosity by taking the 5 to 7 IQ challenge, it provided the ideal opportunity for the sales reps to talk with them about increasing their coverage. Additionally, when the insurer followed up after the trade show, this need for more insurance would be top of mind (see Chapter 15).

HOW THE US NAVY PROMPTED THEIR TARGET AUDIENCE TO SEEK ANSWERS— AND EMPLOYMENT

Now imagine you work for the US Navy's cryptology division, the group that makes and breaks codes. It's your job to find and engage potential recruits suited to this very specialized type of work. The ideal candidates would be intelligent, determined problem solvers. And because you would be looking for this very specific kind of person, they would not be easy to find.

Ad agency Campbell Ewald took on this challenge for their client, and solved it brilliantly. Since the Navy cryptologists were code makers and breakers, and they were looking to find like-minded others, perhaps it's no surprise that the campaign they ran was all about filling gaps in information—the very thing a cryptologist does.

Campbell Ewald's solution was to develop an alternative reality game called Project Architeuthis. Its storyline involved the "mysterious enemy abduction of the chief architect of a top-secret weapon" (Ewald, nd). They created Facebook pages and Twitter accounts for fictitious characters, and a main character named Maria, a Navy cryptologist who had supposedly snuck aboard the enemy ship.

From her position on the ship, Maria would send "coded messages, complex puzzles, ciphers, stenographs, and more" via social media, over the course of 18 days. The audience members, who worked alone or collaborated in groups, needed to solve the challenges in order to unlock the clues that would ultimately let them win the game.

The campaign demonstrated an ambitious, innovative, and on-the-money use of the information-gap theory tactic. It seemed tailor-made for an audience of puzzle solvers and code breakers who, perhaps even more than other people, are driven to fill in missing information. And it was a success. Campbell Ewald reported that Project Architeuthis exceeded the Navy's recruiting goal for cryptologists, and I watched it win the Diamond Echo at the marketing industry's international Echo awards show, which recognizes superior strategy, creative, and results.

Novelty as a complement to information-gap theory

People are drawn to things that are new. They try new restaurants, travel to new places, line up for the new iPhone, buy new clothes when the styles change, and check out new movies when they're released. Kids gravitate to their new toys. And adults like to show off their new purchases.

There is something about the new and novel that humans can't seem to resist. To be sure, people do have their old favorites—the products and services they return to again and again. The ones that are familiar and comfortable. Easy even. People know what to expect, and they won't be surprised or disappointed. Nevertheless, there is an unmistakable allure to something that is new.

The reason is not because people are fickle or easily distracted or even impossible to satisfy. It's that they are human. Humans are hardwired to crave the new and novel. When people find something they think is new, it activates the reward center in their brains. That releases dopamine, which is often referred to as the feel-good chemical. As a result, people are constantly on the lookout for the next new thing, because when they think they've found it, they experience that next hit of dopamine. Scientists have proven it fosters curiosity and prompts us to search for information.

In fact, in a study published in *Neuron*, researchers showed that "novelty motivates the brain to explore, seeking a reward" (Dean, 2019). In the experiment they conducted, the researchers showed subjects different pictures and monitored their brain response. Usually the pictures were of common, ordinary things, such as faces and outdoor scenes. However, there were times when the researchers deliberately slipped in a novel, unexpected picture.

When they did this, they saw that the brain's reward center was activated and dopamine was released. The researchers found that specific areas of the brain do "respond to novelty, and these responses scale according to how novel the image was."

According to neuroscientist Russell Poldrack, "The brain is built to ignore the old and focus on the new. Novelty is probably one of the most powerful signals to determine what we pay attention to in the world." He goes on to explain, "This makes a lot of sense from an evolutionary standpoint, since we don't want to spend all of our time and energy noticing the many things around us that don't change from day to day" (Poldrack, 2011).

When you think about our earliest ancestors, you can appreciate the role that novelty must have played in their lives. It would have been necessary for them to try new foods, new tools, and new environments, among many other experiences. This desire to seek out new information helped those early humans survive. And today it drives the current generation.

That's why the concept of "new" is so valuable to marketers. That single word immediately signals that there is a gap in a person's information. If something is new, it hasn't yet been learned or experienced. And that alone can make a product or service desirable.

When people see the word new, it raises their expectations and they anticipate a pleasurable experience. As Dr A.K. Pradeep says in his book *The Buying Brain: Secrets for selling to the subconscious mind*, "novelty contributes to interest, surprise, and attraction, and can even contribute to a decision to purchase" (Pradeep, 2010). Perhaps that is why *Copyblogger* lists "new" as one of the five most persuasive words in the English language for copywriting. And why *Brainfluence* author Roger Dooley refers to it as a "magic word," noting that its appeal is hardwired into the human brain (Dooley, 2012).

How novelty drives sales

People respond to things that are new. And those things don't have to be brand new. They can simply be new to the person, or new twists on an existing product or service, as these next two examples show.

HOW A NEW VERSION OF AN OLD PRODUCT DROVE SIGNIFICANT SALES

The first example is for a company that was introducing a new disability insurance product to resident physicians. For years, the industry treated doctors and residents the same way, offering them the same kind of policy using the same kind of qualifying criteria. And while doctors and residents both do need disability insurance, their situations are quite different. Doctors have higher salaries, and therefore qualify for more coverage.

Residents, on the other hand, have lower salaries. As a result, they do not qualify for much coverage—certainly not enough to take care of themselves were they to become disabled and unable to practice at this early stage in their careers.

The new product the company was introducing for residents would allow them to obtain significantly more monthly coverage, regardless of their current income. This was news. It was a twist on an existing product. And that twist meant the target was offered something different than they had previously been able to get.

The multichannel, multi-touch campaign drove that fact home. The copy emphasized words such as "until now," "introducing," "finally," and "new" in high-read pieces of communications real estate, such as headlines, subject lines, and lead sentences. To underscore the news, one email even closed with the reminder that the company had never made this offer before.

And despite the fact that resident physicians are extremely busy, and that insurance is not a top-of-mind topic for them, the campaign's message broke through and connected with its audience. It drove a 614 percent lift in sales over the prior campaign that targeted the same segment, proving once again that people are drawn to what's new.

FIGURE 9.1 "New" drives sales

↑ 614%

Novelty helped drive a triple-digit lift in sales for an insurance product.

HOW A SaaS COMPANY USED NEWS ABOUT THEIR TARGETS TO INTRIGUE THEM

This second example is for a software-as-a-service company. This company sold subscription marketing services to small businesses. The company's products helped their clients improve their online marketing efforts, so they would be more apt to be found by potential customers who were searching in their local area.

They did this by doing four things: building their clients a website optimized for mobile and search engine marketing, registering their clients' business with different directories, providing online reputation management, and handling the client's social media presence.

However, many small business owners feel they can rely on referrals alone to grow their business. They don't think they need to do online marketing. Other small business owners have had less than stellar experiences with lead generation services—the kind that require them to share leads with three or four competitors and pay for the leads whether or not they close the sale. Although this particular service was different, these business owners might confuse the marketing subscription offer with the lead generation services they were familiar with. Finally, some small business owners are not convinced that the time and money required to do online marketing would be worth it for them.

The company needed to put a campaign into the market that would overcome each of these concerns. It would have to quickly capture the target's attention, and then make a strong, succinct case for the subscription product they were selling.

A key component of the campaign they launched involved sending the target a personalized market assessment. It contained information that was new to the target. For example, the assessment included the average number of Google searches for the services the target's company offered, their Google ranking, and their website effectiveness score. It also displayed the available growth potential for the target's business. The small business owners received a printed copy in the mail, as well as a link to go online and view real-time updates to the data, effectively providing new news.

You can imagine how this might intrigue a small business owner. It was the kind of information they were not likely to see anywhere else. And this emphasis on new information paid off. The company saw a 40 percent lift in leads over their previous campaign. Additionally, the personalized URL had a 37 percent conversion rate, with each unique visitor averaging 3.3 visits to the site. The allure of new news was especially compelling.

Powerful ways for marketers to use information-gap theory and novelty

- Start headlines, subject lines, teaser copy, and bullet points with the words: who, what, where, when, why, or how. Journalists use this technique to attract readership. It works for marketers, too. Robert Bly, author of *How to Double Your Response Rates at Half the Cost*, refers to them as fascinations—ultra-specific bullets that get your target to read further and order.

- When using the 5 Ws + 1 H technique (above), make sure your copy appeals to your target. For example, "Why we provide great service" is not as compelling as "How you can expect to be treated."

- Tee up an information gap using superlatives, such as the best, worst, most, last, biggest, only, etc. Keep in mind that an Outbrain study found that negative superlatives outperform positive superlatives.

- Begin a story but delay the conclusion to prompt people to continue reading.

- Use ellipses in your subject line (example: And the winner is…). A May 2021 study by Worldata finds this tactic can lift email opening rates by 31 percent for B2B marketers, and by 28 percent for B2C marketers (Worldata, 2022).

- Pique people's curiosity by posing a question or challenging their assumptions. Consider taking a contrarian view.

- Invite your target to interact with an app or game that will reveal something about themselves, a subject you can count on people to be interested in.

- Create a quiz that lets people measure their knowledge about a favorite topic.

- Use a numbered list (example: Top 10 SaaS Providers) to offer information.

- Pop the word "new" in your headlines, titles, subject lines, and teasers. You can also use other words in the "new" family, such as introducing, announcing, now, finally, soon, innovative, debuting, latest, emerging, never before seen, and at last. For a verb, choose discover over learn, because learn sounds arduous and discover suggests fun.

- Lead off your communications with what's new. Don't bury news.

- Use violators, labels, and other visual cues to flag new products, features, and extensions so people can easily spot them.

- Create a separate area on your website or in your marketing communications to highlight your new offerings.

- Find and market new uses for your existing products.

KEY TAKEAWAYS

1 If there's a gap in people's information, they will take action to close it.

2 People are motivated to satisfy their curiosity because it is rewarding.

3 When people are about to discover something new, their brains release dopamine, which produces a pleasant feeling. Humans are hardwired to seek information.

4 Marketers who tee up an information gap in their communications should pay it off. Do not mislead or resort to clickbait because that can backfire.

5 When highlighting an information gap, choose a topic your target knows something about, but is not deeply familiar with.

6 Frame the information you want to present in a way that piques your audience's curiosity.

7 Your customers and prospects will be drawn to the new and novel.

8 Novelty can spur interest, attraction, and purchase decisions.

9 Trigger an information gap by using the 5 Ws and 1 H, superlatives, numbered lists, questions, quizzes, challenging statements, and delayed payoffs.

10 Use terms such as new, announcing, finally, soon, never before seen, and discover to signal novelty. Flag new products and new uses for products. Lead with what's new.

In conclusion

Curiosity is a powerful driver, because discovering news prompts the brain to release dopamine, which can make people feel good. As a result, people are driven to seek out news and information. By spotlighting an information gap, a marketer can create engagement with their customers and prospects. These people will feel compelled to find answers—to obey their innate desire for knowledge.

People also feel compelled to obey outside authorities, which is another hardwired behavior marketers can harness, as you'll see in the next chapter.

References

Bly, R (nd) *How to Double Your Response Rates at Half the Cost*, https://www.bly.com/Report.pdf (archived at https://perma.cc/59NN-BX7W)

Bromberg-Martin, E and Hikosaka, O (2009) Midbrain dopamine neurons signal preference for advance information about upcoming rewards, *Neuron*, 16 July https://www.cell.com/neuron/fulltext/S0896-6273(09)00462-0?_returnURL=https%3A%2F%2Flinkinghub.elsevier.com%2Fretrieve%2Fpii%2FS0896627309004620%3Fshowall%3Dtrue (archived at https://perma.cc/X78K-BFBS)

Dean, N (2019) The importance of novelty, *BrainWorld Magazine*, 05 September, https://brainworldmagazine.com/the-importance-of-novelty/ (archived at https://perma.cc/8THJ-YU3S)

Dooley, R (2012) *Brainfluence: 100 ways to persuade and convince consumers with neuromarketing*, John Wiley & Sons, New Jersey

Ewald, C (nd) US Navy—"Project Architeuthis", *Adforum*, https://www.adforum.com/creative-work/ad/player/34509511/project-architeuthis/us-navy (archived at https://perma.cc/MRR5-5SC6)

Kang, MJ, Hsu, M, Krajbich, IM, Loewenstein, GF, McClure, SM, Wang, JT and Camerer, CF (2008) The wick in the candle of learning: Epistemic curiosity activates reward circuitry and enhances memory, *Psychological Science*, 27 November, https://ssrn.com/abstract=1308286 (archived at https://perma.cc/ML7Y-LFFX)or http://dx.doi.org/10.2139/ssrn.1308286 (archived at https://perma.cc/7YJE-DUX3)

Loewenstein, G (1994) The psychology of curiosity: A review and reinterpretation, *Psychological Bulletin*, **116** (1) https://www.cmu.edu/dietrich/sds/docs/loewenstein/PsychofCuriosity.pdf (archived at https://perma.cc/S2PU-KYTA)

Poldrack, R (2011) Multitasking: The brain seeks novelty [Blog] *Huffpost*, 17 November, https://www.huffpost.com/entry/multitasking-the-brain-se_b_334674 (archived at https://perma.cc/4PYK-KH36)

Pradeep, AK (2010) *The Buying Brain: Secrets for selling to the subconscious mind*, John Wiley & Sons, New Jersey

Reynolds, E (2021) Preschool children choose to learn about topics where there are gaps in their knowledge they want to fill, *The British Psychological Society Research Digest*, 05 August, https://digest.bps.org.uk/2021/08/05/preschool-children-choose-to-learn-about-topics-where-there-are-gaps-in-their-knowledge-they-want-to-fill/ (archived at https://perma.cc/3F59-MCM8)

Weibe, J (2014) Should you use a curiosity gap to persuade your visitors to click? *Copyhackers*, https://copyhackers.com/2014/04/curiosity-gap/ (archived at https://perma.cc/E9TY-QAF7)

Worldata (2022)…= Suspense: "…"]At the end of subject lines = higher average open rates BtoB: 31%, BtoC: 28%, https://www.instagram.com/worldata/channel/?hl=en (archived at https://perma.cc/2A6B-XYH5)

10

Tapping into the authority principle to stand out and prompt responses

Behavioral scientists know that people are conditioned to respect and respond to authority. As a result, tapping into the Authority Principle is an easy way for you to prompt automatic action, as well as to differentiate your marketing message from your competitor's.

They say that multichannel shoppers are worth more than single-channel shoppers. They say that a follow-up email or direct mail piece will deliver incremental lift, even if you only change the subject line or the outer envelope teaser copy. They say that a customer's past behavior is the best predictor of their future behavior.

Of course, we as marketers believe them. But who are "they"? They are the people we turn to, the ones we trust to know, the providers of the information we take at face value. They supply the collected sources of marketing wisdom that help guide our decisions. They save us time and effort. And they make us feel reassured that we are making the right move—a move we just assume is based on someone else's trial and error or their months of painstaking research.

As marketers, we not only like to learn on someone else's dime, we have become accustomed to it. We depend on what "they" say to inform our marketing decisions, justify our game plans, and sell in our campaigns. If challenged, we are able to supply a ready answer: "Yes, but they say this is the method that works," or "Well, actually they say that will tank response." And to be truthful, this approach has served marketers well. Over the course of your career, you will probably base hundreds if not thousands of decisions on what you've heard from others. Many of those decisions will be relatively small, such as how to write a subject line or how to structure a blog post. Some of the decisions may be bigger. But what they will all have in common is that you heard that they were the right way to do something. And who you heard it, or read it, from made all the difference.

Why? Because those are the people to whom you accord authority status. The source of the information you obtain is important. It can influence whether you question that information, dismiss it outright, or readily embrace it. The people you think of as authorities can be the original discoverers of the information, or they can simply be the ones curating it and passing it on to you. But they are the ones you trust and believe. Sometimes you will know these people personally. Often you will not. And sometimes you may simply know of them. You may have heard of them. You may be familiar with an organization they are associated with. Or you may know their title or occupation and find that to be enough. That is how authority works.

Based on certain signals that some people project, we defer to them as authority figures or subject matter experts. We typically listen when they speak, are more apt to believe what they say, and are more likely to do what they tell us to do. This response is a hardwired, human one.

Ever since we were children, we were taught to recognize and respect authority. We were surrounded by people who we were expected to obey, starting with our parents, and then extending to our teachers, coaches, crossing guards, life guards, school bus drivers, camp counselors, family physicians, and the myriad other adults who populate a child's life. As a result, by the time we are adults, responding appropriately to authority is ingrained in us. The direction provided by an authority can, and often does, shortcut our own decision-making. When the source of information or instructions is an authority figure, we are less likely to argue or disagree. And we are more likely to accept and act accordingly. For these reasons, you want to use the authority principle in your marketing. You may even want to be the "they" your target market references.

> Behavioral scientists have proven that humans have a powerful need to respond to authority. Marketers can use that to your advantage.

People can feel compelled to respect and respond to authorities

Considerable scientific research has shown that humans respond to authority. Scientists believe that people are hardwired to do so. Of course, not every person does every time. But generally speaking, people have a tendency to do what those in positions of authority request. In fact, an interesting experiment reported in the April 2016 issue of the *Journal of Economic Behavior and Organization* supports the use of the word "request" in that last sentence. People in positions of power and authority don't always have to mandate behavior in order to bring it about.

In this particular experiment, two people played a game with made-up money called guilders (Karakostas and Zizzo, 2016). During the game, each player had to decide whether or not to destroy some of the other player's guilders. Researchers found that when the authority figure, who in this case was the person leading the experiment, explicitly but politely requested that a player reduce his partner's income because it would be "useful," but did not offer any explanation as to why, the destruction rate more than doubled. The researchers noted, "If the request is phrased as an order, the increase is not as large."

Additionally, when a reason was tacked on to the polite request, with the researcher saying that reducing the other player's earnings at that time "would help us achieve a scientific objective of the experiment," compliance rates went as high as 70 percent. (Read more about providing reasons to trigger compliance in Chapter 13.) The researchers concluded that "compliance to a cue by an authority is a powerful motivating mechanism." In other words, when an authority figure suggests that a person take a specific action, that person very often will.

Of course, this experiment took place within the confines of a game, with players using fake money. You may think it was not a big deal to comply if the person running the experiment requested you play a certain way. However, an earlier experiment designed to measure authority also found humans appear to have a hardwired tendency to obey. And this experiment was not couched in a game. In it, people obeyed both milder requests from an authority as well as more forceful exhortations to behave in a particular way. In this experiment, the participants did not think they were simply reducing another participant's stash of fake currency. Rather, they were led to believe that they were inflicting pain on another human being.

The Stanley Milgram shock experiment

The experiment took place in the '60s, and was led by Stanley Milgram at Yale University. Participants were recruited to take part in research that was purported to test memory and learning, along with the related effect of punishment. In the experiment, the participant and the researcher sat in a room in front of a large machine designed to generate electric shocks. The machine had 30 switches, which could deliver shocks starting at 15 volts and progress incrementally to 450 volts. Under groupings of switches were labels that began at Slight Shock and continued all the way to Danger: Severe Shock, and then simply XXX.

The participants, who believed they were randomly assigned to the role of teacher, were instructed to read a series of word pairs that could be heard by the "learners," who were in the adjacent room, strapped to a chair with electrodes attached to their wrists. In actuality, the "learners" were not participants in the experiment, but rather part of the research team.

Once the participant read the word pairs, they would then read the first word of a pair along with four other words, and the "learner" was supposed to indicate which of those four was the correct answer. The participants were instructed to deliver a shock if the wrong answer was given, and to increase the voltage with each wrong reply. The "learner" had been privately instructed to provide the incorrect answer at predetermined times. Additionally, by the time the shocks hit the 300-volt level, they were to not only scream out in pain but to pound on the wall. Eventually, they were to go completely silent.

As you might imagine, when the research participants heard the pounding and screaming from the adjacent room, they looked to the research leader for guidance. The leader told them to continue. He also instructed them to consider no reply from the learner as a wrong answer, which would require a shock. The language the researcher used to encourage the participants to continue started with "Please continue," followed by "The experiment requires that you continue," and then "It is absolutely essential that you continue," and finally, "You have no other choice—you must go on."

What Milgram reported was that of 40 participants, 26 fully obeyed the researcher and delivered shocks all the way to the maximum amount on the generator, labeled 450 volts—XXX. He noted that none of the participants refused to administer the shocks until they reached the 300-volt mark, when the learner banged on the wall. At that point, the participant had already delivered 20 shocks, starting at 15 volts and escalating by 15 volts for each subsequent shock.

While the participants did obey the authority in the room, it was not easy for many of them. Milgram reports that they "were observed to sweat, tremble, stutter, bite their lips, groan, and dig their fingernails into their flesh." Moreover, he described these responses as "characteristic rather than exceptional." Yet, as he observed, "they obeyed," which does "suggest that for many persons obedience may be a deeply ingrained behavior tendency" (Milgram, 1963).

FIGURE 10.1 The power of authority

Milgram found that 65% of research subjects continued to deliver electric shocks up to the maximum amount—labeled "450 volts XXX."

Newer experiments find similar findings to the Milgram research

Other researchers have subsequently conducted similar studies to investigate how strongly people are influenced by authority figures. According to a March 2009 *American Psychological Association* post, social psychologist Jerry M. Burger, PhD, ran a modified version of the Milgram experiment which showed compliance rates that "were only slightly lower than those found by Milgram" (Mills, 2009). A July 2018 *Behavioral Scientist* article reports that, in another similar study led by Dariusz Dolinski, compliance rates were even higher (Greenwood, 2018). That same post also references a 2012 *European Review of Applied Psychology* report about a French television game show that also staged a similar experiment. They, too, found equally high levels of obedience.

This latter is notable if only for the fact that a television game show host was viewed as an authority figure in that context. Position and title are two possible indicators of authority. But there are others, as well. In his "Behavioral Study of Obedience," Milgram pointed to several other indicators of authority in his experiment. One was Yale University, and its "unimpeachable reputation." Another was the researcher himself, who had a "stern" appearance and was clad in a "gray technician's coat." A third was that the research itself was an effort to further a field of scientific inquiry, which the participants may have deemed a "worthy purpose." Clearly, authority can be conveyed by many means. As a marketer, you're not about to shock your customers into buying. But appropriately harnessing the authority principle can trigger the hardwired reaction to comply.

Projecting authority with the wall of power

My first job out of Boston University was at Mullen Advertising. I entered the marketing world as a public relations assistant/writer. I got laid off about nine months later, when some clients cut back on their business. But I loved those nine months. Which is just one of the reasons I was delighted to return to the agency 13 years later, tapped to head up their direct marketing creative offering. At that time, the agency had stood up and then dismantled two previous attempts to get into the direct marketing space. They were at their heart a general agency, and an extremely good one at that. But for business reasons, they had decided it made sense for the agency to once again offer direct marketing services.

So off I go, excited to be returning to this wonderful agency. Only this time, I was coming in as an outsider. General agency people know how to build brands, and do funny television commercials, and write witty head-lines. Direct marketing people work in a different way. Or maybe it's more accurate to say we work in a different world. And I had spent the last dozen years in that world. But now I was firmly in a general advertising agency environment.

And I sensed some hesitancy about me on the part of my new colleagues. It was understandable. The account people, who managed the client rela-tionships, were protective of those clients. They didn't want to advise them to try something new, like a direct marketing campaign, unless they felt confident that advice would be good. And the creative people, who all had to be at the top of their game to earn a spot at this powerhouse agency, didn't really know how to judge direct marketing creative.

For a while, I didn't know what to do. How could I convince them I knew my stuff, when they didn't yet have a frame of reference for what I did? Even the words we all shared seemed to have different meanings. When I would talk about response to a campaign, I would mean calls made, coupons redeemed, leads generated, or some similar metric. When they used the phrase, it was often to convey a client or marketplace reaction.

And then one day, it dawned on me what our common language might be. The agency was well-recognized in the business. Each year at the adver-tising award shows, they would haul home dozens of bowls and certificates, recognizing all their wins across various clients and categories. I, too, had accumulated my own stash of award plaques and framed certificates from my time working at previous agencies. So, I dragged in a few boxes of them and hung the awards on the wall behind my desk. Anyone who came into my office to talk to me would be looking at them as they did so.

My friends jokingly referred to it as my wall of power. It certainly did convey authority. And to this day, I believe it helped establish my abilities in a way my colleagues could easily get. The awards projected expertise. They carried independent, third-party validation. And even if they were from award shows that were different from the ones the agency had been enter-ing, they were awards. And awards recognized excellence. They served as an objective measure of my authority.

CASE STUDY
Leveraging the look and tone of authority

As Marshall McLuhan famously said, sometimes the medium is the message. That turned out to be the case for one client who came to the agency where I was working with a particularly thorny B2B challenge. The client was a mutual fund provider, and their target market was financial advisors, who would then sell those mutual funds to individual investors.

The mutual fund business is extremely competitive, with thousands of funds for advisors to choose from. Often, those advisors selected funds not just for performance alone, but also based on their perception of the company behind them, their understanding of that company's product offerings, and their general trust and comfort in doing business with that company.

The problem was, the advisors typically got their product information and research from third-party providers such as Morningstar. In doing so, they weren't developing any affiliation with our client's brand. They also weren't in a position for our client to easily update them about new products and services. In fact, they were downright difficult to reach. Because financial advisors were a very busy group of professionals, their preference was to interact with our client's company by speaking directly to their wholesaler there, with whom they had a relationship. Realistically, however, wholesalers can only contact so many advisors.

So, our client created a password-protected, advisor-only section of their website. There, financial advisors could access up-to-date product and performance information, as well as tools and thought leadership content, at their convenience. But very few advisors chose to do so. Our challenge was to find a way to double the number of monthly registrations to the password-protected portion of the site. It was a tall one.

As such, the creative team explored a number of options. One revolved around the idea that registering at the site would help the financial advisors in their job. Because it provided immediate access to fund information, along with thought leadership content, registering could actually deliver a competitive advantage. While this was true, it was also true that the financial advisors were already accessing both fund information and thought leadership content from other sources. We decided this approach didn't seem persuasive enough to get them to change their habits.

Another concept highlighted loss aversion (see Chapter 2). The idea was to list the six kinds of information that were available only behind the password-protected portion of the site, and then caution financial advisors that they could not get access to it unless they registered. However, since the client had earlier tried promoting the availability of this content without much success, we feared that even with the loss aversion spin, the message might not be powerful enough.

A third idea played off of the exclusivity half of the scarcity principle (see Chapter 3). The team proposed sending an invitation that said the advisor had earned the right to access the site, and simply needed to accept it by signing in. This would elevate the idea of having access, and position it as something of value. The concept had possibilities. Unfortunately, one of them was that the financial advisors might view the invitation as a sales pitch, and that would be bad for the relationship.

Finally, the team landed on an approach that would trigger the authority principle. Because the financial advisors were time-starved, the team decided to keep the message brief. They chose not to go into detail about all the convenient information and smart content on offer. Instead, they would simply focus on the action the financial advisor needed to take—registering for the password-protected portion of the site.

The medium they selected to deliver that message was a snap pack, the kind of mailing a W-2 form, personal identification number, paystub, or other official notification might arrive in. An authoritative package that cuts through the clutter and gets noticed. The team used a stripped-down, black-and-white look, which appeared very serious, and not like typical advertising mail. They also kept the copy short and to the point. In a non-promotional tone, it notified the financial advisor that, as of a specific date, the mutual fund company had not yet received their registration. The copy then informed them that registration was required in order to gain full access to the site, including the proprietary advisor-only content.

The entire message was six sentences long, including the thank you line. But those six serious sentences, delivered in that official-looking snap pack, packed quite a punch. They didn't just double the monthly registrations at the site, they blew them away. The piece beat previous efforts by 673 percent.

In fact, the response was so strong that the operations team at the client couldn't keep up with the back-end processing that was required. The client had to delay the next wave of the mailing until they had caught up. That was the power of an authoritative approach. The official look got the piece noticed and opened. And the no-nonsense tone and message got it responded to. When the financial advisors saw that snap pack arrive in the mail, they felt compelled to open it and to comply with what it asked.

How a vehicle protection plan provider harnessed the authority principle

When delivering a sales message, marketers should think strategically about how they can use the authority principle. Very often, the same message can be perceived differently depending on who it's from. When customers evaluate a message, they consider both the content and context, which includes the source of the information.

One company that harnessed the authority principle in a smart way is Service Payment Plan (SPP), a company within the automotive protection industry. They came to us at HBT Marketing with the request that we develop a large email campaign to help them market vehicle protection plans. Drivers typically buy these plans to help cover the cost of repairs their vehicle may need, especially if their manufacturer's warranty has expired. SPP's idea was to have the email come from the dealership where the target had purchased their vehicle. "We believe that drivers regard the person or dealership that sold them their vehicle as being something of an authority on that vehicle," said Charlie Hymen, President of Service Payment Plan, Inc. "As a result, drivers should be more likely to follow their advice."

In this context, the dealership personnel—who know what they sold a person and who may also continue to service that vehicle—are in fact authorities. And we were able to leverage that authority status in our campaign for SPP. Emails included insider tips that could help customers save money and avoid certain missteps, mentions of repairs the dealership commonly saw and their associated costs, advice that revealed the best times to obtain a vehicle protection plan, and other relevant information that reinforced the dealer as the authority.

Imagine you're the driver being asked to purchase a plan. You receive an email from a company you've never heard of—one that has never seen you or your car, yet tells you that you should get a plan. Or you receive an email from your dealership—the same one that reminds you to come in for service or gives you the heads up when they are about to have a sale, and they recommend you get a plan. Who are you more likely to listen to? As *Influence: The psychology of persuasion* author Robert Cialdini has observed, "Information from a recognized authority can provide us a valuable shortcut for deciding how to act in a situation."

MISTAKE

Not taking advantage of contextual authorities. Your authority does not have to be a household name. Someone can be considered an authority based on where they work or the experiences they've had.

Authority comes in many forms. Here's how you can leverage four of them

- When marketers first think of using the authority principle, it's only natural to think of authority figures. And that's a good place to start. Properly using an authority figure in your marketing can help prompt sales. Look into generally accepted authorities, such as doctors (perhaps you can recall a cigarette company that once used a doctor in their marketing, or a chewing gum company that cited dentists), judges, university academics, captains of industry, think tanks, large research firms, best-selling authors, and Nobel Prize winners. Also think about authorities in the context of your message, like SPP did. And don't forget that sometimes people will accord authority status to celebrities, even if the celebrity's expertise is not directly connected with the product or service they endorse (see Chapter 5).

- Subject matter experts are another form of authority, and they can be an individual person or an organization. For example, people seeking information about wine may turn to Robert Parker or the *Wine Spectator* Top 100 List. Consider the role of the *Good Housekeeping* seal of approval, the A.M. Best rating company, *Consumer Reports* and other established media outlets. They are all examples of subject matter experts who, by virtue of that expertise, are authorities. Your target market will consider them independent experts whose job it is to know their specific field. For example, my friend Joanne was on the fence about buying a particular summer condo on the beach. But when her real estate agent said he'd buy it if she decided not to, that made her more certain she should make the purchase.

- People wearing uniforms are also often considered authorities—everyone from a police officer to a pilot to a security guard. In fact, according to a March 2019 report in the *Oregon News*, two men dressed up as security guards put an "out of order" sign over the night deposit slot at a Wells Fargo bank, and collected hundreds of dollars from unsuspecting customers before taking off with the cash. And the uniform in question doesn't have to be on a guard. For example, one day my friends Sharon and Colleen got into a parking dispute with another driver while visiting New York City. My friends were attempting to save a coveted spot on the street for their friend Lyn, who needed to move her car from a nearby garage. While they were standing in the spot, another driver pulled up and prepared to back in. Just as my friends were beginning to explain the spot was already spoken for, Lyn drove up and began to pull in. Suddenly, there was a parking standoff. When it seemed like the other driver was not going to move on, Sharon set off down the street to find someone in a position of authority to help settle things. She returned with the bellhop from a nearby hotel. When I asked her why that was who she chose, she said she'd been unable to locate a police officer, and she thought at least the bellhop was wearing a uniform.

- Certain props can also convey authority. A stack of leatherbound law books, a framed diploma, a lifeguard's whistle, and a marcher's bullhorn are all examples. An embossed seal on an envelope or letter can suggest authority. Similarly, a text-only email may project seriousness and authority. Additionally, the way a person is attired can project authority. UK fundraising consultancy Bright Spot reports that researchers in Texas conducted a study involving a man who crossed the street against the light. Sometimes he was dressed in a suit and tie. Other times, he wore more casual clothes. The researchers found that when the man was wearing the business suit, three times as many pedestrians followed him off the curb and into the traffic.

More powerful ways to leverage the authority principle in your marketing

- Use important titles, such as Doctor, Attorney, President, Director, Dean, etc. These can be especially potent when used in the corner card of a direct mail piece (the upper left-hand corner of an envelope where the return address often appears), the sender line of an email, or in the signatures of communications you send. And you can be creative. For example, if your company's president does not wish to sign a direct mail letter or an email, have it come from the Office of the President. Years ago, I worked on a health newsletter that was marketed to businesses, so they could distribute it to their employees. It was written by a doctor. The long-standing subscription control for it used his name, followed by M.D., in the corner card.

- Make sure to mention if your product, service, or company was written about in business publications or professional journals, or was featured in popular magazines, blogs, or television news programs.

- Pop any awards or certifications your company, company's founder, or product has won and any recognition bestowed on them. (example: Ted

Talk speaker, *Forbes* contributor, Mensa member, *NY Times* best-selling author, Nobel Prize recipient, CES Innovation award winner). For example, my friend Amy Schrob co-owns the visual design studio, ONE80 Visual. I always mention they're Emmy Award winners when I recommend it, to signal how good they are.

- Include trust badges, such as safe payment and accepted payment badges, on your landing pages and website. These will contribute to the perception of your authority.

- Highlight lists your company's been included on, such as Inc. 500, Amazon bestsellers, or any trade or industry lists that your customers and prospects will recognize.

- If you're not yet widely known, partner with a well-known brand. Potential customers will infer that brand vouches for you (example: co-present, sponsored by, in partnership with).

- Feature endorsements you receive (example: rated by Moody's, Michelin starred) or associations you belong to (example: Better Business Bureau).

- Point to the years you've been in business, the number of patents your company holds, the number of clients you've served, or other successful companies you've started or products you've launched.

- To establish your personal authority, mention your background (example: companies worked at, years of research conducted, experts studied under, Ivy League schools attended, degrees attained).

- Use clothing, power poses, and props to convey authority (example: conversion scientist Brian Massey is pictured in a white lab coat on his website; John Sisson, my business partner at HBT Marketing, often wears an "I'm Irrational" lapel pin to client meetings—nodding to his expertise in behavioral science).

- Create content that positions you as an expert (example: Orbit Media Studio's Andy Crestodina published an article entitled "How to Design A Blog: The 13 Best Practices of the Top 100+ Marketing Blogs").

- Choose language like world-renowned, recognized expert, definitive authority, proven, time-tested, best of breed, established, reference brand, often quoted, and award-winning.

- Feature positive star ratings you've earned.

- If you're in professional services, highlight recognizable clients you've done work for.
- Include pictures of authority figures or props where appropriate (example: a company that sells employee health plans could show a picture of a doctor or a stethoscope in their marketing).

KEY TAKEAWAYS

1 People are hardwired to recognize and respect authority.

2 Your customers are more apt to listen to what an authority says, and do what an authority asks.

3 Scientific research shows many people feel a strong need to obey authority.

4 Marketers can use authority figures or symbols of authority in their communications to prompt response.

5 Marketing communications that look and sound authoritative can trigger compliance.

6 Some authority figures are widely recognized and others are contextual. Don't overlook contextual authority figures as you develop your marketing messages. The key is to choose someone your audience perceives to be an authority.

7 Your customers will use information from authorities as a decision-making shortcut.

8 Marketers can tap authority figures, subject matter experts, uniforms, and other authority props in their campaigns in order to signal their expertise and convey their authority.

9 Include important titles, media mentions, awards won, trust badges, lists you've been named to, and endorsement you've received to your marketing messages to project authority.

10 Consider clothing and symbols that convey authority when creating your marketing assets.

11 Position yourself or your company as an authority by publishing content that demonstrates your command of a subject.

In conclusion

Defaulting to authorities and subject matter experts is a common decision-making shortcut. Your customer or prospect will assume those people have done the work for them, saving them time and effort. They typically believe these authorities are knowledgeable and should be listened to.

In addition to authority figures, a marketer can also leverage authority symbols to increase compliance and trust. Experts and authorities signal an easier way to make decisions, which is an approach that humans often seek.

Another way to make it easy for your customers and prospects to make a decision is to guide them to it, with the choice you want them to select being at the end of the path of least resistance. In the next chapter, you'll see how you can use Choice Architecture to do just that.

References

Cialdini, R (1984) *Influence, The psychology of persuasion*, Quill William Morrow, New York

Greenwood, J (2018) How would people behave in Milgram's experiment today? *Behavioral Scientist*, 24 July, https://behavioralscientist.org/how-would-people-behave-in-milgrams-experiment-today/ (archived at https://perma.cc/J9Q9-FZLF)

Karakostas, A, and Zizzo, D (2016) Compliance and the power of authority, *Journal of Economic Behavior and Organization*, https://www.sciencedirect.com/science/article/pii/S0167268115002590 (archived at https://perma.cc/BP2Z-ZFVM)

Milgram, S (1963) Behavioral Study of Obedience, *The Journal of Abnormal and Social Psychology*, **67** (4), pp 371–378, https://doi.org/10.1037/h0040525 (archived at https://perma.cc/456X-CTMZ)

Mills, KI (2009) More shocking results: New research replicates Milgram's findings, *American Psychological Association*, https://www.apa.org/monitor/2009/03/milgram#:~:text=More%20shocking%20results%3A%20New%20research%20replicates%20Milgram's%20findings,-March%202009%2C%20Vol&text=Burger%2C%20a%20professor%20at%20Santa,than%20those%20found%20by%20Milgram (archived at https://perma.cc/W7ZX-E4CZ)

11

Choice architecture and status quo bias: how to use inertia to get things moving

People prefer the status quo to exerting the energy to act. This can sound like dismal news to a marketer unless that marketer uses Status Quo Bias to their advantage, presenting the desired behaviors as the default or the path of least resistance. By thoughtfully architecting choices, marketers can use the predilection for inaction to actually drive action.

So far, if you've been reading each chapter of this book in succession, you've discovered a number of ways to influence your customers and prospects. You've seen the important role that emotion plays when people make either a B2B or a B2C buying decision (Chapter 1). You've seen that some motivating emotions include the fear of loss (Chapter 2), the feeling of being special (Chapter 3), the guilt if you don't repay what someone has done for you (Chapter 4), and the security that comes with doing what other people are doing (Chapter 5).

You have also found that stories are an ideal vehicle to stimulate emotions (Chapter 6). Additionally, you've seen that people like to feel autonomy (Chapter 7), that they experience a certain comfort when they act consistently (Chapter 8), and that when they feel the itch of curiosity, they usually scratch it (Chapter 9). Most recently, in the previous chapter, you learned that humans feel a strong obligation to obey those who appear to be in charge.

If you've been reading in succession, you have also encountered another way to influence behavior. Social scientists call it choice architecture. Researchers have found that the way choices are presented actually influences the decisions a person will make about them. I chose to present the behavioral science principles in this book in a particular order, and numbered the chapters accordingly. If you've read each chapter in succession, you were influenced by my choice architecture. Of course, you don't need to read the chapters in that way, and I'm completely aware that some readers may choose not to. That is absolutely fine. You are free to dip into whichever chapter topic you wish, and throughout the book you'll see references to appropriate chapters that come before or after the one you elect to read so you can easily locate related information.

But if you've read the chapters in order, you were influenced by my choice architecture. Similarly, the way you as a marketer present information and choices will affect the behavior of your customers and prospects. Everything from how you construct the fields on your landing pages to the way you design your products is an opportunity to thoughtfully deploy choice architecture.

As Richard Thaler and Cass Sunstein, authors of *Nudge: Improving decisions about health, wealth, and happiness*, observe, "there is no such thing as a 'neutral' design."

How you display information, and how you offer options, will influence how your customers and prospects ultimately make decisions about them. This can include the number of choices you provide, the order in which you list those choices, what information your design and visual cues draw attention to, the words you choose to describe various options, and the ease or lack thereof that customers encounter when completing your order form.

Even if at first blush you believe these are of no significant consequence, you should reconsider. Because as you will see, science has shown that they can have a measurable impact on the performance of your marketing. While people certainly do, as you may point out, make choices based on their preferences and past experiences, there are also other factors at play. And a key one is choice architecture.

Research has shown that people's decisions are impacted by the way their choices are served up to them. How you organize your options is important.

Choice architecture can exert a strong influence on how people decide

In their book, Thaler and Sunstein explain that "A choice architect has the responsibility for organizing the context in which people make decisions."

They go on to explain that "small and apparently insignificant details can have a major impact on people's behavior." A number of research studies have proven this to be the case. One they cite, conducted by Eric Johnson and Dan Goldstein (2003), involves organ donor rates. The researchers found, using an online survey, that when people were asked to indicate whether or not they wanted to be an organ donor, 79 percent said that they did. However, when people were told that in the state they'd just moved to, the default was not to be an organ donor, and if they wished to be a donor, they needed to change their status and opt in, only 42 percent did.

On the other hand, when they were told that in their new state it was presumed that people would be organ donors and if the person did not wish to be one, they needed to actively opt out, 82% of the people remained donors—even more than the 79 percent in the neutral (no default) version of the question, and considerably more than the 42 percent in the opt-in version. As Thaler and Sunstein note, "Many organizations in both the public and the private sector have discovered the immense power of default options."

German researchers ran an online study that also supports the impact of defaults in the decisions people make. It was referenced in "A systematic scoping review of the choice architecture movement: Toward understanding when and why nudges work," published in a December 2014 issue of the *Journal of Behavioral Decision Making* (Szaszi et al., 2014). The study measured whether German households "would purchase their energy from renewable sources for a slightly higher price or not (Ebeling and Lotz, 2015)."

The study found that in the opt-in condition, only 7 percent of the survey participants chose to purchase the higher-priced, renewable energy. However, in the opt-out condition, a substantial 70 percent did. This study suggests that if you, as a marketer, want to get people moving in a specific direction, you should carefully consider your defaults.

Descriptions, order, novelty, imagery and ease can all be used to influence a person's choice

Of course, defaults are not the only way to architect choice. Descriptive words, plus the order in which people encounter available choices, can also impact decisions. One study conducted in school cafeterias in North Wales found that choice architecture could be employed to motivate children to eat more fruit by, among other things, positioning the fruit before the desserts in the cafeteria line, and using descriptive names that kids would find attractive, such as "Superpower Satsumas" (Marcano-Olivier et al., 2019).

Another experiment showed that people could be prompted to take the stairs, the presumably healthier alternative, instead of an escalator. The fun study, sponsored by Volkswagen and conducted in Stockholm, Sweden, turned the stairway leading out of the Odenplan subway station into an oversized piano keyboard. Stepping on each step would actually play a note. The experiment's organizers found that the musical steps prompted 66 percent more people than usual to take the stairs (Bates, 2009).

A third experiment demonstrated that the background an ecommerce site displayed on their splash page could influence which product a shopper preferred (Mandel and Johnson, 2002). In the study, people saw either a blue background with clouds, or a green background with coins. Seeing the clouds primed purchasers for comfort, and they were more likely to prefer the more comfortable, *more expensive* couch. Seeing the dollar signs primed them to think of cost, and as a result, people were more likely to choose the less comfortable, less costly couch.

Finally, behavioral economists have shown that giving people an easy way to choose an action that would happen later, and then relegating that action to autopilot status, can motivate more of them to commit to that specific action. This 2004 experiment was conducted by Richard H. Thaler and Shlomo Benartzi, and involved employees' decisions to save for their retirement.

While some employees never sign up for their company's retirement plan, others do enroll but then never change their contribution amounts. Neither of these situations is optimum for saving.

Thaler and Benartzi created the Save More Tomorrow (or SMarT) program to try to change those behaviors. In the program, employees "commit in advance to allocating a portion of their future salary increases toward retirement savings." Employees who joined the program agreed to have the amount of money they contributed to their company-sponsored retirement savings plan increased by a set percentage after their next pay raise, which would happen at some point down the road. That amount would increase again by a specific percentage after subsequent pay raises until a preset maximum was reached.

In their paper, "Using behavioral economics to increase employee saving," the authors report that in the first of three implementations they tested (the first having been in place the longest—for four pay raises), 78 percent of the employees who were offered the program signed up for it, the "vast majority" had continued with it, and "the average saving rates for SMarT program participants increased from 3.5 percent to 13.6 percent over the course of 40 months." Thaler and Benartzi observed that "the

SMarT plan takes precisely the same behavioral tendency that induces people to postpone saving indefinitely (i.e., procrastination and inertia) and puts it to use."

Why choice architecture works

These studies show that what a person decides to do can be heavily influenced by choice architecture. Many other studies also support this finding. And it is one that can be extremely useful to marketers. As we've seen, research shows the use of defaults can be particularly powerful. One reason is that people have a tendency to stick with them. For example, think about the number of people that you know who use their laptops and mobile phones with the same defaults the manufacturer originally set up—never changing them. Thaler and Sunstein (2009) write that "In many contexts, defaults have some extra nudging power because consumers may feel, rightly or wrongly, that default options come with an implicit endorsement from the default setter." This suggests that consumers may accept the defaults a marketer sets for this same reason.

Architecting choices by making one option appear to be the more fun or novel one is an additional tactic marketers can employ. It can both attract attention and appeal to the human need for novelty (see Chapter 9).

Another effective choice architecture tactic is for a marketer to position the desired option as easy, simple, beneficial, and requiring little effort. All of these are quite likely to appeal to your customers. Why? Because, as Thaler and Sunstein point out, those customers are typically "busy people trying to cope in a complex world in which they cannot afford to think deeply about every choice they have to make." As a result, their decisions are often driven by choice architecture.

It is important to note, however, that choice architecture is not about forcing a person's hand. They should always be able to make a different decision, for example opting out of an organ donor program, selecting a less expensive fuel source, choosing to take the escalator, buying a different couch, passing on participating in a retirement savings program, etc.

HOW CHOICE ARCHITECTURE INFLUENCED THIS AUTHOR'S CONTRIBUTION
TO THREE DIFFERENT CHARITIES
My exercise of choice is a "shog." That's my personal combination of a shuffle and a jog, with more emphasis on the former than I care to admit. So, I was understandably impressed when Megan, a petite account supervisor at

the agency where I was working, announced that she was running the Boston Marathon, perhaps the most legendary of the 26.2-mile-long running competitions. Not only was Megan running the race, with its infamous Heartbreak Hill literally a short "shog" from where I lived, she was running to help raise money for a charity she volunteered for. Called Back on My Feet, the charity's mission is to combat homelessness across the country—a very good cause. Naturally, I was more than happy to support her run with a pledge.

A few months later, I got an email from Leslie, a former colleague from another agency. She wrote to say that her husband was taking part in the Pan Mass Challenge, which is a demanding bike-a-thon that covers 168 miles over the course of two days—rain or shine. Leslie is a breast cancer survivor. And the Pan Mass Challenge helps raise money for cancer research and treatment at the Dana-Farber Cancer Institute, where she had been a patient. In her email, she included some of her personal story about getting diagnosed with the disease, and what it was like to go in for her follow-up checkups. There was no question I wanted to support her husband's ride with a pledge, too.

Although both of my colleagues are marketers, there had been no choice architecture involved in their fundraising requests. They had simply mentioned what they were doing, and I had wanted to support their causes. Given my clear lack of athletic ability, that support was obviously going to be financial. And that is where the choice architecture came in. I had decided to make a $100 donation to each of them.

When I got to the Back on My Feet pledge confirmation page, they showed my $100 donation, followed by a $4.50 charge that I assume covered the administrative and processing costs of my donation, for a total of $104.50. To be fair, there was a small orange "edit" link next to the $4.50 charge, so I could have clicked it to remove the charge and bring my total down to the $100 I had originally pledged. But there was a large orange "donate now" button beneath the $104.50 total, and that was very easy to click, so I did. In a blink, my credit card was charged $104.50 for the Back on My Feet pledge I'd made to Megan.

When I got the Pan Mass Challenge pledge confirmation page, the information was displayed differently. It showed my $100 pledge followed by a $100 total. Beneath that, there was a small, unchecked box. The copy next to it invited me to add the cost of covering the credit card fee for my donation by checking the box. However, I did not. Now I want to stress that I believed both causes were worthy. And that I was not favoring one colleague over the other. I was just moving quickly and not exerting a lot of mental effort. As a result, I did what behavioral scientists have found many people do. I did not opt out. I did not opt in. I opted for what was right in front of me. I followed the defaults.

In the first case, I paid the little bit extra to cover the cost of processing my donation because it was the quickest, easiest, least effortful thing to do. And in the second case, I did not—for the very same reasons. I wasn't really thinking. I was just doing. And as a result, the way the choices were served up to me influenced how I responded to them. It was only later, when I was gathering landing page samples for a presentation about behavioral science in marketing, that I realized what I had done.

These days, whenever I make a donation, I try to remember to check what kind of choice architecture is being used on the confirmation page. Whether they saw my marketing presentation or not, I have noticed that the Pan Mass Challenge has changed their approach. The confirmation for my most recent donation showed my pledge, the credit card fee, and my total, which included that fee. At the bottom of the page was an unchecked box that I could choose to tick if I wanted the Dana Farber Cancer Institute to pay the credit card fee for my donation. In case you're wondering, I left it unchecked.

Several years ago, when a good friend's mom passed away, I encountered another clever use of choice architecture on a donation page. My friend's mom had died of Alzheimer's disease, so I decided to make a contribution to the Alzheimer's Association. If I had sent flowers to the wake, I would have spent $100, so I thought a $100 donation would make sense. But when I got to the site, the donation options I was presented with went from $60 directly

FIGURE 11.1 Choice architecture in fundraising

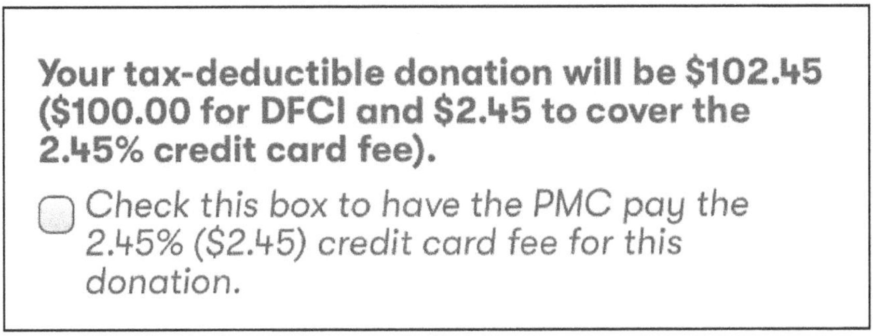

> **Your tax-deductible donation will be $102.45 ($100.00 for DFCI and $2.45 to cover the 2.45% credit card fee).**
>
> ☐ Check this box to have the PMC pay the 2.45% ($2.45) credit card fee for this donation.

The credit card fee is automatically added to my donation unless I opt to check the box telling the charity to pay it instead.

to $120, with no $100 choice. There was a spot for me to type in a custom amount. But as you've probably guessed, I did not. That would have required more effort than I was willing to make right then. The $120 button seemed close enough to the $100 amount I had been planning to give, so I just clicked that. And it would not surprise me if that is what a lot of people do. In fact, the last time I checked, I saw the same donation options were in place, with no $100 choice listed.

CASE STUDY

Using choice architecture to boost sales meeting attendance

In Chapter 5, there's a case study about hard-to-sell insurance, and the role social proof played in the successful multichannel campaign. However, that was just one behavioral science principle that the marketing leveraged. As you may recall, the client markets voluntary workplace benefits, specifically insurance designed to help cover disabilities, accidents, and critical illnesses—policies that the employee would pay for on their own. An important component of the sales process is a meeting held at the workplace, where a representative from the insurance company talks with the employee about the various kinds of coverage available and how they could be helpful.

Typically, employees find out about the meeting through an email that the human resources department sends out. The email would explain that the insurance company representative would be coming in on a particular day, and invite employees to sign up to meet with that representative to learn more and, if interested, purchase the coverage. One goal our client had was to increase the number of employees that attended a meeting at their workplace. The agency team got on it, thinking of ideas that would get the largest number of employees to a meeting.

One way, of course, would be to tap into the authority principle (see Chapter 10), and mandate attendance. But employers may not have wanted to require their employees to go to a meeting about voluntary benefits. Another idea would have been to provide snacks and beverages, and frame (see Chapter 12) the meeting as more of a social occasion. Most employees would welcome a break in their day, and in my experience, people are usually attracted to free food at work. However, this approach didn't feel consistent with the purpose of the meeting. And it could have resulted in a number of employees attending a meeting with the sole goal of grabbing a snack, which means they would not have been in the right frame of mind for the message.

Since the meeting was about specific kinds of insurance, leveraging loss aversion (see Chapter 2) could have been a logical avenue to pursue. But that seemed more of an angle for selling the coverage versus selling attendance at the meeting. With that in mind, the team stepped back a bit and explored using information gap theory (see Chapter 9) to point out what people might not know about their potential risks, as well as ways to help protect themselves from them. While people don't like to think that they may ever get injured or sick, used properly the information gap theory concept could have worked well.

However, in the end, the client and agency landed in a different place, one that was actually closer to the idea of leveraging the authority principle. But this concept used choice architecture. Employees received an email from their company's human resources department that notified them that because their benefits were important, a time had been reserved for them to meet with the representative from the insurance company. The email included the date, time, and place of that meeting. There was even an "add to calendar" button. There was also a link for the employee to reschedule the meeting if for some reason the proposed time was not convenient.

Suddenly, attending the meeting was easy. It became the path of least resistance. The employee did not need to do anything but show up. Everything had already been taken care of. In fact, it would require more effort to reschedule. As a result, meeting attendance soared, increasing by 418 percent. All because of the smart application of choice architecture.

HOW A PROFESSIONAL JOURNAL INCREASED SUBSCRIPTIONS USING CHOICE ARCHITECTURE

The key fact marketers should remember about choice architecture is that the way choices are presented influences how customers will decide about them. This next example demonstrates that nicely. A professional journal had a long-standing subscription control that had been impossible to beat. But it was fatiguing. The publishers came to the agency where I worked and asked if we could help them. Our plan was to identify and keep the parts of the messaging that seemed to be the strongest performing, and to look for areas that could be improved.

Two jumped out at us right away. The first involved how prices were displayed. The control messaging showed a box with the original price, under which was a box indicating the amount of special savings being offered, and under that was the amount the subscriber would pay. Three vertically stacked boxes with prices. We eliminated that middle box, so the way we presented the information made the contrast between the original price and the sales price more evident. And it made the pricing message clearer. The other thing we noticed involved payments. In the control messaging, subscribers were given two options, a pay by credit card price, and a non-credit card price that was $20 more expensive. The two appeared together. We decided to make the credit card payment the default way to order. We highlighted it in a box, and relegated that non-credit card option to a small tick box beneath the main pay by credit card box. This guided people to pay with a credit card, and also opened up the ordering area to make it easier to scan.

When the client tested our changes, they consistently saw increased subscription rates of 18–21 percent. Perhaps even more important, they had more subscribers paying by credit card. From experience, they knew that this would lead to higher conversions at full price, as well as increased retention rates. A couple of small tweaks to their choice architecture yielded significant results.

MISTAKE

Leading with your lowest price. Instead, put your highest price first. It will serve as the anchor or reference against which all your other prices are evaluated, and those other prices will appear more attractive as a result.

HOW A POPULAR SINGER ENFORCED THE CHOICE ARCHITECTURE OF ALBUMS ON SPOTIFY

In the fall of 2021, Spotify fans encountered a difference when listening to albums on the streaming service. While the default for an album had been auto-shuffle, Spotify switched to automatically playing the songs in the order they appeared on the track list.

According to an NPR report, they did so in response to a request from British singer-songwriter Adele, who was quoted as saying, "We don't create albums with so much care and thought into our track listing for no reason. Our art tells a story and our stories should be listened to as we intended" (Cills, 2021).

As a result of Adele's request, albums now automatically play in the order the artist architected. Prior to it, Spotify listeners needed to toggle off the shuffle icon in order to hear the songs chronologically. Now, listeners who prefer a shuffled experience have to take the extra step of turning on the shuffle icon. It is no longer the default.

Marketers can tap status quo bias to get the behavior they seek

While the expression "change is good" is a common one, the sentiment is not always readily embraced. In fact, humans have proven themselves to be creatures of habit. Despite our quest for novelty (see Chapter 9), and our reluctance to leave something that we started incomplete (see Chapter 8), we usually prefer not to change what we have or the way we do things. We like to keep everything as it is. As Thaler and Sunstein observe, "For lots of reasons, people have a general tendency to stick with their current situation."

One of those reasons may be familiarity. People feel comfortable with what they know and can count on. Another reason could be that they are driven by the fear of loss. If a person tries something new and does not like it, they feel they've given up the previous product or service that made them happy. Sticking with what they know guards against this potential loss.

Another of the reasons people don't change may be that they have invested a lot of time, effort, or money into a project, product, or cause. Having sunk all those resources into it, they are reluctant to walk away. And yet another reason may simply be habit or convenience. Once a person is used to doing something, it can easily become second nature—something they do with little thought or consideration.

Researchers William Samuelson and Richard Zeckhauser (1988) coined the term "status quo bias" to describe this kind of behavior. In a series of experiments, they showed that "status quo framing was found to have predictable and significant effects on subjects' decision making." They went on to state that "Individuals exhibited a significant status quo bias across a range of decisions."

In one of the experiments they conducted, some subjects were told to imagine that they had inherited a large sum of money. They were then asked to choose from four different portfolios that they could invest it in. Other subjects were given the same scenario, but with one difference. Among the four investment alternatives, there was one that was described as the investment portfolio that the money was currently in. It represented the status quo.

In the experiment, researchers told the subjects to assume they had a decent level of financial knowledge, and that there were no appreciable tax consequences or brokerage fees attached to any of the four portfolio choices. At the conclusion of the experiments, Samuelson and Zeckhauser reported that the research participants indicated a strong preference for the status quo option.

As a marketer, you can tap status quo bias to help bolster customer loyalty and retention. Remind people of how long they've relied on your product or service, and how many years they've invested in the relationship with your company. Point out to them that remaining with you is easy, and requires no additional effort. Or suggest that switching to a competitor could leave them feeling dissatisfied and missing the convenience you offer.

STATUS QUO BIAS IN TELECOMMUNICATIONS

A colleague of mine, Pat Peterson, created some very effective messaging using status quo bias to win back customers. She was trying to convince people who had recently switched phone companies to return to their original carrier. She headlined her piece, "Change is good," and told the target it was good they had changed companies so they could see for themselves how much better their original phone provider was. Then she included an offer to welcome them back if they wanted to return. A good percentage of them did, exhibiting a preference for the company they knew and had relied on for some time.

HOW ONE FINANCIAL MARKETER USED STATUS QUO BIAS TO THEIR ADVANTAGE

A financial services firm needed to send a series of emails to people who had 401(k) money parked in the firm's accounts. These customers appeared to have left the employer where they had originally started the retirement savings account some time ago. The account had shown no activity for over a year, and the customer may have forgotten that they even had the money there.

Naturally, the financial firm would prefer that the customers keep that money right where it was. However, by reminding them of the funds, they ran the risk that the exact opposite would happen. The emails would make the money top of mind. Once it was, the customers might think about moving their cash to another retirement account, perhaps one they may have started at their new place of employment.

In order to prompt customers to keep the money where it was, we used language to trigger the status quo bias. Customers received a series of emails that reminded them about the money. In those emails, we invited customers to see how their account was still working for them, and assured them it continued to be a great way to save for retirement.

The emails included a link to a landing page. If customers chose to visit it, they immediately saw a message that reassured them that their money was safe and growing tax-free. They also were told that no action was necessary on their part. However, if they wished to speak with a representative to review their account or discuss other options, they could. The email contained both a phone number and a button to schedule an appointment. Essentially, customers got the message that their money was doing what it should be where it was, and they weren't doing anything wrong leaving it there. In short, it was perfectly fine to do nothing.

Effective ways to use choice architecture and status quo bias with customers

- Frame the choice you want your customers to make as the standard one—the one that is typically chosen.
- Position the desired customer action as popular and attractive.
- Have the path of least resistance lead directly to what you want your customers and prospects to do, whether it's to enroll, subscribe to a particular service level, repurchase a product, etc.
- Make it easy for customers to do what you want them to do, and harder for them to do what you don't want them to do. For example, you can make it easy for a customer to purchase an extra supply of a needed item by including a one-click option next to the original purchase button.
- Remove points of friction that might interrupt or derail your customer from completing an action you want them to take.
- Carefully consider your defaults. Because no design is neutral, make sure your defaults favor your marketing goals.
- Precheck desired options, such as include me on your email list, contact me with updates, pay the credit card fee (fundraising), etc.
- When communicating with customers, include the number of years a customer has been with your company.
- Have inertia work in your favor. Make "doing nothing" actually result in the behavior you seek.
- Create "sticky" products or situations. For example, banks should focus on getting checking account customers, and subscription companies should strive to get a credit card on file for auto renewal.
- Overcome status quo bias by providing a strong reason or a compelling incentive to act.

KEY TAKEAWAYS

1 The way a marketer presents choices to a customer will influence that customer's decision about them. This is known as choice architecture.

2 Examples of choice architecture include the number of choices you provide, the order of those choices, what information your design and visual cues draw attention to, and the way you describe various options.

3 Preferences and previous experiences are not the only factors that determine what someone chooses to purchase.

4 The defaults you set up will have a strong influence on your customers' decisions. Rather than opting out or opting in, people will often opt to just go with the flow—which will be the default.

5 People tend to stick with defaults. Research shows they may think of the default as an implicit endorsement.

6 Positioning the desired option as fun and easy can make it more likely to be chosen.

7 People often don't have the time to think through options, so they'll take the path of least resistance.

8 When employing choice architecture, marketers should never force their customers' hands. Customers should always be able to make a different choice than the one you want them to.

9 Removing friction and simplifying options can help people make the choice you hope they do.

10 Your customers will have a strong preference for the status quo—for the way things are. It might be due to familiarity, loss aversion, time and effort already invested, or habit.

11 Marketers can tap status quo bias to increase customer loyalty and retention.

12 Overcoming status quo bias can require a strong reason or incentive.

In conclusion

How choices are presented can have a sizeable impact on the selections people make. Opt ins, opt outs, and defaults all influence choice. This is particularly true given the human preference to leave things as they are versus actively making changes. Your customers and prospects will have a natural tendency to go with the flow, or with the suggested or easier choice. As a marketer, you should factor this into the options you make available and the way those options appear.

Another way to prompt people to make the decisions you want them to is to label your customers and prospects as being part of a group that would likely decide that way. As you'll see in the next chapter, when someone believes they are part of a particular group, they will begin to behave accordingly.

References

Bates, C (2009) Scaling new heights: Piano stairway encourages commuters to ditch the escalators, *Daily Mail*, https://www.dailymail.co.uk/sciencetech/ article-1218944/Scaling-new-heights-Piano-stairway-encourages-commuters-ditch-escalators.html (archived at https://perma.cc/7YYE-BFCG)

Cills, H (2021) Adele asked Spotify to remove the default shuffle button for albums, and they obliged [Blog] *NPR*, 22 November, https://www.npr.org/ 2021/11/21/1057783216/adele-spotify-shuffle-30 (archived at https://perma.cc/ K5WQ-695Q)

Ebeling, F and Lotz, S (2015) Domestic uptake of green energy promoted by opt-out tariffs, *Nature Climate Change*, 5, pp 868–871

Johnson, E and Goldstein, D (2003) Do Defaults Save Lives? *Science*, 21 November, https://www.science.org/doi/10.1126/science.1091721 (archived at https:// perma.cc/7ETQ-A3L7)

Mandel, N and Johnson, E (2002) When web pages influence choice: effects of visual primes on experts and novices, *Journal of Consumer Research*, 29 (2), pp 235–45

Marcano-Olivier, M, Pearson, R, Ruparell, A et al (2019) A low-cost behavioural nudge and choice architecture intervention targeting school lunches increases children's consumption of fruit: a cluster randomised trial, *International Journal of Behavioural Nutrition and Physical Activity*, 16 (20), https://doi.org/10.1186/ s12966-019-0773-x (archived at https://perma.cc/F3CP-94KZ)

Samuelson, W and Zeckhauser, R (1988) Status quo bias in decision making, *Journal of Risk and Uncertainty*, https://citeseerx.ist.psu.edu/viewdoc/ download?doi=10.1.1.632.3193&rep=rep1&type=pdf (archived at https:// perma.cc/3BM5-6ET4)

Szaszi, B, Palinkas, A, Palfi, B, Szollosi, A, and Aczel, B (2014) A systematic scoping review of the choice architecture movement: Toward understanding when and why nudges work, *Journal of Behavioral Decision Making*, https://onlinelibrary.wiley. com/doi/full/10.1002/bdm.2035 (archived at https://perma.cc/H3AZ-G8H7)

Thaler, RH and Benartzi, S (2004) Save more tomorrow: Using behavioral economics to increase employee saving, *Journal of Political Economy*, https://www.journals.uchicago.edu/doi/full/10.1086/380085 (archived at https://perma.cc/6RQJ-UEZP) [Last accessed 29 January 2022]

Thaler, RH and Sunstein CR (2009) *Nudge: Improving decisions about health, wealth, and happiness*, Penguin Books, London

12

Labeling and framing: making people see things your way

The terms marketers use to describe their audience and their products can impact buying decisions. When people are labeled as part of a group, they behave consistently with that group. To increase sales, label your target as part of a group that would naturally buy your product or service. And when describing that product or service, use words that frame it in a way that makes it more appealing, or that prompts your prospect to view it in a new light.

Marketing would be so much easier if people just did what you wanted them to do. Isn't that right? It could be so simple. You are the seller. They are the buyers. Act accordingly. Sellers sell. Buyers buy. So please just hand me your credit card!

Unfortunately, it's usually not that easy (otherwise, why would you be reading this book?). The truth is, many factors can get in the way, even when you have a really good product or service. Often people still have to be convinced they need what you are selling. And, perhaps even more important, that they need it now. On the other hand, if you're selling something that people already know they want, you still have to persuade those people to buy it from you. As you've no doubt experienced, there are many other companies out there working hard to win those prospective customers away from you.

As a competitive marketer, you too will do your best to position your products and services as the ideal choice. But sometimes even that will backfire. Take, for instance, the fact that people have been cautioned not to believe everything they hear. While generally speaking that can be good advice, it can actually be harmful to your marketing efforts. It can make prospective customers skeptical that your product will be as good as you say it is. Injecting some social proof (read more in Chapter 5) is one way to apply behavioral science to help in that case. So, too, is tapping into the authority principle (read more in Chapter 10), or harnessing the power of storytelling (read more in Chapter 6).

The point is, it's always important to keep in mind what could be in your prospect's mind when they encounter your marketing message. But savvy marketers can go one step further. You can use behavioral science to put an idea in your prospect's mind. By using a specific behavioral science tactic, you can impact someone's immediate receptivity to your message, and to their belief that it is right for them. This can actually result in their purchasing a product that they previously didn't think they were even in the market for. Behavioral scientists refer to the tactic as labeling.

> Marketers can use labeling to motivate behavior. Once a person is told they belong to a particular group, they start to act the way the other group members do.

Labeling can help marketers direct their prospects to the desired action

When people are labeled as part of a group, they begin to take on the characteristics of that group. They behave in a way that is consistent with other members of the group. What's more, this can be true even in situations where a person had not originally thought of themselves as belonging to the group in question. In other words, even if your prospect hadn't identified themselves in a certain way, once you plant that idea in their head with the appropriate label, their behavior can change so as to live up to that label.

Before asking someone to make a purchase, suggest to them that they are a good candidate for your product or service. This could get them to see themselves that way, especially if you employ labeling in that suggestion. Labeling can be a very powerful tool to get people to view themselves the way you want them to. According to Donna L. Roberts, PhD, "when we believe that something is real, we can make it real with our attitudes and behaviors. Nobody is immune to the influence of labels. The labeling theory indicates that our identity and behaviors are determined or influenced by the terms that we or others use to describe us" (Roberts, 2019).

Labeling has been shown to increase voting, charity donations, and political preferences

Researchers Alice Tybout and Richard Yalch (1980) showed this in a study they conducted in Chicago. Prior to a local election, they talked to a group of voters about their "political attitudes, knowledge of issues related to the upcoming election, past political behavior, voting intentions for the upcoming election, self-perceptions regarding voting, and demographic characteristics." Afterwards, they randomly assigned each person they'd spoken with to one of two groups. One group was told they were "average citizens with an average probability of voting," and the other group was told that they were "above-average citizens with an above-average probability of voting." Again, these labels were given arbitrarily.

However, when the election was held one week later, 15 percent more of the people who'd been labeled as above average actually went to the polls. The researchers concluded that "Individuals labeled as above-average citizens were more likely to perceive themselves as voters than those labeled as average citizens."

Robert Cialdini, author of *Influence: The psychology of persuasion* (2006), describes an experiment that also supports the effect of labeling. It was conducted with two groups of people who were asked to contribute to a cancer charity. One week before the donation was requested, the people in one of the groups had been given a cancer awareness button to wear for the week. When the researchers subsequently asked for a donation, the people in this group donated more. The button could be considered a labeling device, which got those people to think of themselves as people who were supportive of the cause.

Labels can also influence whether or not someone will agree with a stated idea. In an experiment conducted in Germany, researchers found that supporters of a particular political party were more likely to agree with statements that were labeled as being endorsed by that party versus not (Neumann et al., 2020). People who did not agree with the political party were less likely to agree with the labeled statements versus the non-labeled ones. The researchers concluded that "labelling of the *very same* political statements changes voters' agreement with these statements," and that people may agree or disagree with an idea simply based on its source.

In the United States, a similar observation can be made. In the US, when someone inherits the property of a person who has died, the inheritor must pay taxes on it if the value of the estate is over a certain amount of money. This tax had traditionally been called an estate tax.

However, the Republican party, which is not a fan of the tax, began referring to it as a death tax. According to a report in *Business Insider*, a messaging consultant for the political party conducted focus groups and found that "68% of people opposed the estate tax, but that number shot up to 78% when he called it the death tax." Clearly, the label impacted people's reaction to the tax. In fact, the article observed that the "Use of the term soon became an indicator of which side of the political football you were on" (Abadi, 2017).

Labeling someone can influence their perception of themselves, and their subsequent behavior based on that perception. Additionally, attributing information using the labeling technique can influence a person's acceptance of it. As a marketer, you can use these findings to help motivate the action you want from your customers. Label those customers in a way that is consistent with the request you're about to make of them. And take care to ensure that any supporting sales arguments you provide come from people or organizations your customers would agree with.

The way you refer to, or label, products can also influence buyer behavior

There is a bakery outside of Dallas, Texas called the Collin Street Bakery. And their specialty is fruitcake. People who try their fruitcake really love it, and they get a good amount of repeat business. Their challenge, as you might have guessed, is getting new people to try it. After all, fruitcake is the dessert that often finds itself the butt of jokes.

Gary Hennerberg, a marketing consultant who was working with the bakery, did some research and found that people liked the taste of his client's confection, but were turned off by the word fruitcake. In conversations with his client, he discovered that their fruitcakes were made with a very special kind of pecan. That inspired Hennerberg to suggest not calling the desserts fruitcakes, but instead labeling them native Texas pecan cakes. When the bakery tested the new name, mail orders shot up by a significant 60 percent. The recipe did not change. Nor did the price of the fruitcakes. The difference sprang from how the product was labeled and promoted.

Additional research also supports the idea that product descriptions influence people's attitudes toward those products. In a study involving menu item descriptions, researchers found that labels such as "grandma's

FIGURE 12.1 Descriptions make the difference

Shawn's *Famous* Special Bloody Mary...$12.
*Black peppercorn, lemon peel & pepperoncini infused
vodka with our homemade bloody mary mix*

Provincetown's The Lobster Pot takes advantage of labeling when describing their Bloody Mary.

zucchini cookies" and "succulent Italian seafood filet" increased sales by 27 percent, and improved people's attitudes toward the food, the restaurant, and their intention to return (Wansink et al., 2002).

With this in mind, I headed over to my favorite Cape Cod restaurant, the Lobster Pot in Provincetown, MA. I wanted to know if the family-owned dining destination thought that the "Shawn's Famous Special Bloody Mary" on their menu sold better than if they had just listed it as a Bloody Mary. Julie, who works the front of the house with her brother Shawn, told me she was "positive" it did. "People see Shawn's famous, and they say I have to try it," she explained. "The same thing happens with 'Tim's Award-Winning Clam Chowder,'" she added, referring to the soup named for her brother, the chef.

HOW AN UNEXPECTED LABEL INFLUENCED SOME OF MY PURCHASE DECISIONS
During the summers, I spend a good number of weekends at the beach. On a particular Saturday, I had met some friends at Herring Cove beach to enjoy an afternoon of swimming and sunbathing. The beach is beautiful, considered one of New England's finest, but it does have a certain drawback. There can be quite a lot of stones on the packed sand leading into the water. As a result, any trip down to the waves, or back up to the blanket after a swim, typically involves a kind of contorted walk, with beachgoers twisting, turning, and "ouching" their way out of the surf and along the beach, as the tender soles of their feet land on the unforgiving stones. Anyone already comfortably returned to their spot under the umbrella looks on with a mixture of empathy and amusement.

It was on one of these returns to my blanket that my friend Annette observed that I have runner's legs. As you may recall from the previous chapter, I have never considered myself to be much of an athlete. In fact, my self-described exercise of choice is a "shog," my word for the cross between a shuffle and a jog that I tackle most mornings, weather permitting. Annette, on the other hand, is an athlete. In fact, she is a runner. If she says I have runner's legs, I can only assume she knows what she is talking about. When I returned home from the beach that day, I appraised my legs in the mirror. "So," I thought, "I guess that's what runner's legs look like."

But from that day on, something happened. I began to think of myself less as a "shogger" and more of a... beginning runner. I started timing my daily three-mile efforts, and worked on increasing my speed. I began posting on my social media pages about runs I had just returned from. And I paid the registration fee and signed up for my first 5K fun run.

Perhaps most notable from a marketing perspective, my purchase decisions evolved. While in the past, I would have bought any pair of sneakers that looked good and were reasonably priced, I suddenly found myself researching "best running shoes for women." I went to a store that specialized in running shoes and got fitted for a pair. And after spending way more on the footwear than I ever previously had, I added a pair of running shorts to my cart as well.

These changes in my behavior, both my physical behavior as well as my purchasing behavior, were all driven by the runner label Annette had given me. While I had not formerly thought of myself in those terms, her labeling me in that way drove the difference. Because I was told I was part of a group, I began to act in ways that were more consistent with the members of that group. The label influenced my perception of myself, and my resulting behavior.

CASE STUDY
A credit provider used labeling to effectively sell their product

What should the marketing say when the product you sell benefits the buyers' end users more than the buyers themselves? That was the challenge I received from one client while working at a Boston-area agency. The client marketed payment plans which dental professionals could offer to their patients who were having elective dental work, such as implants, done. These loans could help the patient cover the cost of the expensive dental services, since their insurance most likely would not.

Most of the dental practices the client was targeting already had some form of financing solution in place for their patients. Typically, once the dental office decided upon a solution, they had little desire to revisit it. Additionally, there was a belief among dental office managers that all patient payment plans were basically the same.

This was the marketing environment in which we needed to deploy some effective messaging. The creative team explored a few different ways to do so. One approach was to focus on the offer, which was free lunch for the dental office when they registered with the payment plan service. Leading with the offer is often a good idea, because offers can be very motivating. This can be particularly true if they involve receiving something for free. However, we knew the dental office managers and the dentists themselves were very busy people. And since they likely already had a financing solution in place, they did not have an urgent, unmet need for our client's service. As a result, we thought the draw of a free lunch as the lead message might not be enough to overcome inertia (see Chapter 11) and convince the offices to register.

The team also explored highlighting why our client's service may be better than the dental office's current solution. It did offer high approval rates for the patient loans. And the practice fees associated with it might even be lower than those the dentist was paying with a competitor. While these were compelling points, they seemed too rational to drive a large response rate. People usually make decisions for emotional reasons and then justify those decisions with rational reasons (see Chapter 1). We decided leading with these rational reasons would not be convincing enough.

Ultimately the team landed on a powerful concept that used the free lunch offer and the rational reasons to sign up for the service as key support points. But the lead message employed labeling. It labeled the target as someone who puts patients first. Once the office manager or dentist was labeled in that way, the foundation was set. It became harder for them to claim they were not interested in a payment plan that could be very beneficial to their patients—one that offered those patients high approval rates, and attractive terms that could let them start their dental work sooner. The emotion-laden label was intended to prompt the target to behave in a way that was consistent with it. And they did. The messaging outperformed the client's previous pitch by 64 percent.

Other ways companies strategically use labeling

As a marketer, you want to choose labels that put your target in the right mindset to act on your message. You want them to see themselves as a member of a group that would naturally buy your product or service. For example, I've used labeling in communications for several different types of clients:

- A business services provider labeled their target as a promising business in town.

- A life insurance company labeled their target as the type of person who always takes care of their loved ones.

- A financial services firm labeled their target as someone who intended to feel confident they'd have money waiting for them when they retired.

Once the target accepted the label, and identified with it, the actions they should take were self-evident. For example, if you're someone who always takes care of your family, it only makes sense that you'd purchase life insurance. You'd want to make sure your loved ones were not left financially strapped after you passed away.

As powerful as labeling can be, however, there will be times when a marketer will want to use a related behavioral science principle to trigger customer action. That trigger is framing.

Framing can change people's perceptions and behaviors

Behavioral scientists have found that the way something is described, or framed, can influence the decisions people make about it. As Daniel Kahneman, author of *Thinking, Fast and Slow*, explains, "Different ways of presenting the same information often evoke different emotions." And as Thaler and Sunstein, authors of *Nudge* (2011), note, "The idea is that choices depend, in part, on the way in which problems are stated."

As a marketer, you should know that the words you choose for your marketing messages can make a significant difference in the reaction your customers and prospects will have to your sales proposition. You want to pick words that are easy to understand, that are meaningful to your target, and that prompt people to see things in a new way—or at least in the way you want them to.

Psychologist Elizabeth Loftus ran an experiment that proved how important the choice of one word over another could be (Loftus and Palmer, 1974). In it, she showed people a video of a car accident. Then she asked them to estimate how fast the cars in the video were going. However, when she asked the question, she tested using several different verbs. And the responses she received were telling.

When some people were asked to estimate how fast the cars were going when they smashed, those people estimated 40.8 miles per hour. However, when other people were asked to estimate how fast the cars were going when they contacted, the speed estimate dropped to 31.8 miles per hour, a difference of over 28 percent. Everyone had watched the same video. Everyone had been asked the same question. The only difference was the verb that was used in it. The experiment revealed that the framing of a question can be critical.

Researchers at the Canadian software company Unbounce also tested the effect of framing. When describing an online sweepstake, they found framing it as a giveaway outperformed framing it as a promotion by 50 percent. The test involved two similar words, but produced two very different responses.

Finally, in another experiment, researchers found that people who were dieting ate more of a confection when it was framed with a healthier name. The same sweets were either called fruit chews or candy chews. When they were described as fruit chews, the dieters consumed more of them, even though they had read the ingredients list and knew exactly what they were eating (Irmak et al., 2011).

As a marketer, you have an ideal opportunity to inject some framing tactics into your online calls to action. And that opportunity comes when using yes or no buttons. The key is to frame the no option in a way that points out the folly of not saying yes. For example, one button could say "Yes, I want the white paper now." And the other button could say, "No, I don't need to know what my competition is doing." When the choices are framed that way, it can be much more difficult for your prospect to say no. According to research reported in the *New Neuromarketing* blog, properly framed yes or no buttons have increased conversions by 40 to 125 percent (Van Bommel, 2016). By framing the options to underscore what someone may miss out on, you can trigger loss aversion (see Chapter 2) and prompt a positive response.

Framing can help marketers shape how prices are perceived

Marketers should note, framing isn't only about the descriptive words you include in your marketing copy. It's also an important tactic to consider when dealing with percentages and prices. You've no doubt been to the supermarket and seen 95 percent fat-free yogurt, ice cream, or ground beef. Imagine the consumer reaction if the container said the product contained 5 percent fat instead. Similarly, you have probably seen prices expressed in a per month amount instead of an annual one. Naturally, marketers would prefer to get all their money upfront. But framing a purchase as costing $10 a month seems much more affordable to prospective buyers than saying it will cost an immediate $120.

Additionally, behavioral science research shows that even when prices are small, it still may be worth pointing that fact out—particularly to some types of customers. In one experiment, people were told they could pay an overnight shipping fee in order to receive their merchandise faster (Rick et al., 2008). The fee was either framed as a $5 fee or as a *small* $5 fee. When it was framed as small, 20 percent more people chose to pay it. The researchers note that these people were classified as tightwads as opposed to spendthrifts. This distinction is significant, because "tightwads overall outnumber spendthrifts by a ratio of 3 to 2," which means you are likely to find more of these price-sensitive people among your customers and prospects.

Researchers at Stanford University, however, have found that in many instances, framing your product in terms of the experience someone will have with it can be more effective than framing it in terms of its price or affordability (Mogilner and Aaker, 2009). "Because one's experience with a product tends to foster feelings of personal connection with it," they say, "referring to time typically leads to more favorable attitudes—and to more purchases."

The researchers arrived at this finding after conducting five experiments. The most unusual one involved two six-year-olds, a lemonade stand with three different signs, and a park in San Francisco. Every 10 minutes, the sign on the lemonade stand was changed, so different park passersby would be exposed to a different message. One sign said, "Spend a little time and enjoy C&D's lemonade." Another sign said, "Spend a little money and enjoy C&D's lemonade." And the third sign simply said, "Enjoy C&D's lemonade." When a person stopped to buy a drink, they were told they could "pay anywhere in between one dollar and three dollars," and that this price included the logo-embossed plastic cup. After purchasing their lemonade, they were asked to complete a short customer satisfaction survey.

Researchers found that more people stopped to purchase lemonade when the sign that invited them to spend a little time was on the stand. They found that these people also offered more money for their drink. And that in the customer satisfaction survey, they reported more favorable attitudes toward the lemonade. This led the researchers to conclude that "In the context of a real business, conducted among a variety of consumers, this experiment shows that merely mentioning time, rather than money, in a product's marketing materials can make the very same product more alluring and better liked."

MISTAKE

Missing the opportunity to recast your message. If your target thinks that you're like everyone else, or that they don't need your product, or that it's too expensive, adjust their frame of reference. That can change their thinking and their behavior.

SOMETIMES YOU NEED TO REFRAME, OR REPOSITION, A PRODUCT IN YOUR PROSPECT'S EYES

Framing can be a smart strategic tool to employ when you need to get people to think about your product or service differently. This is especially true when people assume they know what you're selling, and because of that, believe they're not in the market for it.

Early in my career, I witnessed an excellent example of reframing in order to overcome this kind of resistance. I was working for a small direct marketing agency. The founder was young, charismatic, ambitious, and smart. He wanted to work with some well-known, blue-chip companies. However, those companies were sought after by many different agencies. And each company already had a large, established direct marketing agency on its roster. So, they would have the perfect excuse to turn down his inquiries.

As I recall, when he approached them, he wouldn't describe his company as a direct marketing agency. Instead, he framed it as a cross-industry marketing company. It was certainly true. The agency did set up successful partnership marketing programs. And then after we did, we created all the direct marketing materials needed to promote them. The way he initially framed his services to prospective clients got him in the door. He made them see the company as different from the other agencies they already had on retainer. They likely did not have a company on their existing roster that did what he described. And because of that, they were willing to talk to him.

His company went on to do extremely well, and to count a large number of blue-chip companies among its clients. While not the only reason for his success, I believe the way he initially framed his company played a key role. In fact, at the time, I recall thinking it was especially smart. And this was long before I discovered the power of behavioral science in marketing.

CASE STUDY
How a financial literacy organization used framing to encourage their target to view them differently

Once kids head off to college, they spend a lot of time studying and socializing. The thing they don't really focus on is how they'll repay their student loans once they come due. That's why one of the more interesting challenges I've tackled in marketing came from a US organization that emphasized financial literary for college students, with the ultimate goal of helping them to repay their student loans on time.

The organization's previous efforts to get college kids to prepare to pay off their student loans were not as successfully as they'd hoped. So, when they came to the agency where I was working, we decided to frame their messaging differently. Instead of talking about money owed, we framed the program as one that would help students find money. By using a frame that was more empathetic to their current situation, we were able to attract attention, and talk about other elements of the program, including scholarships, internships, and job search assistance, as well as help to stay on track to pay off student loans. As a result, campus activation rates doubled and student participation soared.

Using framing to increase beer consumption and to think about time

A few years later and approximately 8,000 miles away, a beer brewer employed the same framing technique as the financial literacy organization. Their challenge was quite different. People were not drinking enough of the New Zealand-brewed lager, DB Export. The agency Colenso BBDO used framing to solve the problem. They framed the act of drinking the beer as one that would help save the world.

DB Breweries created Brewtroleum, a biofuel made from the leftover yeast that resulted from brewing their beer. And they encouraged people to drink the beer, because the more they drank, the more of this cleaner alternative to petrol that would be created. And the more that was created, the more vehicles it could fuel. According to a 2018 report in Australia's *Marketing* magazine, the "first two batches of Brewtroleum turned 116,000 tonnes of yeast slurry, from the DB Export brewing process, into 330,000 litres of Brewtroleum and prevented 75,000 kilograms of carbon from entering the atmosphere." The article summarized the award-winning initiative by saying "DB Export Brewtroleum changed the perception of drinking beer—from a selfish indulgence into a selfless act of environmental heroism." Additionally, sales of the beer reportedly increased by 10 percent in a declining market. Now that is an example of framing marketers can drink to.

Another exemplary example of framing comes to us courtesy of Tamsen Webster. Early in her career, the author and independent marketing consultant moonlighted as a Weight Watchers leader. Some of the people she coached saw themselves as "night eaters." They could control what they consumed during the day, with a careful eye on the points that the weight management program allowed them, but after dinner they felt they needed to keep eating, which would blow their daily allowable points.

So Tamsen reframed the day. She told the members of the program to start their day—their 24-hour period—at night. As she explained, "*nowhere* in the program did it ever say that the points had to start in the morning, and we could all agree that *any* span of 24 hours is a 'day'." This creative bit of framing worked, allowing members some latitude at night when they needed it, and prompting them be more stringent during the day when they felt more in control (Webster, nd).

While working on the account of a major long-distance phone company, I heard my colleagues cleverly reframe time in a different way. If customers called to cancel their service, the call center representatives were trained to offer them 60 minutes of free long-distance calls to entice them to remain. However, if the customer declined the offer of minutes, the representatives would then move to a response that came to be known as the horizontal flex. They would ask the caller if they would remain a customer if the company gave them a full hour of free long-distance calls. Framing the offer this way successfully retained a number of customers, even though 60 minutes and an hour are the same amount of time.

Strategic ways that marketers can use labeling and framing tactics

- Refer to your prospect with a label that is consistent with the behavior you're seeking. For example, if you're selling high-end cookware, call your prospect a foodie or a gourmet. Similarly, label your best customers as such. As marketing strategist Gregory Ciotti points out, "People who are labeled as 'superior' consumers tend to spend more, and those in the 'regular' class aren't affected" (Ciotti, nd).

- When choosing labels to use, make sure your target would not be offended by them. Calling a Democrat a loyal Republican, or calling a vegetarian a discerning carnivore, would be a mistake.

- Labels that flatter can work well. So, too, can labels that attribute certain relevant characteristics to your target. For example, a charity may want to refer to their prospects as generous individuals. A clothing brand may want to refer to their target as a trendsetter. And a business conference may want to label prospective attendees as influential executives.

- Consider labeling techniques when naming your products and services to help differentiate them from others in the market, and to make them more appealing to your audience. Imagine the difference between someone receiving an "application" or a "quick decision form."

- Use framing to change the way people think about a product, service, or need. One of the more interesting examples I've seen was a company selling air fresheners. When you think of an air freshener, you may think of using it to cover up unpleasant odors. However, they framed using the product as akin to experiencing an immediate getaway, because people could make different rooms in their houses smell like different locales.

- When you're the incumbent, frame the thought of leaving your company in terms of the risk of change, and the things your customer may lose. When you're the challenger, frame your message in terms of the fear of staying, because the prospect won't gain all you have to offer if they stay where they are.

- Reframe potential drawbacks so they're viewed in a more positive manner. For example, a cramped restaurant could be framed as an intimate one. A basic version of a product could be framed as having all the necessary functionality without any of the distracting add-ons.

- Use framing to influence how customers and prospects view things. For example, refer to the cost of your service as an investment versus an expense. Or, if you run a conference that can't afford the big-name speakers, you can frame it as the conference where attendees won't hear the same things from the same names that show up everywhere, and instead will hear from real practitioners revealing the day-to-day details of successful efforts.

KEY TAKEAWAYS

1   When you label a customer as belonging to a group, they will begin to act in ways that are consistent with it.

2   People will accept labels that they'd not previously considered applied to them, as long as the label is not one they find disagreeable.

3   Labels can change how people view themselves and how they subsequently behave.

4   How you label the source of information can impact a person's receptivity to it.

5   The way you refer to your products can influence how customers perceive them.

6   Label prospective customers in a way that is consistent with the actions you're asking them to take.

7   Framing the same information differently can drive different reactions to it. For example, people may seek out a 95 percent fat-free product and avoid a 5 percent fat product. A cheap product can be framed as a bargain. An older style can be framed as a classic. And a company that offers limited services can be framed as a specialist.

8   Choose your descriptive words carefully, because they will influence your target's perceptions and actions.

9   When using yes and no buttons, use the copy on the no button to frame the consequences of not saying yes.

10 Test framing your product in terms of the experience that customers will have with it versus the money they'll save on or with it, because experiencing a product can foster an emotional response to it.

11 Use framing to get people to see things in a new way or in a marketer's preferred way.

In conclusion

You can increase your target's likelihood to purchase with the use of labeling and framing. The first influences how they view themselves, and the second influences how they view what you are marketing. Both can trigger automatic buying decisions. People will behave in a manner consistent with the group they've been told they belong to. And they will respond to messages framed to direct how they see and think about a product or service.

For example, they may buy a new-to-market item because the marketer labeled them a trendsetter. Or they may purchase a product that's been around forever, because the marketer framed it as a classic that's always in style. In each of these examples, the word "because" figured prominently as part of the explanation. In the next chapter, you'll see how providing the reason why can trigger automatic agreement, and how that word "because" plays a key role.

References

Abadi, M (2017) Republicans say 'death tax' while Democrats say 'estate tax' — and there's a fascinating reason why, *Business Insider*, 19 October, https://www. businessinsider.com/death-tax-or-estate-tax-2017-10 (archived at https://perma. cc/U6KL-KZ4Y)

Cialdini, R (2006) *Influence: The psychology of persuasion*, Harper Business

Ciotti, G (nd) Understanding consumer behavior to convert more customers [Blog] HelpScout, https://www.helpscout.com/consumer-behavior/ (archived at https:// perma.cc/2UTM-CSF5)

Irmak, C, Vallen, B and Robinson, SR (2011) The impact of product name on dieters' and nondieters' food evaluations and consumption, *Journal of Consumer Research*, 38 (2), pp 390–405, https://doi.org/10.1086/660044 (archived at https://perma.cc/68F2-SXKS)

Kahneman, D (2011) *Thinking, Fast and Slow*, Farrar, Straus and Giroux, New York

Loftus, EF and Palmer, JC (1974) Reconstruction of automobile destruction: An example of the interaction between language and memory, *Journal of Verbal Learning & Verbal Behavior*, 13 (5), pp 585–589, https://doi.org/10.1016/ S0022-5371(74)80011-3 (archived at https://perma.cc/WN84-2MXB)

Marketing (2018) Thinking outside the bottle—revitalising a dying culture by saving the world with beer, 27 June, https://www.marketingmag.com.au/hubs-c/ case-study-brewtroleum-db-exports/ (archived at https://perma.cc/PX45-EXLE)

Mogilner, C and Aaker, J (2009) "The Time vs. Money Effect": Shifting product attitudes and decisions through personal connection, *Journal of Consumer Research*, https://academic.oup.com/jcr/article-abstract/36/2/277/1942869?redir ectedFrom=fulltext (archived at https://perma.cc/CYB7-VLXY)

Neumann, H, Thielmann, I and Pfattheicher, S (2020) Labelling affects agreement with political statements of right-wing populist parties, *Plos One*, https:// journals.plos.org/plosone/article?id=10.1371/journal.pone.0239772 (archived at https://perma.cc/2KB7-K9NE)

Rick, S, Cryder, C and Loewenstein, G (2008) Tightwads and Spendthrifts, *Journal of Consumer Research*, https://academic.oup.com/jcr/article-abstract/34/6/767/1845388 (archived at https://perma.cc/Z955-LZGM)

Roberts, D (2019) Labeling Theory: How do the labels we use change our reality? [Blog] *Media Psychology*, 07 July, https://mediapsychology101.com/2019/10/07/labeling-theory-how-do-the-labels-we-use-change-our-reality/ (archived at https://perma.cc/8H5U-BRC4)

Thaler, RH and Sunstein, CR (2009) *Nudge: Improving decisions about health, wealth, and happiness*, Penguin Books, London

Tybout, AM and Yalch, RF (1980) The effect of experience: A matter of salience? *Journal of Consumer Research*, www.jstor.org/stable/2488741 (archived at https://perma.cc/VSL2-GJWJ)

Van Bommel, T (2016) Restructure your CTA with this simple technique and more than double your conversion rate [Blog] *New Neuromarketing*, 02 December. https://www.newneuromarketing.com/restructure-your-cta-with-this-simple-technique-and-more-than-double-your-conversion-rate (archived at https://perma.cc/7ABF-ACJR)

Wansink, B et al. (2002) How descriptive menu labels influence attitudes and repatronage, *Advances in Consumer Research*, **29**, https://www.acrwebsite.org/volumes/8588 (archived at https://perma.cc/C7HW-3W7Y)

Webster, T (nd) Message in a Minute: To change what people do you have to change how they see, https://tamsenwebster.com/change-how-people-see/ (archived at https://perma.cc/A3ZK-E6E4)

13

Increasing action through automatic compliance triggers and reasons

Behavioral scientists have shown that people are more likely to comply with a request if it's accompanied by a reason. Marketers, therefore, should include the reason why their customers should respond to their messages, even if you think it's obvious. Marketers can also tap into other triggers involving both language and graphics to automatically prompt a particular response in people.

Do you know why focus groups can't always be trusted? Because people will tell you why they would or would not buy a product, or why they would or would not respond to an ad, but they will often give you the wrong information. Not wrong as in deliberately mislead you. It's not as if they walk into the focus group with a Machiavellian desire to deceive. But wrong nonetheless. And that then leaves you, the marketer, operating with data that is less than accurate.

So why do people do that? Why aren't they honest when answering the questions? Do they feel as if it's an invasion of privacy? Do they get flustered when they find out there's a bevy of marketers behind the two-way glass? Do they succumb to peer pressure, and follow the lead of the most vocal person in the group? Or, in an attempt to be kind, do they tell marketers what they hope to hear?

All of these are good guesses. And to a certain extent, they can impact the response you'll collect at a focus group. However, a good researcher or focus group moderator can usually control for these variables, so they do not become a significant factor. Which brings us right back to our question. Why would focus group participants lie to us? They're being compensated for their time. And they have been screened for their suitability to address the subject. So why don't they just answer the moderator's questions truthfully?

Well, here is where it gets interesting. The participants actually think that they are being honest. They really don't realize that the answers they supply are not completely truthful. As far as they know, they are fulfilling their end of the bargain, and providing their genuine opinions and reactions to each question or exhibit.

This is because very often people do not know why they do things. As we covered in the first chapter, they are influenced by factors they are not aware of. While they believe they know why they make certain buying decisions, the truth is often they really don't. Or, as behavioral scientist Susan Weinschenk (2019) reports, "research shows that most of our decisions—big or small—are made unconsciously and involve emotion."

However, even if most decisions are made unconsciously, that does not stop people from thinking they do know why they did what they did. As a result, when asked, they will provide a reason—a reason they truly believe. But one that may not be of much use to marketers. As David Ogilvy, founder of Ogilvy and Mather, once observed, "People don't think what they feel, don't say what they think, and don't do what they say" (BrainSigns, 2019).

And yet, people have a powerful need to feel like they are doing things for a reason. They also have a powerful need to feel that they are in control (see Chapter 7). As a result, the human mind will essentially manufacture a reason that suitably explains the action. Have you ever found your misplaced set of keys, for example, and told yourself, "Oh, I must have put these here because…"? The human brain will fill in the missing information in a way that makes sense and fits the narrative, even if the reason it's supplying is not the actual one. People like to have a reason for what they do. While this may not be the best news for researchers (it's one of the reasons I prefer in-market testing), it is actually very good news for marketers who are trying to accomplish a different goal.

That goal is prompting people to take action. Why? Because behavioral science research shows that if you give someone a reason to do something, they are more likely to do it. And that means that if marketers include the reason why a customer should buy, or otherwise reply, those marketers will be more likely to get the response they seek. People will feel they have a reason for taking the action, and as a result it can trigger an automatic, hardwired human response.

> Marketers can use certain prompts to get people to agree or comply with a request automatically—without giving the matter much, if any, conscious thought.

Marketers can prompt response by offering the reason why

In his book *Influence: The psychology of persuasion*, Robert Cialdini describes certain elements that can trigger "an automatic compliance response" from people—a pattern of response that he likens to a "mechanical, tape-activated" one. It's as if a button is pushed and the person responds with a corresponding taped script or rote behavior.

One such automatic compliance trigger is the word "because." As Cialdini notes, "A well-known principle of human behavior says that when we ask someone to do us a favor, we will be more successful if we provide a reason why." Research has shown that introducing that reason with the word "because" can trigger the response the requester is looking for (Langer et al., 1978).

Imagine this. You're in the library, lined up at the photocopier with some papers you need to copy. Just as you reach the head of the line and place your papers on the machine, a stranger comes up to you and asks if they can cut in front of you. What would you do? Maybe you think the biggest factors in your answer would be what else you had to get done that day, and whether or not you were in a generous mood. That could very well be. Assuming the request was phrased politely, however, would the specific words the person used to ask the question make a substantial difference?

According to Langer's experiment, they would. She arranged to have an experimenter approach a person as they prepared to use the photocopier, and instructed the experimenter to say "Excuse me, I have five pages. May I use the Xerox machine?" When this happened, 60 percent of the people who were asked agreed to let the experimenter cut in front of them. Think of this as the baseline. Langer also instructed the experimenter to phrase the request in two other ways. One was "Excuse me, I have five pages. May I use the Xerox machine, because I have to make copies?" And the other was, "Excuse me, I have five pages. May I use the Xerox machine, because I'm in a rush?"

As you read this last version, you may assume that more people allowed the experimenter to make copies ahead of them when the question was posed this way. In fact, Langer did indeed find that the 60 percent number climbed to 94 percent in this case. After all, the experimenter had said they were in a rush, right?

What was surprising was the response the experimenter received when they explained their request with the phrase "because I have to make copies." The 94 percent number did fall, but only to 93 percent. Clearly everyone standing in line at the photocopier had copies to make. They weren't standing in that line to get a coffee. Langer identified the word "because" as a cue that can get people to agree without thinking. "It may not be that a person weighs information and then proceeds, but that he or she more often just proceeds on the basis of structural cues," she noted.

FIGURE 13.1 The power of "because"

Providing the reason why delivered a significant increase in response during Ellen Langer's copy machine experiment. Even a nonsense reason performed well, with a 93% response rate compared to the baseline 60%.

Langer demonstrated that providing a reason for a request, and cueing up that reason with the word because, can be a very powerful way to gain agreement. But, before marketers assume that any nonsensical reason will be enough to get people to take their desired action, first consider her follow-up experiment. In that one, the number of pages was increased from 5 to 20, a heftier ask. When this happened, the legitimate reason did a get a much higher compliance rate (42 percent versus 24 percent). However, the "no reason" reason did not produce an increase.

What this suggests is that as a marketer, you should provide the reason you're asking people to take action, and that you are better off making that reason a legitimate one. Additionally, you should tee up your request with the word "because." Doing so can greatly increase the likelihood your customers and prospects will automatically say yes.

How providing the reason why drove significant growth for one marketing agency

If you've already read Chapter 9, you may recall my tale of picking up a contract creative director position at a small agency during an economic downturn. I'd been laid off from a larger agency around Christmastime, and was grateful to have the part-time work. You may also recall I'd been delighted when, a few weeks into the job, one of the parent company's sales guys wanted to talk to me about going full-time—and that his plan for making that happen wasn't going to work. But the story did turn out to have a happy ending.

Like most agencies during a recession, this small agency had been working hard to grow their business. They had smart, talented people, who provided good service and effective creative to their clients. But now they were competing in an environment that was exceptionally tough. Larger agencies who typically wouldn't go after smaller accounts were suddenly interested in them. Other smaller agencies were reducing fees to attract clients. And it became increasingly important to offer a strong reason why a prospective client should choose this agency.

Neal, the agency's president, asked me to work with him on what that reason should be. As you might imagine, we considered a few. One idea was to focus on the fact that we could offer big agency experience at a small agency price. Since nearly everyone there had worked at a large, well-known agency previously, that was a solid claim we could make. Unfortunately, so could several of our competitors.

Another area we explored was the link to our parent company. That company offered printing and production services, which meant we could position the agency as having preferred access to expertise in printing and mailing. Few, if any, of our competitors could offer this as a reason to hire them.

However, if a prospective client were looking for an agency that could handle their digital needs, they might not think we did that work, even though we did. And if they did want offline work done, there was the possibility they'd worry that the concepts the agency presented might be limited, because they'd be designed to run only on the kind of presses that our parent company had. While not the case, it could have been the perception.

As Neal and I continued to talk, though, something clicked. It became apparent that both of us shared a strong interest in and healthy respect for behavioral science. For the last half a dozen or so years, I'd been learning more and more about the field, and trying to apply any findings I thought relevant to the creative work my teams produced. And the results had been promising. In a statement that turned out to foreshadow my next position as co-founder of HBT Marketing, I told Neal that if I were running an agency, I'd say the reason clients should hire it was that we added behavioral science prompts into our work.

Neal decided to take the idea and run with it. We were both convinced that using behavioral science in marketing made sense. We weren't aware of any of our competitors making that claim. And we felt it offered a strong reason why a prospective client should consider awarding their account to us. (With the kind of money involved in creating marketing campaigns, we knew we'd need a legitimate reason to follow our "because." Clients were not going to hire the agency "because we did marketing.")

Did our reason why pay off? As the saying goes, "Success has many fathers, but failure is an orphan." As such, it wouldn't be accurate to point to this one reason as the sole driver of the agency's fortunes. But I will say that in the next 36 months, prior to the agency being sold, Neal was able to report that the business grew by over 100 percent. And that agency was named one of the top 35 direct marketing firms in the United States.

MISTAKE

Assuming it's obvious why your prospect should respond, so there's no need to mention it. Always include a reason why, because people are more likely to do what you ask when you do.

CASE STUDY
The 'reason why' that one local bank offered to open a checking account

Banks want people to open checking accounts. Once they do, they are more likely to remain customers. This is even more true if the customer sets up a service such as direct deposit or online bill pay, or uses the bank's debit card. The hassle factor to change banks then becomes higher.

Small, local banks can have a harder time attracting clients than the large banks do. The larger banks have bigger advertising and marketing budgets, and sometimes offer more services. As a result, when a community bank approached the agency where I was working and asked for help attracting more checking account customers, we knew it would take some smart strategizing.

One area we immediately explored was the local angle. The bank branch would be conveniently located near the prospect's home. And it would be staffed by people who were familiar with the community. But we were not convinced this was a compelling reason to open a checking account with them. The big banks had ATMs all over the place; plus, with online banking, the location of the branch seemed less important. And while an understanding of the local community might be a factor in obtaining a loan or mortgage, it seemed less relevant to opening a checking account.

Next, we looked at using the bank's offer as the reason why someone should open an account. They were offering to deposit a certain amount of money into the customer's new checking account. While it was a competitive offer, it was not so unusual that it alone would likely sway someone to switch their checking account to a different bank.

Naturally, we also considered focusing on excellent customer service. But what business doesn't claim to provide great service? It's true that customers have been known to switch banks because of a horrible experience, but unless a prospect were in the middle of one, the promise of service people love would probably register as marketing white noise.

In evaluating the competitive landscape, however, we learned that several big banks had recently begun raising their fees. Our community bank client also charged fees, but did not intend to increase them. This provided an angle we thought we could create some strong messaging around. In constructing our 'reason why,' we believed it would be even more effective if it were about the person and not just the financial institution. So, we crafted our lead message around the idea that because big banks were raising fees, the target was probably looking to join their neighbors and reevaluate where they did their checking.

The reference to the neighbors added some social proof (see Chapter 5), implying that people like the target were switching their accounts. By suggesting that the target was probably already considering this, it actually put the idea into their head.

And by avoiding a direct message that said the bank was not raising their fees, it prevented a skeptical "yeah, for now" reaction. We didn't want to provide a reason that sounded too good to be true. The marketing copy then went on to position the bank, its ongoing commitment to low fees, and the offer it was extending to the target, as creating the ideal time to open a checking account with them. And it worked. The client reported a 31 percent increase over their control.

When providing the reason why, you may also need to supply the reason to believe

You know science has shown that people are more likely to do what you ask if you give them a reason. And you know that larger asks (for example, copying 20 pages versus 5 at a photocopier) require legitimate reasons, not just the "because I have copies to make" kind. One additional factor a marketer should consider is offering the reason to believe. If your reason why raises questions, it can stop your prospect in their tracks, negating that automatic response you hope to trigger.

Consider this scenario. Imagine I have a store that sells raincoats. I want people to buy them, so the reason I give is that they are now 50 percent off. At first blush, that may sound like a big motivator. However, it might also backfire. Prospective customers might wonder if there is something wrong with the raincoats to make me sell them at such a discount. They may wonder if the styles are really old, or if the raincoats are not really water repellent.

However, if I tell people to buy a raincoat because they are half price, and explain that I need to get my spring merchandise off the salesroom floor in order to make room for the incoming summer merchandise, now I've supplied a reason why and a reason to believe. Instead of being suspicious of my sale, people will think they're about to get a good discount at my expense. They may think I had too many raincoats in stock to begin with. Or that because the spring was exceptionally dry, there wasn't a lot of demand for them. Either way, they won't think there's anything suspicious about my discount—my reason to buy.

Not every reason why will require a corresponding reason to believe. The key is to put yourself in the mind frame of your prospect, and evaluate the marketing message the way they will. If your message or offer may elicit a "sounds good, but…" reaction, make sure you overcome it by providing the context—the reason to believe. A good reason why backed up with a convincing reason to believe can deliver the reflexive compliance you want.

Five more ways to appeal to the automatic ways your customers make decisions

Providing the reason why using the word "because" is one way to influence people's decisions, and get them to agree with what you're saying without giving it a lot of thought. As a marketer, you can also take advantage of other triggers that increase the likelihood that people will automatically behave the way you want them to. And those behaviors include important ones like reading and believing your marketing message.

THE DASHED LINES OF COUPONS ATTRACT READERSHIP

For example, coupons attract readership. Advertising research company Roper Starch Worldwide found that an ad with a coupon gets 13 percent more readership than the same ad without a coupon. And this is regardless of what the coupon actually says. People are so accustomed to finding something of value inside those dashed lines that their eyes just automatically go to them. I have advised clients who really wanted their prospects to read certain information to put dashed lines around it, even if that information is not about a discount. In fact, I mentioned this at a conference I was speaking at, and someone from a large nonprofit was in the audience. He went back to the office and decided to try it. They were so pleased with their results, they ended up hiring us.

In addition to attracting attention and driving readership, coupons offer marketers another advantage. According to neuroeconomist Paul Zak (Dooley, 2012), when online shoppers receive a coupon, they experience a surge in the hormone oxytocin—which is related to feelings of happiness, love, and trust. In fact, his research showed the increase in oxytocin was higher than what people experience when they kiss! So not only can a coupon prompt a purchase, it can prompt feelings of love and trust that your customers associate with your brand.

Pictures, graphs, and equations suggest credibility

If you want to increase the likelihood that your customers will believe your marketing copy, run a picture with it. Researchers in New Zealand found that when photographs accompanied statements, those statements were more often judged as true than when no photo was present. For example, people were shown a sentence that said, "Macadamia nuts are in the same evolutionary family as peaches" (Jarrett, 2012). When a picture of the nut appeared with the statement, people were more likely to believe it, even though the picture of the nut provided no evidence of the truthfulness of the claim. The mere presence of the picture was what produced the effect.

GRAPHS AND CHARTS SUGGEST ACCURACY

If you want to improve the persuasiveness of your marketing copy, adding a picture is not your only option. A similar study conducted by researchers at Cornell University found that including a graph along with text made the text appear more credible (Tal, 2015). Researchers had subjects read about a new medication that was ostensibly being developed to help fight the common cold. The copy was not very long. In fact, the researchers actually likened it to the amount that would be found in a press release or ad. When some people read the information, it included a graph. When others read it, there was no graph.

After people read the information, they were asked to rate how effective they thought the new medication would be. Researchers found that when people saw the text alone, 68 percent rated the medication as effective. But when the graph was present, the effectiveness ratings increased to 97 percent.

It's important to note that the graph did not supply any additional information. Nor did it make the written information easier to understand. It simply suggested scientific veracity. Since the copy was supported by a graph, people assumed it must be accurate. As the researchers observed, "graphs have a scientific halo—we associate them with science and objectivity. As a result, graphs give an aura of truth to the information they accompany." The researchers went on to say that "the presence of even trivial graphs significantly enhances the persuasiveness of the presented claims."

While marketers shouldn't make up information to put in graphs, there are certainly times when the content you present would lend itself to a chart or graph. By creating one and including it with your marketing message, you could benefit from your prospect's automatic assumption that what they've just read is true. My team did this for a newspaper client that was looking to increase subscribers. With a bar chart, we illustrated what a new subscriber would pay using their introductory discount compared to the typical subscription cost. Seven years later, although some of their other messaging has changed, they still use this tactic.

EQUATIONS CAN BOOST BELIEVABILITY

Similar to the scientific effect of graphs and charts, adding an equation to what someone reads may also boost their belief that what they've read is correct (Eriksson, 2012). Researcher Kimmo Eriksson conducted an experiment involving the abstracts of two scientific papers. In one abstract, he inserted a line of nonsense text, a sentence from another report that had nothing to do with the topic of the paper in which he inserted it. In the other, he inserted a meaningless equation. Then he asked people with postgraduate degrees, who were familiar with reading research reports, to read the abstracts and evaluate the quality of the research.

Eriksson found that the abstract with the meaningless equation in it was rated higher. This did not hold true, however, for people who had advanced degrees in math, science, technology, or medicine. These people rated the papers similarly. Eriksson concluded that for people who had not mastered mathematics, "the use of mathematics may be held in too much awe."

As a marketer, you may have opportunities to take advantage of the awe that people have for mathematics. If your product or service could logically feature an equation in its marketing messages, this research suggests including one could be a good idea. And one that lends credence to your copy.

BEFORE AND AFTER IMAGES CONVEY EFFECTIVENESS

One more way to bolster the believability of your marketing messages is to support them with before and after pictures, or with product and result pictures. Showing these is a quick way to demonstrate the effectiveness of your product. Even without reading the copy, people can see the promise you're making. And the pictures offer visual proof, which makes your promise seem more concrete.

When using this tactic, however, you want to be sure you position the pictures to gain the most impact. Researchers from the University of British Columbia and the National University of Singapore conducted experiments to determine the effect the placement of the two pictures had on people (Chae et al., 2013).

In the experiments, people were shown pictures for a variety of products, including acne cream, bug spray, and fabric softener. Researchers found that "The spatial proximity between visual representations of cause and effect in an advertisement can influence consumer judgments of product effectiveness. The closer the distance between an image of a product (an acne treatment) and that of its potential effect (a smooth face), the more effective consumers will judge the product to be."

In other words, all things being equal, your customers will automatically think your product claim is more believable if your before and after or product and result shots appear close together.

How input bias prompts automatic assumptions

Behavioral scientists have found that people often use the amount of time or effort that is put into something as an indicator of the quality of that thing. Called input bias, it's a shorthand way humans have of evaluating value. The amount of input becomes a proxy for the resulting quality. While in some cases, there is a direct relationship between how much time and energy is put into a project, in other cases there is not. Yet people are not always good at discerning the difference. As a result, they can automatically assume more effort equals better output.

Researchers proved this when they asked people to watch a presentation on electronic ink and another one on optical switches (Chinander and Schweitzer, 2003). Sometimes they told people that the ink presentation took eight hours and 34 minutes to prepare, and the switch presentation took 37 minutes to prepare. Other times they reversed it. Then they asked people to rate the two presentations on a 10-point scale. The researchers found that the presentation that was described as taking longer to prepare was rated significantly higher, regardless of which one it was. If people had been told the ink presentation took longer to prepare, they rated it better. If they had been told that same presentation took less time to prepare, they consistently rated it lower. The presentation didn't change, but the amount of effort they were told was attached to it did. And that is what made the difference. Although people think they make evaluations based on objective measures, this is not always the case. They may believe they are not influenced by anything other than the actual product, but this experiment indicates otherwise.

Since people just naturally equate input with output, this presents an opportunity for marketers. You can increase the perceived value of your products and services by including a mention of the time and effort it took to create them. Keep the mention succinct, and always remember people are more interested in themselves than in you. For example, "We tried over 100 configurations to bring you the most comfortable one," keeps the message short and focused on the customer, while also triggering input bias.

How you can use the reason why and other automatic compliance triggers in your marketing

- Tell customers why they should respond, even if it seems obvious to you.
- Provide a good reason, but remember it does not have to be an amazing one. For example, a financial newsletter that asks people to subscribe because reading it will make them millionaires is an amazing reason, but not one the newsletter can likely substantiate. However, inviting people to subscribe because reading it will make them smarter about money is a good reason, and it's truthful. Even inviting prospects to subscribe because "our readers really like it" could qualify, especially if signing up was free or inexpensive (not a significant ask).
- Link your reasons why to other behavioral science triggers, such as social proof (Chapter 5), the endowment effect (Chapter 2), information gap theory (Chapter 9), or the authority principle (Chapter 10). To continue the financial newsletter example, a marketer could say because people like you have found it beneficial, because you're entitled to it as a member, because the next issue reveals how ordinary people double their savings, or because *Money Magazine* called it a must-read.
- Tie your reason why to timing (example: a charity might say because all donations will be matched this month).
- Personalize your reason why (example: because you're a new customer, or because customers like you requested).
- Keep in mind that marketers can tee up a reason why using words other than because. Try since, as a result, due to, so, and therefore. A colleague of mine, Michelle Martineau, started an acquisition letter with this

powerful opening: "You haven't responded to our previous mailings and I think I know why."

- Use the reason why to neutralize objections (example: although our company is new to the area, our employees have all lived here for over a decade, so they're familiar with the geographical nuances).

- Immediately legitimize your request by beginning with a reason (example: because it's important to stay in touch with customers, we're asking for your email address).

- Pair your reason why with a reason to believe that adds context.

- Call attention to key copy points by putting a dashed line around that section of your marketing message.

- Feature pictures or before and after shots in your marketing where appropriate. If your product or service doesn't lend itself to a before and after shot, you can show a person—unhappy before becoming your customer, and very happy after doing business with you. Don't forget to caption your photos, because captions are usually read.

- Support your messaging with relevant equations or charts and graphs. Look for pieces of content that can easily be translated into these formats.

- Trigger input bias by including a bullet or callout that highlights how many years it took to develop your product, the amount of research or effort that went into it, or the number of people who helped develop it (example: ten years in the making, completely stitched by hand, input from over 1,000 executives across three continents).

KEY TAKEAWAYS

1 People like to think they have reasons for what they do.

2 Your customers are more likely to do what you ask them to if you give them a reason why.

3 Teeing up your reason using the word "because" can prompt automatic compliance.

4 The reason you give doesn't have to be bulletproof. For easier asks (watch a short video), simply including some kind of reason can trigger people to agree (because it's informative). For bigger asks (purchase a product), be sure to use a legitimate reason (because it will reduce preparation time by 30 percent).

5 When constructing your reason why, consider how differentiating and motivating it is.

6 Sometimes it makes sense for marketers to pair their reason why with a reason to believe, to provide corroborating context.

7 When writing your reason why, try linking it to other behavioral science triggers, timing, or personalization.

8 Marketers can increase the chance customers and prospects will automatically read and believe their messages by using pictures, before and after shots, dashed coupon lines around key content, and the scientific halo that graphs and equations provide.

9 People will use the time and effort put into the creation of a product or service as a proxy for the actual quality of that product or service. While the two are sometimes related, they are not always. Yet people will rely on this information as a way to make a short-hand decision.

10 Marketers can trigger input bias, and therefore increase the perceived value of their products and services, by mentioning how much went into the development of them.

In conclusion

Providing the reason why can get people to make the decision you want them to, without their really thinking about it. When people are provided with a reason for doing something, they often just default to the requested behavior. Interestingly, the reason provided doesn't always have to be especially sound. Research shows, for example, that when people hear the word "because" they begin to agree before even processing the words that come next.

That said, marketers should not underestimate the importance of words. As you'll see in the next chapter, choosing one set of words over another can mean the difference between making a sale or not.

References

Chae, B, Li, X and Zhu, R (2013) Judging product effectiveness from perceived spatial proximity, *Journal of Consumer Research*, 40 (2), pp 317–335

BrainSigns (2019) David Ogilvy said that "consumers don't think how they feel, they don't say what they think and they don't do what they say". People don't know what are the criteria based on those who make a decision. Learn more about how neuromarketing can help us, https://twitter.com/BrainSigns/status/1090636075750572037 (archived at https://perma.cc/4TXH-UNRR)

Chinander, KR and Schweitzer, ME (2003) The input bias: The misuse of input information in judgments of outcomes, *Organizational Behavior and Human Decision Processes*, **91** (2), pp 243–53, https://doi.org/10.1016/S0749-5978(03)00025-6 (archived at https://perma.cc/RS6H-F2B6)

Cialdini, R (1984) *Influence: The psychology of persuasion*, Quill William Morrow, New York

Dooley, R (2012) Coupons: Better than kissing, *Forbes*, 21 December, https://www.forbes.com/sites/rogerdooley/2012/12/21/coupons-kissing/?sh=268a38005d38 (archived at https://perma.cc/4J54-J32L)

Eriksson, K (2012) The nonsense math effect, *Judgement and Decision Making*, http://journal.sjdm.org/12/12810/jdm12810.html (archived at https://perma.cc/PY7U-W5AL)

Jarrett, C (2012) How the presence of an uninformative photo makes a statement more believable, *British Psychological Society Research Digest*, 17 September, https://digest.bps.org.uk/2012/09/17/how-the-presence-of-an-uninformative-photo-makes-a-statement-more-believable/ (archived at https://perma.cc/XK84-QXZ7)

Langer, E, Blank, A and Chanowitz, B (1978) The mindlessness of ostensibly thoughtful Action: The role of "placebic" information in interpersonal interaction, *Journal of Personality and Social Psychology*, https://jamesclear.com/wp-content/uploads/2015/03/copy-machine-study-ellen-langer.pdf (archived at https://perma.cc/JEA6-ZJ3G)

Tal, A (2015) Beware the truthiness of charts, *Harvard Business Review*, 19 November, https://hbr.org/2015/11/beware-the-truthiness-of-charts (archived at https://perma.cc/289W-3QW3)

Weinschenk, S (2019) How people make decisions, *Smashing Magazine*, 7 February, https://www.smashingmagazine.com/2019/02/human-decision-making/ (archived at https://perma.cc/Z7EW-PPFW)

14

Maximizing the impact of your marketing copy and language

Marketers can often convey the same information in several different ways; however, some of those ways offer more advantages. Choosing certain words and phrases can make messages more memorable, more believable, and more persuasive.

Words matter. Sometimes it can be tempting to think that as a marketer, if you just put the basic idea out there, you're good. You may think that so long as your marketing message conveys the necessary information, there's no real need to search for a synonym here, or replace a modifier there.

After all, your audience gets it. They understand they're reading marketing copy. It's not as if they expect it to sound like a work of literary wonder, or even the latest best-selling beach read, right? Shouldn't it be enough to tell them what they want to know—basically what you're selling and why they might be interested—and get on to your next ad, email, letter, blogpost, or video script? Shoot for something above huckster and below Hemingway, make sure there are no typos or factual inaccuracies, and consider the job done?

Not quite. It's true that your target market will not approach your marketing copy with the same expectations they bring to a novel. But that's not the point. The real reason marketers need to remember that words matter is because doing so results in more successful marketing copy. You want to pay attention to the language you use not because you want your audience to think you're a fantastic wordsmith, but because you want them to be more likely to behave the way you hope they will.

Words can be incredibly motivating. If you've read Chapter 5, you may remember the story that had a happy ending because an ashtray was referred to as a statue base. And in Chapter 12, you saw the sizeable difference the modifier "small" made. In that same chapter, you also discovered the surprising effects that labeling and framing can have. And the power of words does not stop there. The word choices you make in your marketing copy can have a significant impact on the way your customers and prospects respond to it. What they read or hear not only delivers factual information, but also conjures shades of interpretation, nuance, and implication. Just like your tone of voice can convey more than the actual words you speak, the selections and substitutions you make when choosing your words also carry a subtext.

Words have connotations and denotations. The denotation is the actual definition of the word. But the connotation is much broader, and can carry with it associated meanings, both negative and positive. For example, you could describe a product as being affordable or cheap. Both suggest the price tag won't be too high. But each carries a different connotation. You could refer to a product feature that's different as being unique, which seems more positive, or as odd, which seems less so. And you can call your customers guests, members, subscribers, or shoppers. Each suggests something slightly different.

As a marketer, you can write copy that people will find easy to absorb. Or copy that requires more mental effort to understand. You can choose words that naturally attract the human eye, words that stir specific emotions, and words that rile your readers up or hold them safely at arm's length. Consider the difference the switch from active voice to passive voice produces with "You entered the wrong size" and "The wrong size was entered."

Perhaps best of all, you can craft sentences to sound more memorable, or more motivating, or even more believable than similar sentences that convey the same information. It is for these reasons that the language you use in your marketing materials is so important. Your words won't simply tell, they will sell. Or not.

Rhyming copy is not just more memorable. People also feel that it's more truthful. This effect can give marketers with rhyming slogans a clear advantage.

Rhyme as reason effect can prompt an automatic assumption that is quite helpful to marketers

One of the most curious impacts of word choice can be found in the Rhyme as Reason Effect, which is also known as Eaton-Rosen Phenomenon or the

Keats heuristic. When your copy triggers the Rhyme as Reason Effect, your audience will find it to be more memorable, believe it to be more accurate, and feel more confident in their ability to make a decision about it. So how do you hit this marketing trifecta? By choosing words that rhyme.

The fact that rhyming phrases are easier to remember is not surprising. However, a study conducted by Matthew McGlone and Jessica Tofighbakhsh, and reported in a September 2000 issue of *Psychological Science*, showed an additional impact of rhyming phrases. The researchers took certain aphorisms that were not well-known and modified them by changing a rhyming word to a non-rhyming one. For example, "woes unite foes" was altered to read "woes unite enemies," and "what sobriety conceals, alcohol reveals" was reworded to say "what sobriety conceals, alcohol unmasks."

People were then shown the pairs of sayings, and asked to rate them for accuracy. The researchers found that the rhyming phrases were the ones people judged to be more accurate and truthful. They concluded that "this effect is a product of the enhanced processing fluency rhyme affords," referring to the fact that the human brain finds it easier to process phrases that rhyme. When the brain has an easier time processing something, it feels right. And when something feels right, it's not a big leap to assume that it is right.

The researchers added, "Although we have explored the rhyme as reason effect within the narrow domain of antiquated sayings, it clearly can occur in contemporary communications as well." They then went on to cite the line defense attorney Johnnie Cochran became known for in the 1995 O.J. Simpson trial: "If the glove doesn't fit, you must acquit."

TWO MODERN DAY EXAMPLES

An even more contemporary example of the rhyme as reason effect can be found in a campaign that Ogilvy Consulting created for England's National Health Service in 2020, during the Covid-19 pandemic (Jenkins and Buck, 2020). The team was challenged to "rapidly deliver effective and practical, behaviourally informed ideas across a number of briefs." One of those briefs was to ensure that at NHS Nightingale Hospital, the first of a number of emergency field hospitals set up to treat coronavirus patients, "the staff stay hydrated throughout their 12-hour shifts."

The Ogilvy team created a hydration poster with a headline that read "Keep your pee between 1 and 3." The poster showed eight different shades that could describe the color of one's urine. The medical staff was reminded to "have a drink in the next 10 minutes if your urine is coloured between 4–8 to boost hydration." The poster also included a prominent callout that harnessed the rhyme as reason effect. The words Drink Right, Think Right were shown surrounding a glass of water, to remind the hospital staffers that dehydration could impair their ability to think clearly.

Arguably one of marketing's best-known, and most effective, rhyming phrases is for coffee. In a *Contagious* interview, retired Procter & Gamble Group Vice President Pete Carter said, "I remember, in the early days, Folgers Coffee was a distant number two brand. You know 'The best part of waking up is Folgers in your cup'? We launched that campaign and the brand started growing against Maxwell House and eventually overtook it. Folgers then continued to grow 3–4% a year. Even the new owners today are still running that campaign" (Dodd, 2021).

Rhyming phrases take advantage of cognitive fluency

When behavioral scientists talk about how easy it is for the human brain to process information, they refer to it as cognitive fluency, or processing fluency. Because rhyming phrases are easier to process, they are considered to be more cognitively fluent. Perhaps not surprisingly, scientists have found that people prefer things they feel are easier to think about and easier to understand. Not only do they prefer them, people are more confident in their ability to make decisions about them.

On the other hand, when things don't feel easy to think about—when they are disfluent—that disfluency "functions as a cognitive alarm that gets people to slow down and reassess a situation," according to UX researcher Colleen Roller (Roller, 2011). That can lead them away from their initial decision to buy a product or sign up for a service.

Fortunately for marketers, injecting a bit of poetry into your messaging is not the only way to make sure your communications are cognitively fluent. You have other options at your disposal, and they broadly break into two types—the language you use and the way you lay out or art direct that language in your communications. You want to choose words that are common and don't confuse your readers, or force them to consult a dictionary. In fact, some research suggests that unfamiliar terms could negatively impact your bottom line.

According to a 2003 study conducted by Princeton University psychologists Adam L Alter and Daniel M Oppenheimer, the pronounceability of stock names actually influenced stock performance in the marketplace (Boutin, 2006). The researchers looked at how easy or hard it was to pronounce both the name of the stock and the stock's ticker symbol. What they found was that those stocks with names that were easier to pronounce performed better after their initial public offering. And this remained true even after accounting for factors such as company size and industry.

"This research shows that people take mental shortcuts, even when it comes to their investments, when it would seem that they would want to be most rational," said Oppenheimer. It's probably rare that someone would claim to choose a stock based on how easy its name was to pronounce, but that's exactly what seems to have happened. If the name was cognitively fluent, it was easier to process, and as a result, it felt like a good pick.

Another example of the importance of choosing a word that is clear and does not confuse your audience comes from Apple. According to a *Mashable* report (Binder, 2021), Apple began the process of changing the call to action for its podcasts from "subscribe" to "follow." The reason? Apparently "subscribe" signaled to people that there would be a cost involved. The article quoted Edison Research, a market analysis company, as saying "that 47 percent of people who *don't* listen to podcasts thought it cost money to 'subscribe' to podcasts" (Binder, 2021). By changing "subscribe" to "follow," Apple hoped to clear up that misperception. As a result, they could put themselves in position to add a substantial number of listeners.

How you display information can influence how people react to it

While the words you choose are important for cognitive fluency, so too is the way you display them. Cluttered layouts, not enough white space, and typefaces that are difficult to read can also impact people's ability to process your marketing messages. This means marketers should resist the urge to cram as much information as possible into an ad, letter, or email, as well as the temptation to use unusual typefaces for large swaths of text. While an unusual font can attract attention, it can also impair readership, as these next two studies show.

Researchers Hyunjin Song and Norbert Schwarz ran an experiment that involved exercise directions (Song and Schwarz, 2008). People read about the steps to do an exercise printed in either an easy-to-read typeface such as Arial, or a more difficult-to-read typeface such as Brush. Then they were asked to estimate how long they thought it would take to do the exercise, and whether or not they would incorporate it into their daily routines. People who read about the exercise in the easy-to-read typeface estimated it would take about eight minutes to complete. But people who read about it in the more difficult-to-read typeface thought it would take almost twice that amount of time, about 15 minutes. The people who had an easier time reading the directions were also more likely to say they'd

FIGURE 14.1 Cognitive fluency in font choice

How to complete the exercise in Brush

How to complete the exercise in Arial

Because your customers will believe information displayed in a difficult-to-read typeface will be difficult to do, it's usually a good idea to choose a font that's easy to read.

add it to their routines. The researchers observed that "people misread the ease of processing instructions as bearing on the ease of executing the desired behavior." In other words, if something is hard to read, people assume it will be hard to do.

A different study, conducted by researchers from Yale University and the University of Southern California, found similar results related to purchasing decisions (Novemsky et al., 2007). People were shown descriptions of two phones that appeared in either an easy-to-read or difficult-to-read typeface. They were then asked to choose a phone, or postpone their purchase decision and continue looking. While only 17 percent of the research participants put off their purchase decision when the font was easier to read, 41 percent deferred their choice when it was hard to read. The way marketers display information can influence a customer's decision to buy. If a product description is difficult to read, people may assume the product itself will be difficult to use.

I can recall looking at an artificial Christmas tree featured in a catalog. The copy led with how easy the tree would be to assemble, an important consideration when buying a tree of this sort. But because that copy was in a hard-to-read, italic typeface that was reversed out, it communicated a very different message. I remember thinking that the catalog's designer hadn't done them any favors.

Marketers should note that legibility of type is not just a function of the font. The contrast between the color of the type and the color of the page or screen it appears on also makes a difference. And that difference in readability can impact your credibility. In a study that changed the color of statements to make them easier or harder to read against a white background, researchers found that the easier-to-read statements were judged to be more truthful (Reber and Schwarz, 1999). Marketers, of course, want customers to perceive their messages as truthful and not hiding anything.

BEWARE OF JARGON, BIG WORDS, AND TECHNICAL TERMS

As a rule of thumb, you should try to get your message across in a simple, easily absorbed way. Marketers need to be especially careful when writing to a business-to-business audience, or when the products and services they describe are more specialized, scientific, or technical. In those cases, it can be even easier to slip into industry jargon or acronyms. In fact, sometimes marketers can be so familiar with a word or term that it doesn't even seem like jargon to them. And that's why it's even more important to watch out for it.

Ann Handley, author of the best-selling book *Everybody Writes*, describes jargon and buzzwords as "the chemical additives of business writing online: you can use them, and maybe one or two used sparingly don't much matter. But use too many of them and they become toxic."

Another mistake to avoid is trying to impress your audience by using large words and technical terms. Marketers sometimes think this helps to position them as experts. However, it can backfire. It can even backfire when your audience should be familiar with the terms, or when you are targeting highly educated people.

An interesting study out of Rome appears to support this. Researchers Alejandro Martinez and Stefano Mammola of the Italian National Research Council authored a 2021 paper titled "Specialized terminology reduces the number of citations of scientific papers." After analyzing 21,486 research articles, the researchers found that those that included higher proportions of jargon in their titles or abstracts actually received fewer citations from their fellow scientists. In other words, even scientists preferred not to deal with another's scientist's jargon. The paper's authors actually encouraged their readers to resort to jargon only when it was "unavoidable" (Martinez and Mammola, 2021).

If using jargon is actively discouraged in scientific research papers, imagine the effect it could have when used in communications to the general public. A 2020 study from Ohio University suggests it is not a positive one (Shulman, et al., 2020). The study found that when people read articles that used jargon on topics such as self-driving cars, they reported being less interested in science afterwards than people who had read the same articles without the jargon.

The results of another study, this one led by Daniel M Oppenheimer, PhD, suggest that avoiding big words is also advisable (Lebowitz, 2015). When researchers simplified dissertation abstracts by replacing every word of nine or more letters with a shorter synonym, people found the writing easier to understand, and judged the authors as more intelligent. Finally, a 2012 study by Christopher Trudeau that involved legal communications found that the more educated a person is, the more they prefer plain language. Additionally, the more complex the topic is, the greater that preference for simpler wording is.

So, if you think using big words or scientific terms will make you sound smart, or is what your audience will expect, you might want to reconsider. Persuading people starts with making sure they understand what you're saying – by clearly communicating with them. And research shows that starts with simple, cognitively fluent language.

Employing the rhyme as reason effect to attract business

For marketing agencies, one of the hardest assignments is creating advertising for yourself. Often, you'll hear marketers joke that the cobblers' kids go barefoot, explaining they're so busy with client work they don't have time to promote themselves. But when they do turn to the task, it can be a tough one.

That's what happened to John Sisson and me when we started HBT Marketing. We were, as a matter of truth, quite busy with our initial clients. But we knew that as a new agency, we needed to quickly launch a website so people could find us, prospects could check us out, and we could win more business. As we thought about our site, there were two things we were sure of. It would be simple, and it would demonstrate some of the behavioral science techniques that we are known for.

One of the key messages for any business website is the one that tells the world what you do, and how you do it. During some whiteboarding, we distilled our process down to three steps. Next the challenge was to communicate them in the best possible way. That way would have to explain our approach, summarize what someone could expect if they engaged us, and highlight how that experience would be different than working with one of our competitors.

Our three steps involved conducting the upfront research necessary to tackle a challenge, developing the appropriate behavioral science-infused marketing strategies and creative executions to solve it, and then analyzing the results of the effort in order to inform subsequent campaigns. The question was how to best describe that on our site. As you might imagine, we considered—and set aside—a number of ideas. For example, one of them was pithy and alliterative: Discover, Deploy, Distill. Another played off the

B in our name, which stands for behavior, and used repetition. It was Current Behavior. Desired Behavior. Future Behavior.

Finally, we landed on a set of descriptors that we felt did the trick. It was memorable, started with action words, and demonstrated our behavioral science-infused approach to marketing. Not long after its founding, HBT Marketing began advertising our three-point process as Assess the Terrain, Trigger the Brain, Measure the Gain. We took advantage of the rhyme as reason effect, and continue to benefit from the boost in memorability and believability it brings. If you visit the Our Approach section at HBTmktg.com, you can see it there.

CASE STUDY
How cognitive fluency improved a professional services sales proposition

What do you do when even giving away your product doesn't seem to work? That was the challenge a large research and advisory company presented to the agency where I was working. The company was offering a free trial membership of their technology insights service, which would help clients make informed decisions. Normally, a company would need to subscribe to the service and pay for each employee who wanted to use it. The free trial was designed to let them sample the service, providing access to certain research, analyst reports, and other information over a 30-day period, as a way to cultivate prospective customers.

A prospective customer would find out about the free trial membership when they saw a banner ad while visiting the client's website. Although prospective clients did sign up for the free trial, the problem would occur shortly after that. The client reported that nearly half of those prospective clients who had opted in for the free trial would drop out after the initial sign-up, considerably before their 30 days were up. This, of course, severely compromised the trial membership as a cultivation tool.

An analysis of the registration process revealed there was confusion around exactly what potential customers were entitled to during the free trial program. Some assumed they would have complete access to all the resources that the research and advisory company offered, including calls with analysts. Other prospective customers were not sure how to use the service once they signed up, and were unsuccessful at finding the trends and best practices they sought.

Even though the architects of the free trial program had been sure they were communicating all the relevant details appropriately, that seemed not to be the case. There appeared to be an opportunity to improve the cognitive fluency surrounding it. With this in mind, our team went to work.

Changes to banner ad and email copy drove a big difference

Banner ads, by definition, do not provide much room for copy. As a result, the words that do appear in them need to be succinct and spot on. After examining the language on the site's banner ad, we made a key strategic change. Instead of inviting prospective clients to "experience" the service, we changed the copy to invite them to "give it a try." We did this because we believed the word "experience" might have been misleading, and could have implied that the full capabilities and resources of the service would be available to someone. By changing the language to "give it a try," we hypothesized it would better set the expectation that the prospect would not get full access to the research portfolio of thought leadership, but rather an opportunity to try, or sample, it.

Once someone signed up, they received a series of emails, providing instructions and encouragement to use their free trial, and ultimately to convert to a paid subscriber. In reviewing those, we also adjusted the wording to be more clear and cognitively fluent. To start, we separated the first email into two emails, one that welcomed the person, and another that provided detailed instructions about how to use the service. Chunking the information in this way made it easier to absorb, and less likely to overwhelm a new user.

Additionally, we used phrases such as "customized sample of world-class research" and "access up to 30 popular research reports you can use right now." This was to accurately convey the trial nature of the offer as well as the value of it. We also added elements of personalization, loss aversion (see Chapter 2), and social proof (see Chapter 5) to the campaign, and extended the requests to convert to one week after the trial's end, versus stopping three days prior to it. These additional reminders were designed to deliver the information at a time when it might be easier for the prospect to think about it.

Finally, we included both email and phone contact information for a company representative in case the prospect had difficulty finding what they wanted. By increasing the cognitive fluency of the communication stream, and including a way for the prospect to obtain help, we hoped to improve the key performance metrics for the free trial. And we did. While the adjustments we made were small, they were meaningful. The client reported these changes yielded a 10x return on their marketing investment.

Literary devices that aid marketing copy and language

In addition to rhyming phrases, marketers can take advantage of other literary devices, or tools, to increase the effectiveness of their messages. These devices can help make your copy more memorable, more understandable, and as a result, more motivating.

ALLITERATION AND REPETITION MAKE MESSAGES MORE MEMORABLE

For example, you can use alliteration, which is marked by a series of words that all begin with the same letter. Alliteration is a good tool for attracting a reader's attention, because people notice when several words start the same way. It's also a smart strategic step (did you catch that example?) for making what they just read more memorable. Interestingly, your copy doesn't need to be spoken out loud in order to take advantage of alliteration. When people read, they hear the words in their heads. Research has confirmed that alliterative phrases that are read aloud or silently both enhance the memorability of the copy (Haury, 2017).

In fact, while writing this, what springs to mind is a group my friend Gert belongs to. Called Divas Uncorked, it's a women's wine education group. Their tagline is "sisters who sip," a wonderful application of alliteration. Another example, this one written by me, was for an email campaign for a company that specialized in reinsurance. By signing off each email with the alliterative line "fair answers fast," I hoped to help customers remember the kind of service they would get.

Similar to alliteration is repetition, which is when a word or phrase is repeated for rhythm and emphasis. This calls attention to the information, and also makes it more likely to lodge in your customer's brain. Essentially, the more often a person hears or reads something, the more familiar it becomes. Behavioral scientists have found that when something feels familiar, people are more inclined to believe it and think positively about it.

For example, you may recall hearing Dollar Shave Club advertise with the line "Shave Time. Shave Money." Or the United States Marines use the slogan "The few. The proud. The marines." Or Verizon Wireless repeat "Can you hear me now?" multiple times in an ad. These are all examples of marketers using repetition in ways that help drive home a point, and make it more memorable.

SIMILES AND METAPHORS MAKE INFORMATION EASIER TO UNDERSTAND

If you are introducing a product that people may not have a frame of reference for, or you are marketing a service that may be hard for your customers to grasp, you should consider using a simile or a metaphor. Both are ways to make a comparison between two things. A simile draws the comparison using the word "like" or "as", while a metaphor suggests a comparison, similarity, or sharing of qualities without using those words. A simile or metaphor is a powerful way to make a product or service that is abstract feel more concrete and accessible. It can prompt your customer to see things in a new and different way. In fact, when people encounter a metaphor, different parts of their brain are activated than normally would be, influencing their perceptions of the objects being described.

Both of these literary devices can help marketers make boring products more exciting and emotional. Similar to stories, they engage the imagination. For example, if you have ever seen the energy drink Red Bull advertised, you have probably seen the metaphorical line "Red Bull gives you wings." Or if you have come across any messaging from the insurance company State Farm, you have likely seen their tagline which employs the simile, "Like a good neighbor, State Farm is there." Similes and metaphors help your customers create mental images, which can make your message more persuasive.

The curious case of homophones

One other literary device that marketers should find both curious and compelling is the effect of homophones. A homophone is a word that sounds like another word, but has a different meaning and spelling. For example, write and right are homophones. Researchers have found that when people see or hear one, it can cause them to think of the other—and any behaviors that are associated with it.

In one experiment, people were asked to read a travel blog post. At the end of the post, some people saw the words "so long" and other people saw the words "bye bye" (Decision Lab, nd). Next, they were told that a new restaurant was opening that was going to have a name your own price dinner package. Research participants were asked to say what price they were willing to pay for a dinner for two.

The people who had read the blog post that ended with so long said they would spend, on average, just under $30. However, the people who'd read the identical post with the bye bye sign-off said they would pay, on average, just over $45. The researchers found that the word bye had prompted people to think of the word buy, and made them willing to pay more for the dinner package.

This experiment certainly raises possibilities for marketers. For example, imagine you have created a diet program to compete with the market-leading plans. However, your program is easier to use, with fewer restricted foods, or no need to measure portions and constantly count calories. Now it's time for you to name your diet program. Think of the impact a name such as the Way Less Work Diet Plan could have. Not only would it convey that the program is easier than others on the market, it might also get people to think they'll weigh less because of it.

> **MISTAKE**
>
> Over-relying on the words I, we, our company, and our products. Instead, write your marketing copy so sentences begin with you. That will draw readers in.

The power words that make marketing messages more effective

In marketing copy, there are certain go-to words that seem to be imbued with extra persuasive power. Because of that, you should use them frequently, and place them in high-read pieces of real estate such as headlines, subject lines, content titles, and lead sentences.

In Chapter 9, you discovered the brain-craving context of the word "new." And in Chapter 13, you read about the automatic pulling power of the word "because." But there are three other big guns that marketers should stash in their linguistic arsenal.

The first of these words is "you." People are more interested in themselves than in anyone else. As a result, when people are reading, or more typically skimming, their eyes will be drawn to the word you, but will gloss right over words such as I, me, our product, and our company. That's why I tell my clients to use the word you far more often than they use I and we.

My friend Tom Shapiro, in his new book *Rethink Lead Generation*, offers similar advice. He says, "If you want your website to maximize conversions and leads, it should be framed from the perspective of the site visitor ('what's in it for me?')." He recommends "flipping the script" on me language and writing to emphasize the word you.

Copyblogger goes so far as to list you as one of the five most persuasive words in the English language. They actually recommend using a person's name, which I wholeheartedly agree with. However, that is certainly easier in communications like email and direct mail than in others. But when a marketer cannot personalize, your next best substitute is the word you. Your target will recognize it as a stand-in for their own name and will act accordingly. In fact, if you were to limit me to a single word to start every marketing message I write, "you" would probably be my choice.

The next marketing power word is "imagine." This is an incredibly potent word to use when you want your readers to create a mental picture. And you do want your readers to create that mental picture, because once they can envision themselves doing something (like using your product), it paves the way for them to actually do it (see Chapter 17). The word imagine lowers someone's resistance, by switching the scene away from the reality of the here and now. It opens up possibilities. And it lets your prospective customer populate those possibilities exactly the way they wish. The mental image they create is their own. In their mind's eye, they will see themselves successfully using your product or service—and getting the exact results they seek. When they imagine that, it will make them feel good. And once they feel good about your product, they'll be more apt to become your customer.

Your final marketing power word is "free," and it packs a lot of punch. As a marketer, you may have some hesitation about offering something for free. You may worry it will cheapen your brand image. Or that free offers attract the wrong kinds of customers. You are prudent to consider these possibilities. However, you should weigh them against the incredible pulling power of the word free. Dan Ariely, author of *Predictably Irrational*, devotes an entire chapter in his book to it. He explains that free gives people such an emotional charge that they overvalue the free item. Getting something for free becomes irrationally irresistible. People just can't say no.

As a marketer, you can harness that inability and make it work in your favor. If you are worried about the impact on your brand, don't discount your product. Instead, offer a free add-on. Or make sure people know the normal price of the free product, so they can see its value. If you are concerned that you'll attract too many unqualified prospects, make your free item one that would appeal only to someone interested in what you sell. Or one that would be far more useful or enjoyable if the person also purchases your product. Find the right way to use free for your particular situation. But don't overlook the immense motivation tucked into those four little letters.

The impact of nouns and concrete language

Nouns are specific. Nouns suggest identity. And nouns can help marketers get the behavior they seek. For instance, one experiment involving voters in California showed the effect of choosing a noun over a verb (Bryan et al., 2011). People were either asked "How important is it to you to be a voter in the upcoming election?" or "How important is it to you to vote in the upcoming election?" Over 95 percent of those asked the question using the noun construction "be a voter" subsequently showed up at the polls, as compared to less than 82 percent of the people who had been asked the question using the verb construction.

The researchers concluded that nouns create a sense of who someone is, and once that is established, that person knows the corresponding behavior to take. Similar to labeling (see Chapter 12), referring to someone using a noun is more powerful than simply telling them what you want them to do using a verb. For example, it would be more effective for a car marketer to ask, "Would you like to be a new Audi owner?" than to ask, "Would you like to own a new Audi?"

Related to the specificity of nouns is concrete language. Research has shown that concrete language can be more motivating than using abstract terms (Packard and Berger, 2020). A study published in the *Journal of Consumer Research* reports that concrete words (example: blue jeans vs. pants, or t-shirt vs. top) used in a retailer's customer service emails prompted people to spend an average of 30 percent more over a 90-day period. As a marketer, you should replace more vague terms with concrete language. You should opt for specifics over generalities. And you should know that this same study also found that when employees used concrete language with customers, those customers felt heard, and as a result were more satisfied.

More ways to maximize the impact of your marketing copy and language

- Write your company's tagline, call to action, email subject line, or content title using rhyming phrases. For example, your call-to-action button copy could say "Don't delay, sign up today." Or you could craft a benefit-oriented tagline, such as this well-known insurance company slogan: "Nationwide is on your side."

- Review your marketing communications for ease of reading and clarity. Re-word any jargon and define any acronyms or technical terms that you must include.

- Deliver your message using the most easy-to-understand language you can. Keep your copy simple and accessible. Avoid dense paragraphs and minimize complex sentences.

- If you deliberately want to slow down your reader so they do not miss or forget a point, or to prompt them to make a more considered decision, you can introduce some disfluent copy. However, know that your readers will have to be very motivated to stay engaged and you'll risk losing them.

- Make information on your website and in your other marketing materials easy to find. Use clear category headings, descriptive callouts, informative headlines and subheads, and bulleted or numbered takeaways. Use segues between paragraphs that make your copy flow. And select visuals that support your message. Choose obvious over obfuscate.

- Ensure your copy is customer focused, not company focused. Begin sentences using you rather than making the subject I, we, or our company. For example, instead of saying "We carry a full line of widgets," say "You'll find a full line of widgets here."

- To lower a prospect's initial defenses, start your message by having them imagine owning or using your product or service. This can also trigger the Endowment Effect (see Chapter 2).

- Pop the word free in your offers. In fact, Worldata (2020) research shows using free instead of complimentary in a subject line can double your open rates.

- Look for opportunities where priming with homophones can help you deliver your message. For example, an advertising agency could say, "When the copy needs to be right, hire us to write it."

- Lay out your copy in a way that invites readership. Choose common typefaces. Use italics sparingly. And limit knocked-out type to a few words or a short sentence.

- Favor nouns over verbs when addressing your customers and prospects. For example, refer to them as chocolate eaters rather than people who eat chocolates.

- Be specific. Don't let vague terms creep into your marketing copy. For example, if you refer to your product as a solution, will prospects really understand what you are selling? Is it software? Consulting? Something else?

KEY TAKEAWAYS

1 Your customers will find rhyming phrases more memorable and believable.

2 Rhyming phrases are more cognitively fluent, which means they are easier for the brain to process. Things that are easier for the brain to process feel right, and as a result, people often assume they are.

3 People prefer things that are cognitively fluent, and feel more confident in their ability to make decisions about them.

4   The words you choose and the way you lay them out in your marketing materials both affect cognitive fluency.

5   Choose words that are accessible and easy for your customers and prospects to understand, even if you are writing to an educated or professional audience.

6   Watch out for jargon, acronyms, technical terms, and words that may be confusing or unfamiliar to your target.

7   Literary devices such as alliteration, repetition, metaphor, and simile help make your marketing messages more memorable and understandable.

8   Homophones can prompt people to think of the other word in the pair, and actions associated with it. That's why bye-bye or goodbye can prime someone to buy.

9   Power words that marketers should take advantage of include you, imagine, and free, as well as new and discover.

10 Referring to your customers using a noun can be more effective than telling them what you want them to do using a verb. For example, call them an owner versus a person who owns.

11 The use of nouns and other specific, concrete language has been shown to increase customer satisfaction and sales.

12 Maximize the impact of your marketing copy by making it cognitively fluent, using helpful literary devices, and choosing power words for high-read pieces of real estate.

In conclusion

The words you choose to describe your product, service, offer, or company influence your target's response to it. Using rhyming phrases, alliteration, repetition, similes, metaphors, homophones, concrete language, and power words can all have a significant impact on your marketing messages, and make them more noticeable, credible, or motivating.

Additionally, as you'll see in the next chapter, the way your copy sets the stage for your marketing message is also important. Done properly, it can predispose your target to your message—when their initial instinct may have been to pass.

References

Ariely, D (2010) *Predictably Irrational: The hidden forces that shape our decisions*, Harper Perennial

Binder, M (2021) Apple changes 'subscribe' to 'follow' on Podcasts because people think subscribing means paying, *Mashable*, 9 March, https://mashable.com/article/apple-podcasts-follow-subscribe (archived at https://perma.cc/WKN2-VK83)

Boutin, C (2006) Study: Stock performance tied to ease of pronouncing company's name, Princeton University, 29 May, https://www.princeton.edu/news/2006/05/29/study-stock-performance-tied-ease-pronouncing-companys-name (archived at https://perma.cc/S2ZF-SZNL)

Bryan, C, Walton, G, Rogers, T and Dweck, C (2011) Motivating voter turnout by invoking the self, *Psychological and Cognitive Sciences*, https://www.pnas.org/doi/10.1073/pnas.1103343108 (archived at https://perma.cc/3N37-73BU)

Decision Lab [Blog] Why are we likely to spend more after reading the word "bye"?, https://thedecisionlab.com/biases/bye-now-effect/ (archived at https://perma.cc/W8A4-T8V3)

Dodd, KS (2021). Ex-P&G brand 'doctor' Pete Carter comes clean on advertising FMCGs, *Contagious*, 6 December, https://www.contagious.com/news-and-views/pete-carter-comes-clean-on-brand-building (archived at https://perma.cc/9E9K-77K7)

Handley, A (2014) *Everybody Writes: Your go-to guide to creating ridiculously good content*, Wiley, New Jersey

Haury, C (2017) The Superpower of Alliteration: How alliteration can work in marketing, *Medium*, 17 May, https://medium.com/@writingcorissa/the-superpower-of-alliteration-c6bc6c98c4b9 (archived at https://perma.cc/E3MW-2T67)

Jenkins, E and Buck, J (2020) Staying healthy on the NHS front line, *Ogilvy Consulting, The Annual 2019–2020,* https://www.ogilvy.com/ideas/annual-2020-ogilvys-yearly-behavioral-science-collection (archived at https://perma.cc/8LKU-S9DJ)

Lebowitz, S (2015) Science says using big words to sound sophisticated makes you seem less intelligent, *Business Insider*, 17 September, https://www.businessinsider.in/science/science-says-using-big-words-to-sound-sophisticated-makes-you-seem-less-intelligent/articleshow/49003732.cms (archived at https://perma.cc/V4K8-KH25)

Martinez, A and Mammola, S (2021) Specialized terminology reduces the number of citations of scientific papers, Royal Society Publishing, https://royalsocietypublishing.org/doi/pdf/10.1098/rspb.2020.2581 (archived at https://perma.cc/8ZKV-F7UR)

McGlone, MS and Tofighbakhsh, J (2000) Birds of a feather flock conjointly: Rhyme as reason in aphorisms, *Psychological Science*, https://www.scirp.org/(S(i43dyn45teexjx455qlt3d2q))/reference/ReferencesPapers.aspx?ReferenceID=757144 (archived at https://perma.cc/F2QC-HE6Y)

Novemsky, N, Dhar, R, Schartz, N and Simonson, I (2007) Preference fluency in choice, *Journal of Marketing Research*, https://www.researchgate.net/publication/235357162_Preference_Fluency_in_Choice (archived at https://perma.cc/C7RU-ETPK)

Packard, G and Berger, J (2020) How concrete language shapes customer satisfaction, *Journal of Consumer Research*, https://academic.oup.com/jcr/article/47/5/787/5873524 (archived at https://perma.cc/SN5B-5ATU)

Reber, R and Schwarz, N (1999) Effects of perceptual fluency on judgments of truth, *Consciousness and Cognition*, https://www.sciencedirect.com/science/article/abs/pii/S1053810099903860#! (archived at https://perma.cc/L48V-3XE9)

Roller, C (2011) How cognitive fluency affects decision making, *UX Matters*, https://www.uxmatters.com/mt/archives/2011/07/how-cognitive-fluency-affects-decision-making.php (archived at https://perma.cc/8ZM2-368C)

Shapiro, T (2022) *Rethink Lead Generation*, Stratabeat, Massachusetts

Shulman, H et al (2020) The use of jargon kills people's interest in science, politics: Even when specialized terms are defined, the damage is done, *ScienceDaily*, www.sciencedaily.com/releases/2020/02/200212084357.htm (archived at https://perma.cc/E7CX-H3N6)

Song, H and Schwarz, N (2008) If it's hard to read, it's hard to do: Processing fluency affects effort prediction and motivation, *Psychological Science*, https://dornsife.usc.edu/assets/sites/780/docs/08_ps_song___schwarz_effort.pdf (archived at https://perma.cc/2L2P-DHYP)

Trudeau, C R (2012) The Public Speaks: An empirical study of legal communication, *14 Scribes J. Leg. Writing* **121**, Bowen Law Repository: Scholarship & Archives, https://lawrepository.ualr.edu/cgi/viewcontent.cgi?article=1254&context=faculty_scholarship (archived at https://perma.cc/2B5U-GM6D)

Worldata (2020) Free and Complimentary are NOT the same! Using "Free" will generate a 2X open rate increase vs. "Complimentary" Instagram.com, 26 June, https://www.instagram.com/worldata/channel/?hl=en (archived at https://perma.cc/M47Z-FEWL)

15

Increasing desirability through triggering availability bias

People will judge the likelihood of an event happening based on how easily they can recall a relevant example. When the event in question is their need for the product or service you sell, an effective marketing message will make pertinent examples readily spring to mind, which will help convince prospective customers that they should, indeed, make a purchase.

Quick. Answers these questions: Do more people die every year from shark attacks or flying champagne corks? From being accidentally shot or from sunstroke? From car accidents or from falls?

I opened a marketing webinar in 2021 with the first question, and most people chose shark attacks. There were some who, I suspect, sensed a trick question and voted for the champagne corks. But for many people, the first of each of these deadly pairs would be the typical answer. So, if they were your choices, you are not alone.

Not only do you have plenty of company, you also have science on your side. Because there is a very good reason why more people would choose sharks, gunshots, and auto accidents as their respective answers. It has to do with how often someone has heard of something. For example, I live in Massachusetts. Every time I head to the beach on Cape Cod, I'm greeted by a graphic sign showing a large, open-mouthed shark with pointy teeth. The sign has an arresting red and white warning headline, and copy that cautions me that great white sharks hunt in the shallow waters along the coastline. The sign even invites me to download the Sharktivity app, so I can get alerts when sharks are spotted nearby.

That sign, of course, makes me think of my friend Kenneth "Shark" Kinney—marketer, podcast host, and avid diver—who once advised me to always remember you're in the shark's territory when you're diving. This in turn brings to mind the news reports I've heard about shark attacks not only in Massachusetts, but also off the coast of Florida, and even as far away as the waters of Australia. When Australia springs to mind, so does Danika, the conference organizer who flew me to Sydney to deliver a marketing keynote. Over lunch, she told me she is also an adventure travel writer, and has written about her experience being submerged in the frigid waters of southern Australia in a shark cage, with only a mesh barrier between her and nature's "killing machine."

Not far behind those thoughts are my recollections of reading Peter Benchley's classic *Jaws*, watching the numerous shark movies that followed it, and of course the Discovery Channel's annual shark week. To put it simply, I have plenty of shark references to influence me. And that is exactly what happened when I was first asked the shark or flying champagne cork question. I was influenced. A quick check-in with my memory bank gave me lots of material about shark attacks.

But when I plugged in death by flying champagne cork, I came up empty. No news reports, no paperback plots, not even a single cinematic scene. Just some effervescent instances of wedding toasts and new year's celebrations, all safe and homicide-free. Therefore, I was quite sure I knew the correct answer. Although as you have probably guessed by now, I was wrong.

Surprisingly, about 24 people die from flying champagne corks each year, while only 10 succumb to shark fatalities (McCall, 2021). And based on the research of the National Safety Council (NSC, 2019), in the United States, falls edge out motor vehicle crashes in the lifetime odds of death. The Council also reports that sunstroke does indeed top accidental gun discharges, proving again that what people think they know isn't necessarily so. But that does not stop people from assuming they do know. Science has shown that when a person can call something to mind easily, they think there's a greater chance of it happening. As a result, they make decisions accordingly.

This decision-making shortcut presents marketers with an advantageous opportunity. Before asking for the sale, you can lay the groundwork by prompting your prospects to think of instances in their lives where your product or service would have fit in nicely. The quicker they think of them, the more likely they are to also think they'll need what you sell.

This handy tactic also provides great ammunition against the holdouts in your target. When a prospect does not think they are interested in what you offer, they can shut right down and dismiss your entire marketing message. They often deliver the line every marketer hates to hear: "I am all set; I'm not in the market at this time." However, now you have an effective way to ward that off. When you can get your customers and prospects to come to the conclusion on their own that what you are selling is something they should look into, that puts you in a much more powerful position.

> If a person can readily call to mind an event, that makes the event seem as if it happens more often.

Triggering availability bias can pave the path for easier sales

People will use the ease of retrieving an example as a sign of the frequency or probability with which that thing occurs. If it is difficult to think of an occurrence, people will assume the event does not happen a lot, and as a result, will probably not happen to them (therefore they won't need what you're selling).

However, when they can easily think of an instance, when it's readily available in their memory bank, they'll feel this means it's more common-place and has a greater likelihood of occurring to them (cue the cash registers). When behavioral scientists refer to this decision-making shortcut that people so often default to, they talk about availability bias or the avail-ability heuristic.

A good deal of research shows just how common relying on it can be. For example, in one study, people were asked if there were more seven-letter words in the English language that ended with "ing," or if there were more seven-letter words that had "n" appearing as the sixth letter of the word when it was spelled (Farnam Street, nd). Because it is harder for people to think of seven-letter words that have an "n" in the sixth position, a greater number of people assumed there were more words that ended in "ing." However, every seven-letter word that ends in "ing" also has "n" in the sixth position, as do words ranging from abalone to unbound.

FIGURE 15.1 The ease of availability bias

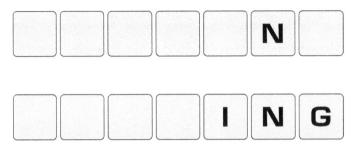

Because it's easier to call to mind seven-letter words that end in "ing," people will assume there are more of them than seven-letter words that have "n" as the sixth letter.

What someone's asked to think about doesn't even have to be as difficult as the occurrence of the sixth letter in seven-letter words to trigger availability bias. It can actually be something that they have firsthand knowledge of. Daniel Kahneman, in his *New York Times* bestselling book *Thinking, Fast and Slow*, describes a study involving spouses and their roles in housekeeping. Each spouse was asked to estimate the percentage of their contribution to keeping their home tidy.

Researchers found the combined total for the couples added up to more than 100 percent, which mathematically cannot be true. But because each spouse found it more difficult to recall instances of their spouse's contributions as compared to their own, they misjudged their percentages. Their own contributions to the chores seemed more vivid. Even though they lived in the house and experienced the results of their spouse's efforts, those efforts were harder to recollect.

On the other hand, when something is easier to think of, that can also skew a person's perceptions. In another experiment, research participants were read a list of 39 names (Bar-Hillel, 2001). The list would either contain the names of 19 women who were more famous than the 20 men on it, or the names of 19 men who were more famous than the 20 women on it. After hearing the list, the research subject was asked to estimate whether there had been more women's names or more men's names read.

Researchers found that when the women's names were more famous, people said there were more female names on the list. But when the men's names were more famous, people said there had been more men's names on the list. Because the famous persons' names sounded more familiar—and as a result those names were more available in the research participant's memory—the gender of the famous names was the one given as having more names on the list.

Frequency, recency, and quantity contribute to availability bias

When people hear about something often, that can factor into their decision-making shortcut. Researchers described two scenarios and asked people to say which was the more likely (Bar-Hillel, 2001). The first was a large flood somewhere in the United States that killed 1,000 people. The second was an earthquake in California that caused floods that killed 1,000 people. Because people associate earthquakes with California, it was easier to imagine the second scenario with its cause and effect as being true. However, logically, a flood killing 1,000 people that could happen anywhere in the country, without having to be caused by a California earthquake, would be the more likely of the two scenarios to happen.

As research has demonstrated, repeated exposure to information, even about an occurrence that does not directly affect a person, can influence that person's perceptions of the information and its likely frequency. For example, people who hear a lot of prescription drug ads come to think that the condition the drug treats is more common than it really is (An, 2008). Similarly, and also drug-related, a 1993 study by Russell Eisenman found that people estimated that drug use in America was going up, even though the National Household Survey on Drug Abuse showed that it was not (Eisenman, 2013). Researchers believed it was the media's ubiquitous reports about drug use that impacted people's evaluations. It was easy for people to recall hearing news stories about drug abuse, and as a result, they surmised drug use must be on the rise.

While frequency clearly contributes to availability bias, so too does recency. Recent memories can be easier to retrieve and because of this, people may overweight them. For example, after a 2019 Southwest Airlines accident that killed one passenger, people were afraid to fly. The airline is reported to have lost between $50 and $100 million in sales, due in part to this fear (Boyce, 2022). While the likelihood of a similar accident was quite small, the possibility loomed much larger in the minds of potential passengers.

Finally, researchers observed an interesting effect of the availability heuristic. They found that the ease of retrieving information was more impactful than the amount of information retrieved (Schwarz, et al., 1991). In a study, people were asked to either list six or twelve instances when they had been assertive. Then they were asked to rate how assertive they thought they were. Almost counterintuitively, the people who listed 12 instances rated themselves as less assertive. The researchers believe this is because, while it might be easy enough to come up with six examples, identifying twice as many is much harder. As a result, when a person has a hard time listing 12 examples of being assertive, they decide that they must not be all that assertive after all.

However, when researchers provided their subjects with an explanation as to why they might have trouble recalling the number of instances, for example that music playing in the background could slow down their ability to think, they no longer came to the conclusion that because it was harder to recount 12 instances, they must not be assertive.

Marketers have a number of ways to trigger availability bias

Marketers can use availability bias to their advantage. You can prompt a customer or prospect to think of a time when having had your product or service would have been really beneficial. For example, if you sell a product that removes difficult stains, get people to think of a time they spilled red wine on a white shirt or tablecloth. Or you can encourage them to recall someone they know that experienced the bad outcome that your product can prevent. For example, if you sell presentation training, ask them if they have a friend or colleague who is terrified of public speaking and worries they'll freeze when they step up to the podium.

You can also get prospective customers to recall a story they recently heard on the news or read on social media that is related to your product or service. For example, if you sell retirement services, reference the latest story of a famous celebrity or athlete that died penniless, even though they had earned a big salary in their prime. Finally, you can ask your target to list the top three ways your product or service could be useful to them. Those three should come easily. Alternatively, ask them to list the 10 reasons they don't need it right now. They should have a difficult time coming up with 10. Either approach could lead people to the conclusion that they do need what you offer.

The key is to trigger availability bias by causing people to estimate the likelihood something will happen that would make your product a smart purchase. As Daniel Kahneman notes, "A good way to increase people's fear of a bad outcome is to remind them of a related incident in which things went wrong; a good way to increase people's confidence is to remind them of a similar situation in which everything worked out for the best."

HOW AN AMERICAN IN HONG KONG RELIED ON AVAILABILITY BIAS
TO NEGOTIATE A BUSINESS DINNER DILEMMA

When I was a young copywriter in Boston, something amazing happened to me. I was working for an agency that landed the Olympic coin collectibles account. That in itself was pretty cool. We were creating direct response print ads that encouraged people to purchase the coins. The ads featured beautiful pictures of the coins along with the back story about them, detailing why they were collectibles, the care and precision that had gone into crafting them, the cultural and sports scenes they depicted, and the exclusive opportunity to own some before the finite supplies sold out.

One morning I walked into the agency and saw my creative director on the phone, looking uncharacteristically agitated. When he finally popped out of his office, he asked if I could recommend any freelance writers. "Sure," I replied, "Why?", thinking perhaps we had gotten a rush assignment, or had been invited to a big pitch. He explained that he'd just heard our Olympic coin client needed us to send a writer to a meeting. The meeting was going to be held in Hong Kong in a few days. And none of the freelancers he had reached out to that morning wanted the job.

"Wait," I said incredulously. "You're sending a freelancer?" I couldn't believe this plum assignment was going to be sent out of house. Now it was his turn to be incredulous. "Why?" he said, looking at me like I'd suddenly grown a second head before his eyes. "Do you want to go?"

I absolutely did. I knew nothing about Hong Kong. I'd never traveled to that part of the world. In fact, I didn't even own a passport. But the idea of jumping on a plane in a few days and winging off to a business meeting in Asia was intoxicating. Wasn't this what working in marketing was supposed to be like? Still not quite believing it, my creative director said the job was mine. Soon after, he handed me a plane ticket. Now I only had to get a passport and pack my bags. Fortunately, this was during a time when emergency passports could be obtained in a day at the Boston passport office.

After a 20-hour flight and a slight taxi snafu, I arrived at the hotel, slept a bit, and found my way to the client's office the next day. Following a day of meetings, the client took his entire team, including the various agency representatives, out to dinner. At the end of the long table, I spied another American, who introduced herself to everyone as Elaine, based in Hong Kong, from the account's New York public relations agency.

After another full day of work, the plan was to fly home the following day. However, the client asked if I'd be willing to stay the weekend and come into the office for a few days the following week. I most certainly was. As 5 pm approached that Friday, and with the realization that I suddenly had an entire weekend to explore, I asked the office secretary to please phone Elaine, hoping she might be up for some sightseeing. This led to a weekend of racing around the island, visiting a variety of ancient temples, scenic vistas, local restaurants, and ex-pat bars. I had an amazing time. Elaine was wonderful company, knew how to get around the city, and made sure I saw the best it had to offer.

As my final night approached, I wanted to repay her kindness. The hotel where I was staying had a very high-end restaurant, so I thought dinner there would be appropriate. It was when the server brought over the wine list that I realized how far in over my head I was. None of the wines were familiar to me. I was a young copywriter from Boston, and I knew you were supposed to order a bottle of wine at a business dinner. But a more experienced colleague had always been the one to review the wine list and make the selection. I didn't even know what I was looking for. To make matters only slightly worse, the prices were, of course, not listed in US dollars.

I stared blankly at the list, not wanting to admit my ignorance. Then suddenly I saw it. As if by divine intervention, my eyes found the Châteauneuf-du-Pape. I sounded it out in my head and realized I had heard of this wine before. Not only had I heard of it, I had heard it referenced in reverential tones. Now I felt confident I could order a good wine (even if I wasn't completely confident I could expense it).

While I didn't realize it at the time, it was availability bias that had come to my rescue. Because Châteauneuf-du-Pape sounded familiar, because I'd heard it mentioned in stories and in various media, I believed it would be a good choice. In fact, if someone had asked me to name a good wine at that point in my career, this was the wine that would've easily come to mind. And Elaine and I had no complaints. Sitting high in the sky in Hong Kong, dining at a fine restaurant, our evolving palates enjoyed every last drop of that bottle.

CASE STUDY

Bar code readers, availability bias, and benchmarks beaten

How do you convince your business target to consider replacing their existing equipment with your new option? More specifically, how do you overcome their "if it's not broken, don't fix it" attitude? This was the challenge a new client presented to the team at the agency where I was working.

Our new client manufactured bar code reader equipment, which is a machine vision product typically bought by logistics people who work at the distribution and fulfillment centers of large retailers. These are companies that pick, pack, and fulfill thousands of orders a day. The equipment helps to inspect or identify packages as they move down the fulfillment line. This particular bar code reader equipment had a lot going for it. It could process images faster than competitive products, it could read labels at difficult angles or labels that had certain rips or tears, and it had less hardware and fewer moving parts.

However, there were two reasons why the sell was far from a slam dunk. The first was that the company was not yet well-known by the target market. Their prospects wouldn't necessarily recognize the brand. While this is something that could be overcome, it certainly would make getting a response more difficult. The second reason was even worse. The target market was very busy and very resistant to change. These people had been running the fulfillment line the same way for years. They had no incentive to change things. Even if it wasn't perfect, it worked. And their jobs were all about keeping things moving.

FINDING THE RIGHT APPROACH

Noting both the product benefits and the target market challenges, the team began to work up some potential angles for our new client's marketing message. One direction we considered pursuing was the novelty one. People are generally attracted to what's new and novel (see Chapter 9). Since the company and its product would likely be new to the target, we thought we might make that work. But then we learned that the target felt this type of equipment is fairly similar from vendor to vendor, and offered only incremental differences. Announcing the product as new ran the risk of getting it written off as a slightly different version of the same old thing.

Next, we considered focusing on increased savings. Because our client's equipment had less hardware and fewer moving parts, companies wouldn't have to spend as much on maintenance and repairs. The issue with that direction, however, was that our target wasn't focused on those metrics. They were primarily responsible for ensuring a smooth operation. Decreasing costs would be great—if the equipment worked as promised. But this was a new product, and inserting anything unproven into the current process would be risky. If it failed, the target would fail in a very public way. In a case like this, a reliable good enough was preferable to a potential better.

Finally, we landed on the messaging we believed was right. We knew we needed to shake the target out of their complacency. And we had to demonstrate from the start that we understood them and their jobs. So, we sent them a box that looked like it had a damaged bar code on its label. We knew that would produce an immediate visceral reaction in them. Damaged and compromised labels were an issue in their line of work. When a package with a ripped or torn label came down the line, it would need to get kicked out and reworked. The target even had a name for this pile of rejects. With grim humor, they called it the jackpot lane.

One look at that label would trigger availability bias. The target would automatically call to mind all the items that hit their jackpot lane recently, and what a giant pain dealing with them was. It would remind them that, while functioning, their current equipment was far from perfect. This would be an ideal mind frame to have them in as they were about to read our message. Beneath the distressed label, we ran a line of copy acknowledging that typically a label like this was bad news, however now there was a fix that was anything but typical. The message was crafted to get their attention in an empathetic way. Once it did that, we were able to make the case that this new bar code reading equipment really was worth a look. And then we incentivized them to respond by offering them a gift.

Was it enough to influence their behavior? To overcome the perception that all these products were similar, and therefore it would be risky to even consider introducing something new to the line? Apparently so. Our client happily reported they beat their benchmark, achieving 266 percent of their goal.

> MISTAKE
>
> Launching into features and benefits without first setting the stage. By starting your message with an availability bias trigger, you can immediately make your target more receptive to it.

Six more examples of availability bias in marketing communications

When your customers or prospects have an easy time thinking of a relevant instance or example, they will feel that what you're describing is more likely to happen. If you describe something they want to avoid, availability bias can work nicely with loss aversion (see Chapter 2). If you describe instances of events that worked out well, availability bias can be coupled with optimism bias, the belief that bad things more often happen to other people.

There are certain conditions under which relevant events and examples will be more apt to be recalled by your customers and prospects. If the event or example was especially noticeable, vivid, or emotional, it will have a better chance of coming readily to mind. Additionally, if it is something that happened recently, or something that the person recently heard about, it will also be more likely to be recalled. Similarly, if the situation is something that your customer or prospect is very familiar with, either through personal experience or repeated exposure, it will also have a greater likelihood of springing to mind easily.

A CONSTRUCTION EQUIPMENT COMPANY

A construction equipment rental company ran digital ads that did a good job of using availability bias in an emotional way. They very succinctly described a construction horror story, during which a critical piece of equipment such as an excavator or scissor lift broke down when a key deadline was looming. The target market could easily identify with the scenario, and feel the dread and stress it would produce. They had likely experienced a similar situation, or heard of a coworker who had, and knew how it could throw the entire job off schedule. Then the equipment company showed that they were the answer, because they had the needed replacement readily available to rent. The ad got prospective customers to call to mind a time when they wished they had used the company, or to imagine using this company should a future equipment issue arise. Then it asked them for their business.

A POLITICAL FUNDRAISER

A political fundraising email I once received used a simple graphic technique to trigger availability bias. The goal of the email was to raise contributions to an election fund before a specific deadline. Anyone who donated in time would be entered to win dinner with the candidate at an upcoming event. However, people receiving the email may have thought their chances of actually winning would be quite small, given all the people who must have been on the email list. To counter this, the email included a picture of a round table with eight chairs around it. At the head of the table was a chair with the candidate's name above it. An arrow pointed to the chair to the candidate's right and was labeled with the prospective donor's first name. Another arrow pointed to the chair to the candidate's left and indicated it was reserved for the donor's guest. This made the possibility of dining with the candidate very vivid. It helped the email recipient envision it. And once they were able to imagine it so clearly, it seemed more probable that it could happen. As a result, they would be more likely to donate.

AN INSURANCE COMPANY

An insurance company that sold hospital indemnity plans was faced with a challenge. If customers had been lucky enough not to have been hospitalized over the year, and as a result, not to have used the insurance, those customers would be more likely to cancel their coverage the following year. Naturally, the insurance company did not want to lose their business. To help increase the chances they'd retain it, they inserted an availability bias trigger into their marketing copy. The insurer told customers they had been smart to obtain the insurance, especially when they thought of all the people they knew who had been hospitalized over the past year. This got the customer to feel that even though they had not needed the coverage, they very well might have—and might still.

A CYBERSECURITY COMPANY

A colleague of mine, a very talented writer named Amy Hunt, used events in the weekly news to trigger availability bias. She was creating banner ads to generate leads for her cybersecurity client. There are, of course, a number of approaches a writer can take to convince a company they need to protect themselves from cyberattacks. She could talk about the growing sophistication of criminals, or the fact that even the best-designed systems have vulnerabilities. Another angle could be the expense and lost productivity if the company were to become a victim. But Amy knew that she needed to find the argument that would motivate her technology and information systems prospects to respond quickly. So, she turned to current events.

The evening news had increasingly been showing stories of large companies that had experienced data breaches, sometimes accompanied by customer and shareholder backlash. Amy positioned the cybersecurity product as the way to keep the target's CEO off the nightly news. The reference would prompt the target to recall the most recent company to suffer that fate. Not only would it trigger availability bias, it would also add urgency to the call to action.

A SOFTWARE CORPORATION

When your target frequently experiences a problem, or knows someone who does, tapping into availability bias is a smart way to set up your sales pitch. A software company that marketed a PDF product did just that. They knew they were challenging the market leader, but for the right audience segment, their product would be a better fit. Their email didn't start by introducing their product, though. Instead, they reminded the reader that they were currently compromising when it came to their PDFs. They pointed out that they were probably paying for functionality they didn't need, or they had been forced to trade down to less power. This made the target think of all the times they'd complained about that very fact, or that they had heard their staff do so. Only after laying this groundwork did the company then talk about the benefits of their new product.

A DAILY NEWSPAPER

Finally, a major metropolitan newspaper wanted to increase subscribers to their daily e-newsletter. They decided a good way to do that would be to encourage their existing subscribers, who presumably liked the product, to purchase gift subscriptions for people they knew. But they didn't just tell them that the subscriptions would make good gifts. Nor did they ask them if they knew someone who might enjoy one.

Instead, they listed 10 different descriptors that would characterize someone who would appreciate the product because of its editorial coverage. They used phrases such as political junkie, travel buff, and sports fan. This use of availability bias prompted the existing customer to think of the people they knew who matched these descriptions. Once they did, it would be easy to come to the conclusion that they knew up to 10 people who might enjoy a gift subscription.

How you can use availability bias to increase the desirability of what you sell

- Prompt people to recall a time when, if they'd already owned your product or service, it would have been advantageous.

- Get them to imagine a time in the future when your product would fit nicely into their work or personal lives.

- Focus your marketing so that you are well-known for one thing. That way, your company will come to mind when people think of that particular attribute.

- Make your messaging consistent. And persistent. You want your product or service to feel familiar to your target.

- Include instances, examples, and stories in your marketing that point to your product as the obvious answer. For example, if you sell trip insurance, remind people of how disrupting—and expensive—it can be when a flight gets delayed or when luggage gets lost.

- Link a common saying to your marketing messaging. For instance, imagine you sell backup parts for a particular product, and you want people to buy them now so they're not caught unprepared later. You could ask them if they've ever noticed that it only seems to rain when they forget to carry an umbrella.

- Take advantage of a current event that connects to the product or service you sell.

- Make sure your marketing paints a vivid, emotional picture of what owning your product would be like. That will make it more easily recalled by your prospects.

- Get people talking about your brand. The more often people hear or see it mentioned, the more familiar it will feel.

- Repurpose your content (example: pull tweets from your blog post, resend emails with a new subject line) to extend your market presence.

- Be where your customers and prospects are. Make sure they encounter your marketing message as they go about their day. Show up in the various places they'll be. And use retargeting to stay top of mind with them.

KEY TAKEAWAYS

1 When your customers and prospects have an easier time calling to mind an event, they believe it's more apt to happen.

2 The harder it is to think of a relevant example, the less likely they are to think it will happen.

3 Hearing about something frequently, or recently, can trigger availability bias. So, too, can having a personal experience with it, or knowing someone who has.

4 Being able to easily recall information is more important than how much information someone can recall when it comes to influencing them. For instance, asking someone to list three ways they might benefit from your product can be more persuasive than asking them to list 10 ways.

5 Before asking someone to buy, first get them to think of a time in the past when your product or service would have really come in handy, or get them to imagine a time in the future when they can see themselves benefiting from it.

6 Marketers can link news stories, current events, and common sayings to their products to make them more readily recalled.

> **7** You can use imagery to quickly and effectively prompt availability bias.
>
> **8** Events or examples that are especially noticeable, vivid, or emotional will have a better chance of readily coming to your target's mind.
>
> **9** The more familiar your brand is to your prospect, the more likely they are to think of you.
>
> **10** Have a consistent marketing message and appear frequently where your target is. This will make you familiar to them and more easily recalled.

In conclusion

Your prospective customers will be more open to your marketing message if it triggers availability bias. Before asking for the sale, first get them to think of a time in the past when having your product or service would have come in handy, or get them to imagine a time in the future when they could see themselves using it. Marketers can trigger availability bias by tapping into events that stand out in their target's mind, including stories they've heard or experiences they've had.

When something stands out, it makes a bigger impression. As you'll see in the next chapter, there are tactics you can use to ensure your marketing messages stand out, and as a result, get noticed and remembered.

References

An, S (2008) Antidepressant direct-to-consumer advertising and social perception of the prevalence of depression: Application of the availability heuristic, *Health Communication*, https://pubmed.ncbi.nlm.nih.gov/19089697/ (archived at https://perma.cc/2DEX-2JYK)

Bar-Hillel, M (2001) Availability Heuristic, *Science Direct*, https://www.sciencedirect.com/topics/computer-science/availability-heuristic (archived at https://perma.cc/ENK7-2QN7)

Boyce, P (2022) What is Availability Heuristic, *BoyceWire*, 18 March, https://boycewire.com/availability-heuristic-definition-and-examples/ (archived at https://perma.cc/W4GP-9SFG)

Eisenman, R (2013) Belief that drug usage in the United States is increasing when it is really decreasing: An example of the availability heuristic, *Bulletin of the Psychonomic Society*, https://link.springer.com/article/10.3758/BF03334920#citeas (archived at https://perma.cc/MW8Y-PNAB)

Farnam Street Mental Modes (nd) 3 things everyone should know about the
    availability heuristic [Blog] fs https://fs.blog/mental-model-availability-bias/
    (archived at https://perma.cc/5TYE-YUER)
Kahneman, D (2011) *Thinking, Fast and Slow*, Farrar, Straus and Giroux,
    New York
McCall, C (2021) Sharks: 18 everyday things that are more dangerous [Blog]
    padi.com, 5 June, https://blog.padi.com/18-things-dangerous-sharks/ (archived
    at https://perma.cc/J66D-8G82)
NSC Injury Facts (2019) Lifetime odds of death for selected causes, United States,
    2019, https://injuryfacts.nsc.org/all-injuries/preventable-death-overview/
    odds-of-dying/ (archived at https://perma.cc/2LNQ-5JP6)
Schwarz, N, et al. (1991) Ease of retrieval as information: Another look at the
    availability heuristic, *Journal of Personality and Social Psychology*, https://
    psycnet.apa.org/record/1991-33131-001 (archived at https://perma.cc/2YU2-
    XRZ8)

16

Creating stand-out marketing communications through context, rewards and unpredictability

Good marketing executions break through the clutter. In doing so, they trigger the Von Restorff Effect—the human tendency to notice and recall things that stand out. Context, surprise, and the pursuit of a reward can each make a message stand out. However, standing out won't always equal success. Marketers must employ the Von Restorff Effect strategically.

As I write this, it's been exactly a week since I broke my right ankle. Fortunately, the doctors say it's a clean break, so that increases my chance of returning to normal mobility once it heals. But for now, I'm either hobbling around on crutches or a knee scooter, with my right foot encased in a large, grey walking boot—which is an obvious misnomer for me, because at this point, I am not allowed to place any weight at all on my right foot, let alone attempt ambulation.

I tell you this because it occurred to me that I am now a living, breathing (I will stop short of saying walking) embodiment of the Von Restorff Effect. Named for German psychiatrist Hedwig Von Restorff, the Von Restorff Effect refers to the human tendency to notice things that are different or that stand out from their surroundings.

For example, last night my friend Beth invited a group of us over for a steak dinner to celebrate our friend Sue's birthday. Naturally, it was a picture-taking occasion. But when people look at Sue's celebration pictures, it will be me in my boot that stands out. At a glance, the boot will make me different from the nine other people in the photo. If a stranger were to look at the picture, not knowing any of the individuals in it, the thing that would immediately attract their attention would be the orthopedic air cast strapped to the limb of one of the people pictured.

The Von Restorff Effect was probably very helpful for our early ancestors. If they woke up in the morning, stuck their heads out of their cave to scan the horizon, and saw everything looked the same as it did the day before, that was good information. It would have suggested that things were probably safe and stable, at least as safe and stable as the previous day.

But if, in scanning the horizon, things looked different—if something were missing that had previously been there, or if something new had entered the environment—that could be cause for concern. And in those days, that concern could literally be of the life-or-death variety. Being able to quickly notice something new or different is what ended up keeping some of our ancient ancestors alive.

Now, many thousands of years later, humans are still hardwired to notice things that are different. As a marketer, you can use that to your advantage. If you have a lot of competition, you can employ the Von Restorff Effect to make sure your marketing messages stand out among the onslaught of your competitors'. You can use it to nudge customers to choose one of your products or service levels over another. You can even tap the Von Restorff Effect to make sure people don't miss your all-important call to action.

But as you will see, properly leveraging the Von Restorff Effect requires more than simply making your message stand out. Being different won't always lead to sales. For that matter, smart marketers know there are times when it actually makes sense to indicate some similarity to your competition. As an example, if you fail to mention a benefit that all your competitors offer, prospects may assume they cannot get it from you. Or, if you're brand new in the field, showcasing some similarity to the leading players can signal that you are a legitimate entry in the category. However, too much similarity in marketing messages will render them ineffective.

So, let's take a look at how the Von Restorff Effect works, and how you can make it work well in your marketing campaigns. There are right ways and wrong ways to make a message stand out. You want to be sure yours get noticed for the right reasons. And that means appreciating the power, and the perils, of the Von Restorff Effect.

People will pay attention to and remember the item that is different from the others around it. As a marketer, you want that item to be your ad, email, direct mail piece, or other marketing communication. That's your first step toward success.

Marketing that stands out from what's around it will get noticed and remembered

When I speak about the Von Restorff Effect at marketing conferences, I sometimes show a row of black wingtip shoes neatly lined up, with a pair of purple high-top sneakers dropped in the middle. Other times I'll show something simple and geometric, such as three yellow circles and one blue square.

The effect is almost always the same. People focus on the purple sneakers or the blue square. It's all about context. The purple high-top sneakers appearing in a row of other brightly colored versions of the identical shoe wouldn't have the same power. Similarly, if the blue square were surrounded by a blue triangle, a blue circle, and a blue rectangle, it would lose its ability to attract attention.

Behavioral scientists refer to this as the isolation effect, or the Von Restorff Effect. The early work that Hedwig Von Restorff did on memorability is what led to the name. In her study, she gave research participants a list of random three-letter nonsense words. Inserted into the list was a single string of three random numbers. So, for example, a list might have looked like the one in Figure 16.1.

A little while after looking at the list, the research subjects were asked to recall what they could remember from it. The string of numbers was what was most recalled.

While this research took place in the early 1930s, other, more current experiments have underscored the efficacy of the Von Restorff Effect. For example, in 2018, Richard Shotton's excellent book *The Choice Factory: 25 behavioural biases that influence what we buy*, was published. In that book, Shotton recounts that he and his colleague Laura Weston ran an experiment in which they showed research participants a list of numbers. Fifteen of the numbers

FIGURE 16.1 The Von Restorff Effect in action

btx

mur

630

ghv

trl

hca

jsd

People will naturally notice things that are different from what's around them. What jumps out at you?

were written in black. One was written in blue. Shortly after seeing the list, participants were asked which number they recalled seeing. Shotton reports that "respondents were 30 times more likely to recall the distinctive number."

Subsequently, Shotton and Weston repeated the experiment, but this time they used brand logos, something closer to a marketer's heart. They showed research participants a list of 11 car brand logos and one fast-food brand logo. The researchers report that "consumers were four times more likely to mention the fast-food brand than the average car brand."

Finally, in a 2019 article entitled "How the isolation effect can boost your conversions," Robin Nichols of the customer experience optimization company AB Tasty writes about an in-market demonstration of the effect. She reports that the Conversio agency used it for one of their ecommerce clients. Because they called more attention to one of the client's products when it was displayed on the website than to the others around it, they drove a 3.4 percent increase in conversions for that item.

The context your message appears in, or what is surrounding it, influences how noticeable and memorable it is. If it looks very much like everything around it, your marketing message can blend right in. However, if there is something different about it, something that makes it stand out from its background or apart from the items it is grouped with, it will have a far greater chance of being paid attention to and, as a result, lodging in your prospect's memory.

People cruise through much of their days on autopilot. Even when they are actively seeking your product or service, they may still be paying only partial attention. Anything you can do to attract their interest or to make your product the default choice will help your business. Your use of size, color, and visual cues will all impact how different or distinct your message is. The goal is to stand out in your immediate environment, where there may be many unrelated messages vying for your prospect's attention, and also to stand out within your product or service category, where appearing too similar to your competitors can sink your sales.

How the Von Restorff Effect could have cost me my job

Early in my career, I had the opportunity to be the creative director on my very first credit card solicitation package. Credit card companies rely on direct mail a fair amount to acquire new customers, and that reliance was even heavier at the time I was working on this assignment, when email and social media were not yet big players.

The card was relaunching itself into the market. Because of that, our client was even more focused on attracting new card holders. Between that fact and the fact that the account was new to the agency, the work we presented would be under stronger than normal pressure to perform. That was not a problem. We welcomed the challenge, and were delighted to be part of the client's direct marketing team.

One of the first things we did was to begin collecting samples of competitive credit card mailings that were out in the marketplace. We knew that the audience our client would target would very likely fall into the target market of some other credit card companies. After all, there are only so many people within a particular FICO score range, which is the indicator credit card companies use to assess credit-worthiness. If someone were receiving our client's direct mail solicitation, there was a good chance they would also be receiving several others. We wanted to experience what those people would experience—to see the marketing messages they'd be sent, as well as the envelopes that those solicitations would arrive in.

We took all the packages we had collected and put them on the wall in one of the agency's war rooms, where the entire team could review them. One of the first things to strike us was the sameness of all the solicitations. There seemed to be very little to differentiate one direct mail package from another. Of course, there were different logos and brand colors, but other than that, the packages could be described as almost interchangeable. Most flaunted a similar list of features. None seemed to stand out at all.

AN OPPORTUNITY TO APPLY THE VON RESTORFF EFFECT

Based on this, we decided that what was needed was an approach that tapped into the Von Restorff Effect. In order to get people interested in a new credit card, we would first have to create a package that stood out in that day's mail and got noticed. Not only that, it would have to be different enough from typical credit card acquisition packages that it didn't immediately get appraised as "same old, same old." If people thought they knew what was inside, we surmised, they would be less inclined to open it.

The teams went to work. Each strove to create an outer envelope that couldn't be missed. When the concepting phase was over, the piece that stood out was a glossy, bright yellow 6x9 envelope. On it was a distinctively distorted picture of a person shot through a fisheye lens, which put extra focus on the face, making it appear to look up at the reader. We were quite sure that no other piece of mail arriving in the target's mailbox would look anything like it.

Feeling certain we'd masterfully applied the Von Restorff Effect on behalf of our credit card client, we were eager to present the concept and hear their reaction. This, however, is where the story took an unanticipated turn. While the client conceded that their target audience had probably never seen an envelope like this one, the agreement between the client and the agency ended there. The client pointed out that the outer envelope contained none of the information credit card seekers look for when considering a new card. There was no display of the introductory or go-to APRs. No mention of the waived annual fee. No mention, in fact, of a credit card at all. In our effort to make the piece appear different, we had gone too far. And I feared the next place I'd go would be out the agency door, never to return again.

THE RIGHT WAY TO HARNESS THIS PRINCIPLE

Fortunately, the clients were forgiving, and graciously gave us their feedback and sent us off to re-concept. Armed with these new mandatories, we focused on delivering the necessary information in a way that would still set the direct mail piece apart from the clutter. We returned with a #10-sized envelope that stood out because it was part navy blue and part white. It sported an over-sized zero to promote the introductory APR. And it included teaser copy that encouraged people to discover what was different about this new card.

The clients approved it. And more important, the target audience responded to it. New cardholders steadily poured in. Over the course of the multi-year relationship, we established seven separate control mailings for the credit card, providing the client with a suite of well-performing packages to rotate through. While all of them could be identified as credit card solici-tations, each was just different enough to stand out from the competition.

The lesson? Appreciate the power, and the perils, of the Von Restorff Effect. For some products, a curiosity-based approach that provides no hint of what's inside is a smart play. But for others, straying too far from the category can be dangerous. It's important to note that this also applies to media other than direct mail.

BEWARE OF VAMPIRE VIDEO

For example, in my early days of doing direct response television, I was warned to beware of vampire video. The term refers to a television spot that has such a powerful storyline, character, or visual that it pulls the attention away from the main product message. Viewers will remember the commer-cial, and possibly the category, but not the brand being advertised.

Because I'm in the marketing business, my friends will often tell me about a television commercial they recently saw and enjoyed. I'll listen to them describe it, and what they liked about it. Then I'll ask them to tell me who it was for. Most of the time, they can't. Standing out is helpful if you want to get noticed. But marketers must make sure their messages stand out strategically. Your best approach is to create something attention-getting that is naturally linked to the product you sell, so that as a result, it underscores your particular marketing message.

MISTAKE

Making your ad so captivating that people pay attention to it and remember it, but not the marketing message associated with it. Instead, stand out in a way that is linked to the message you want people to retain.

CASE STUDY
Separating fact from fiction in a memorable way

How do you convince media planners to run television commercials on programming they don't think people watch? That was the challenge that my team and I were handed at one agency where I was working. The programming centered around science, and included everything from original science fiction series to deep dives into scientific exploration and discoveries.

The media planners who represented potential advertisers, however, assumed the programming consisted of re-runs of old *Lost in Space* episodes that had first aired in the 1960s, dusted-off B movies that had only managed to create cult followings, and dry, deadly documentaries about niche topics that most people had never heard of.

Persuading someone that what they think is incorrect is not an easy task. But that wasn't our only job. We not only had to persuade these potential advertisers they had the wrong impression about our client's programming, we also had to make them open to the possibility of actually running their commercials on it.

When faced with an ask like this, it can be tempting to start with the facts. One approach could have been to list the actual programming and include detailed descriptions that proved the media planners' assumptions wrong. However, in order to do that, we would first have to convince our target audience to engage with our message. Because that audience already had a preconceived idea about our programming, we felt it was unlikely they would take the time to engage, and more likely they would just ignore our attempts.

Another approach could have been to come down hard on the information that media planners use to make decisions. We could have focused on audience size and demographics, as well as the interests and activities that this audience over-indexed on. We could have highlighted the number of hours each week that people typically watched the programming. We could have even included some testimonials from viewers indicating how loyal they were, and how much they liked the shows. However, while it's true that all of these factors are important to a media planning decision, they were again apt to be ignored because our client had been eliminated from the media buyers' initial consideration set.

The more the creative team wrestled with the assignment, the more apparent it became that the answer would have to start with attracting the media planners' attention and then prompting them to engage. If the planners had already written off our client as a potential place to advertise, we would need a message that would stand out and prove impossible for them to ignore. It was a tall order. Fortunately, the team was up to it.

GETTING NOTICED, BEING RELEVANT, MAKING THE POINT
They developed an intriguing two-part campaign that they mailed to a targeted list of media planners. The first mailing was sent in an anti-static bag, which is a silver, translucent ziplock bag. Visible through the bag was an x-ray of a skull, with a hand-drawn arrow pointing to the place where a piece had been removed. The x-ray was labeled with the media planner's name. The mailing purported to come from L.I. Laboratories. Also inside the anti-static bag was a letter, explaining that unbeknownst to the media planner, a small sample of their brain had been extracted for analysis, to determine if they were "susceptible." They were told their results would be mailed to them soon.

A few days later, a large corrugated plastic box arrived. The box also appeared to be from L.I. Laboratories, and had two bright orange stickers on it. One said "Test results enclosed." And the other warned "Fragile: Medical equipment and samples." When the media planner opened the box, they found a microscope, a small box of slides that showed their brain sample findings, a brochure with instructions on how to interpret those slides, and a letter. The letter informed the media planner that their brain tissue analysis had been completed, and they should view the slides under the microscope to see what was on their mind.

When the media planner looked at the slides through the microscope, they saw images of events that were currently featured in the mainstream news. For example, they may have seen a picture related to recent reports about developments in cloning, or the discovery of water on Mars. The point was that these were the topics people were interested in and talking about at the moment. The analysis concluded that there were millions of people who enjoyed television programming about these topics, and that media planners themselves were also "susceptible" to it. The campaign then highlighted some key statistics about the corresponding programming our client ran, as well as the audience it reached, and then popped a call to action.

These curious packages did an impressive job of capturing the attention of the media planners, and of prompting them to come to the realization that our client's programming wasn't dated or niche, but rather topical and popular. Instead of sending a marketing message that insisted the media planners were wrong in their initial assessment, we sent one that used the very programming to demonstrate just how compelling it was. The media planners drew their own conclusion that the way they'd been defining our client's science-related programming was not accurate. And as a result, they became receptive to the idea of advertising on it. The team had created a campaign that not only stood out, but stood out in a way that underscored the marketing message it wished to deliver. In fact, the work was so powerful and distinctive, it was recognized with a London International Advertising Award.

Creating a message that stands out does not have to cost a lot of money

A campaign like the one just described can certainly be costly. The key is to consider the return on your marketing investment. You don't want to launch a campaign that would require unreasonably high response in order to be profitable. Let metrics like your average order size and the lifetime value of your customer inform your thinking here.

While still working at the same agency where we created the x-ray and microscope campaign for our television programming client, we also did some work that heavily leveraged the Von Restorff Effect for one of our high-technology clients. This campaign used self-mailers, which can be ubiquitous in the mail. As a result, our executions really had to stand out. And they did. For example, one was sent in a brown paper lunch bag, and delivered the message that without our client's product, the B2B target was doomed to continue eating lunch at their desks because they'd have no time to go out. Another was sealed shut by a bandage, and contained the message that our client's product could put an end to the band-aid solutions the target had increasingly come to rely on. Successful at attracting attention in a way that reinforced the marketing message, the campaign generated $40 million in revenue on expenses of just $167,975.

HOW TO MAKE YOUR EMAILS STAND OUT IN YOUR TARGET'S INBOX

If you're like most marketers, you're constantly looking for new ways to ensure your emails get opened and clicked through. The subject line plays a key role in persuading people to open their email. Typically, your target will be scanning a long list of messages in their inbox, with subject line on top of subject line competing for their attention. If you can make yours stand out, you will be in a better position to have your email opened. My colleague Jay Schwedelson, president and CEO of Worldata, continually researches what's working in the marketplace. In 2021, he identified the following tactics that increase open rates, often by double digits. Each of them makes good use of the Von Restorff Effect.

- Include an emoji in your subject line. Jay finds this is effective for both B2C and B2B emails. Start your subject line with an emoji, or bookend your subject line with emojis, placing one at the beginning and another at the end of it.
- Add special characters to your subject line, such as >>>> or ////.
- Place the first word or two of your subject line inside of brackets or parentheses.
- Choose one or two words of your subject line to run in all caps. But make sure it's no more than half of the words in the subject line, otherwise you can come across as shouting.
- End your subject line with ellipses. Those three dots spark curiosity. People want to know what comes next. As a result, they'll open your email to find out.
- Start your subject line with a number, but take care to use the numeral. Don't spell out the number because it will blend in with all the other words in your inbox.
- Exaggerate the spelling of one word in your subject line. For example, you could write save as "saaaave" or long as "loooonnnng."
- Display your sender line in capital letters.

Using these tactics will make your email different from most of the ones in your target's inbox. And people are hardwired to notice things that are different from their surroundings. Include one or two of these approaches when writing your subject lines to increase your chance of getting opened. But back off these tactics when you notice too many other marketers adopting them.

Make your message stand out using surprise and uncertain rewards

The human brain is hardwired to predict what will happen next. But when your customer does not see what they expect to, that person will be surprised.

Surprise can be beneficial to marketers in two ways. When people are surprised, it focuses their attention and it intensifies their emotions. Both of these responses will make it more likely the person will remember what it was that surprised them.

Marketers can craft their messages to surprise their customers and prospects by making adjustments to their copy and visuals. For example, I received an email from a clothing retailer with the subject line "dressed to chill." It surprised me, because when I read the first two words, I expected the next word to be "kill," since that is the common expression. When I actually processed the third word and realized it was not "kill," but rather "chill," I was surprised, and my brain was immediately bathed in dopamine, a chemical which aids in memory. This particular marketer had effectively lodged two thoughts in my mind. I came away from the email thinking these clothes would look good on me (dressed to kill), and that I'd feel comfortable wearing them (dressed to chill). The surprising message actually delivered two-for-one results.

Readers familiar with the language learning app Duolingo may recognize this technique. The company deliberately uses some nonsensical sentences in their lessons. Journalist Jane C. Hu spoke with Cindy Blanco, a learning scientist there, for her *Slate* article "Why Are Duolingo's Sentences So Weird?" In the article, Hu writes:

> "When there's a conflict between your expectation and the reality, that triggers responses in the brain," said Blanco. "It forces you to attend more carefully to what you're seeing." For example, when you see a sentence like, "The bride is a woman and the groom is a…," your brain has likely filled in the word *man*, so the actual word Duolingo uses—*hedgehog*—is a surprise. *Voila*, you have been forced to pay extra attention (Hu, 2021).

Your visuals can also be unexpected, and as a result, surprising. For example, I have seen a New England-based bank show a picture of Santa Claus sitting on a sunny beach, as opposed to being shown in the snow of the North Pole (or a New England December). I've seen a social media tourism campaign that pictured a buffalo on a standup paddle board. And another for a big box store that showed a person with a large stuffed animal head instead of a human one. Coming upon images that we are not used to seeing both attracts our attention away from any surrounding content, and makes the message associated with them more memorable.

THE ROLE OF UNCERTAIN REWARDS

Another effective way to surprise people is to offer them an uncertain reward. Contrary to what a marketer might think, uncertain rewards can be more motivating than certain ones. In fact, according to the *Journal of Consumer Research*, researchers from the University of Chicago and the University of Hong Kong have found that people will actually invest more effort trying to win an uncertain reward than they will pursuing a certain one (Shen et al, 2014).

In one experiment, people were asked to drink a large amount of water in two minutes. Some people were told they would receive two dollars for doing so. Others were told they would receive either one dollar or two dollars if they completed the task. The researchers found that 70 percent of the uncertain reward group drank all the water in the allotted time, as compared to only 43 percent of the people in the certain reward group.

Identified as the Motivating Uncertainty Effect, what drives the behavior, according to the researchers, is the thrill of pursuing the reward. In some cases, the excitement can revolve around which reward will be achieved, and in other cases, the excitement can be fueled by whether a reward will be won or not. Both instances incorporate an element of surprise.

TWO EXAMPLES OF THE MOTIVATING UNCERTAINTY EFFECT IN MARKETING
When working on the account of a community bank, my team used the Motivating Uncertainty Effect to help encourage customers to sign up for mobile banking. In the banner ads and emails introducing the product, we promoted a chance to win a smartphone if the customer enrolled in mobile banking. The response came in at 71 percent over goal. The prize made sense given the message, and the chance to win likely provided more motivation to sign up right away than if there had been no sweepstakes.

An even more innovative example of this tactic, however, comes from a cosmetics company. They invited young women to upload a picture of themselves wearing the company's makeup for a chance to have that picture appear on the company's website. While the reward was uncertain for the young women, the payoff was a certainty for the company, because in order for the women to participate in the promotion, they first had to purchase and apply the makeup.

How to use context, rewards, and surprise to make your message stand out

- Look for strategic ways to break out of the expected approach your category takes to advertising. For example, during the 2022 Super Bowl, Coinbase ran a commercial that consisted solely of a QR code bouncing on the screen for the entire 60 seconds. It was arguably one of the most talked-about spots. As *Contagious* observed, "Coinbase's ad was a misfit among the field of polished ads fronted by megastar celebrities, and so it stood out." It was also effective. The spot drove "more than 20 million visitors to its website in the space of a minute" and the company had to "throttle traffic" (*Contagious*, 2022)

- Consider black and white if your competitors always advertise in color.

- Test having your message appear at events and locations where your target goes but does not expect to see you, or at times that will surprise them.

- Make the option you want customers to notice slightly larger than the ones around it. Or frame it in a color.

- Position calls to action with ample white space around them, so they are noticeable.

- Put key messages like "limited quantities" or "free" in violators, which are design elements such as snipes and starbursts that violate the design integrity of your message and as a result, get noticed.

- Add a sticky note to the outside of your direct mail piece or to your insert to attract attention.

- Mail a box, tube, or an oversized, textured, or padded envelope to stand out from the day's mail.

- Choose unusual shapes for your print ads. Or buy a full-page ad but fill very little of it with content. Or make your content into a shape that also underscores your message. For example, a grocer could position all their copy inside the shape of an apple.

- Include an element in your ad's imagery that will make it jump out. One example is the classic 1950s Ogilvy ad known as the man in the Hathaway shirt, where the shirt model wore an eyepatch. My team once created an ad for dental insurance which showed a smiling boy missing his front tooth. The eyepatch and the missing tooth made the man and boy, respectively, different from all the other men and boys in the ads the target would have seen.

- Open a video or tv spot with a screen showing nothing but words, because people will expect to see images.

- If creating a tv or radio ad to run in the United States, consider a British voiceover to stand out.

- Choose striking visuals and distinctive-looking models to appear in your tv commercials, videos, and ads.

- Start subject lines with words proven to attract the human eye, such as alert, new, and introducing.

- Include a GIF in your email or social media post because movement attracts attention.

- If your digital ad will appear on a website other than your own, incorporate motion because that will pull focus to your message and away from the content surrounding it.

- Use contests, spin to win games, scratch to reveal, and other ways to offer uncertain rewards.

- Surprise customers with an unexpected discount or gift when delivering your sales message.

- Write a headline that's contrary to popular opinion or belief.

- Send customers and prospects a mystery offer to create surprise.

- Tie your message to a holiday to make it stand out. Holidays are different than all the rest of the days in a year, so people pay attention to them.

- There is something being celebrated almost every day of the year. Look for a day that matches your message, or match your message to the day. For instance, National Chardonnay Day can be ideal for a restaurant, bar, winery, or alcoholic beverage distributor. But another marketer can also tie a message to it. For example, you could send a message that says, "Before celebrating National Chardonnay Day, read this first."

- Take advantage of special occasions such as birthdays and anniversaries to stand out. If you know your customer's birthday or the anniversary of their first purchase, send them a message marking it. If not, invite them to celebrate your company's birthday or anniversary. To further stand out, consider acknowledging half birthdays.

- Flag holidays and special occasions in headlines, subject lines, and direct mail teaser copy.

KEY TAKEAWAYS

1 People are hardwired to notice things that are different from what surrounds them.

2 Simply making messages stand out won't automatically generate business for a marketer.

3 Used properly, the Von Restorff—or Isolation—Effect can get your message noticed and can nudge customers to the product or service you wish to sell.

4 Use size, color, and visual cues to prevent your message from blending in.

5 Make sure people aren't so captivated by your unusual marketing that they miss the name of your brand or product.

6 For the best results, your attention-getting marketing should naturally underscore your sales message.

7 Think about the context in which your message will be received. For example, if you're sending direct mail, choose a package that will look different from everything else that arrives that day, because of its size, shape, texture, etc. If you're sending an email, construct your subject line so that something about it jumps out from among all the others in your target's inbox.

8 The human brain is hardwired to predict what will happen next.

9 When your target doesn't see what they're expecting to, whether it's a word or an image, they'll be surprised. Surprise focuses attention and intensifies emotion, both of which make what surprised the person more likely to be remembered.

10 Behavioral scientists have found that people are more motivated to attain uncertain rewards versus certain ones, because pursuing a reward is exciting. Offering an uncertain reward is another way marketers can surprise customers and prospects.

11 Make your marketing messages strategically different than your competitors' by paying attention to your choice of color, models, placement, size, language, props, sound, and use of motion. This can make your message stand out, surprise your target, or both.

12 Use contests and other interactive devices to offer uncertain rewards.

13 Take advantage of holidays and special occasions because they naturally stand out from all the other days in the year.

In conclusion

Marketing that strategically stands out will increase awareness, recall, and sales. However, being too different can backfire. Make sure your product and company name register with your target, otherwise you risk sending business to a competitor or simply entertaining your audience without landing your message.

On the other hand, blending in can be similarly deadly. Be aware of the context your message will appear in. Avoid predictability. And consider your timing, which, as you'll see in the next chapter, can also increase your prospect's receptivity to your message.

References

Contagious Edit (2022) Your weekly dose of contagious thinking, 16 February, http://contagious-1725887.hs-sites.com/the-average-bowl (archived at https://perma.cc/E2S4-2QLR)

Hu, J C (2021) Why are Duolingo's sentences so weird? *Slate*, 29 November, https://slate.com/technology/2021/11/duolingo-weird-sentences-linguistics.html (archived at https://perma.cc/NR26-ZVQ2)

Nichols, R (2019) How the isolation effect can boost your conversions [Blog] *AB Tasty*, 3 February, https://www.abtasty.com/blog/isolation-effect/ (archived at https://perma.cc/JHZ4-5ZRN)

Shen, L, Fishbach, A and Hsee, C (2015) The motivating-uncertainty effect: Uncertainty increases resource investment in the process of reward pursuit, *Journal of Consumer Research*, https://academic.oup.com/jcr/articleabstract/41/5/1301/2962097?redirectedFrom=fulltext (archived at https://perma.cc/CN8X-RDB4)

Shotton, R (2018) *The Choice Factory: 25 behavioural biases that influence what we buy*, Harriman House, Great Britain

17

Temporal landmarks and temporal discounting—the effects of time on behavior

Behavioral scientists have found that people are more open to trying new things at certain times. This can be valuable information for marketers, who can sync their solicitations to these times. However, time is not always a marketer's friend. Companies that hope to sell products and services whose benefit is not immediate must first overcome the human preference to focus on the present.

If the old saying is to be believed, timing is everything. And marketers certainly pay a lot of attention to timing. Although when a marketer thinks about time, it's often in a very practical way. Marketers think about the necessary aspects of time, such as how much of it is available to develop a product or a campaign, are promotions proceeding according to schedule, has a coupon code expired, are marketing materials ready for the seasonal peaks, and are any deadlines in danger of being missed?

Marketers also think about time in relation to their customers. You most likely consider the lifetime value of your various customer segments, the signs that signal a prospect may be ready to purchase for the first time, the fact that shortly after an initial purchase is often the best time to market an add-on or an upgrade, that this is also an opportune time to ask for a testimonial or referral, and that there is a high likelihood following a certain number of days, weeks, months, or years—depending on what you sell—that a customer will be ready to buy again.

As a marketer, you probably also think about when to send your messages and what your contact cadence should be. You may test which days result in the best response to your emails and which ones look like they should be avoided altogether, which dayparts are effective for running your television or radio spots, whether your social posts perform better in the morning or the evening, how quickly you can fulfill requests for proposals or meetings, and when you should try to move a customer from a free service to a paid one.

You likely also factor receptivity to your message into all this thinking about time. You know that if you ask for the sale too soon you will lose it. But if you spend too much time trying to lay the groundwork, your competitors could sweep in and steal away your prospect. You may try to time your messaging to correspond with where in the sales funnel or purchase continuum you suspect your prospect to be. You might also experiment with geofencing your offers or with point of purchase promotions. Your goal is for your target to encounter your message when they are most apt to act on it, and not when they are too far away from making a decision or, conversely, when they have just made one.

So yes, as a marketer, you spend a lot of time thinking about, well, time. Because in these very real ways, time is money. Missed deadlines, missed opportunities, and misaligned messages can all hurt your profitability. And as important as it is to consider all these factors, doing so is still not enough.

Here's why. Behavioral scientists have made two discoveries about time that also significantly impact customer behavior. They both involve the rather curious relationship humans have with time. A marketer who pays attention to these findings will see that they make it more likely that customers and prospects will do what you want them to do—when you want them to do it.

The first of these findings sheds light on when people are most likely to act on your marketing message. It should help inform when you choose to market to them. The second finding reveals the less than rational manner in which people look at time. It explains why people often fail to act when they should. Understanding it can help marketers close this intention-action gap.

> Temporal landmarks are transition periods. Marketers will find their customers and prospects are more open to new experiences during these times.

People are more likely to take action when they encounter a temporal landmark

When it comes to motivating people, not all days are created equal. In fact, behavioral scientists have found that some days are far more impactful than others. The scientists refer to these days as temporal landmarks. A temporal landmark is a time that stands out from most other times and is imbued with special meaning. As a result, people are more likely to take action around a temporal landmark. Temporal landmarks can be days that appear on a calendar—days like a holiday that is widely acknowledged—or they can be special occasions that have a more personal significance, such as an individual's birthday. Researchers have shown that days like these can have an almost magical, motivating quality.

THE SURPRISING EFFECT OF BIRTHDAYS

In Daniel H. Pink's book *When: The scientific secrets of perfect timing*, he observes that "when people near the end of the arbitrary marker of a decade, something awakens in their minds that alters their behavior." Pink cites research from Adam Alter and Hal Hershfield (Alter and Hershfield, 2014) that supports this idea. The research found that people whose age ended in nine were "over-represented among first-time marathoners by a whopping 48 percent." It showed that 29-year-olds are almost twice as likely to run a marathon as 30-year-olds. And that 49-year-olds are approximately three times more likely to run a marathon than 50-year-olds. Approaching the end of one decade and the start of a new one serves as a temporal landmark for these people.

As eye-opening as that is, as a marketer, you may not be all that concerned with motivating people to run a footrace. However, other research also shows the effect of a person's birthday on their behavior, and this research involves marketing. Behavioral scientists from Duke University's Common Cents Lab worked with an online company called Silvernest, which matches baby boomers who have rooms to rent with baby boomers looking to rent a room. According to "Behavioral nudges timed to certain days are effective motivator," a 2018 article by Carla Fried, the company ran Facebook ads targeting people about to turn 65. Fried explained:

> The control group for the experiment was served up the somewhat generic message, "You're getting older. Are you ready for retirement? House sharing can help." The test group got a more age-specific nudge: "You're 64, turning 65. Are you ready for retirement? House sharing can help."

he more age-specific copy generated a nearly 5.5 percent click-through rate, compared to the 2.5 percent click-through rate of the generic messaging. And it is not just birthdays that can spur this spurt in behavior. Daniel H. cites additional examples in his book *When*. He explains that research-nalyzed eight and a half years of Google searches and found that hes for the word 'diet' always soared on January 1—by about

80 percent more than on a typical day" (Dai et al., 2014). But that's not all. He reports that the study's authors found that searches also increased on the first days of every month, and the first days of every week, too.

Pink writes that in a different study, these same researchers found that how a day is framed also makes an impact. Referring to March 20 as the first day of spring was more powerful than referring to it as the third Thursday in March. The first day of the new season functioned as a temporal landmark.

TEMPORAL LANDMARKS CAN PROMPT FRESH STARTS

The studies' researchers coined the term the "fresh start effect" to describe the motivating behavior that ensues (Dai et al., 2014). What they found was that people have a tendency to view themselves differently at temporal landmarks. These temporal landmarks act as points of transition. There is the person you're leaving behind, the old you, and there's the one you're on the brink of becoming, the new and improved you. Because you're about to close the chapter on the old you, with all of its shortcomings, and you're faced with the promising blank page of the new you, people feel more confident that they can take on challenges and accomplish their goals. As a result, they are more open to starting new things. It's why you rarely hear someone proclaim, "I'm going to stop smoking on Wednesday," but it's not at all uncommon to hear, "Starting Monday, I'm going to give up cigarettes."

As a marketer, you should factor these fresh start days, or temporal landmarks, into your campaigns. New Year's Day is already a big marketing opportunity, because it's recognized as a day when people resolve to start anew, with a fresh slate in front of them. But as the research shows, other beginnings can also be quite powerful—and they provide you with more frequent opportunities. Think in terms of the beginning of seasons, quarters, semesters, months, pay periods, and weeks. Each of these can be times when people are primed for a fresh start.

Marketers should also not neglect personal milestone events, such as birthdays, anniversaries, graduations, the start of a new job, the move to a new city, marriage, the birth of a child, the purchase of a home, retirement, and other similar events. Each of these functions as a transition point, a time of demarcation, when people will think in terms of their lives before the event and after it.

How approaching a temporal landmark prompted me to make a six-figure purchase

After graduating Boston University, I did what most of the people I knew did. I decided not to return to the town where I'd grown up, but rather to try to start my career in a bigger city. I found a roommate and together we joined thousands of other recent graduates looking for an apartment in a college town. We found something suitable that summer, and moved a jumble of books, beds, and boxes into a small place on the outskirts of the Boston University campus.

I moved again at the end of the following summer, collecting two more roommates and upgrading to a slightly better apartment. And then I spent the next half a dozen years renting an apartment with two or three friends and working in the Boston area. Things were actually going quite well. My roommates were very good friends of mine. We'd settled into a comfortable, convenient apartment that was a considerable bit nicer than my first, post-graduate place. And the rent, split between all of us, was fairly affordable and allowed me to bank some of my salary. There was no particular reason to change any of it. And yet, as I found myself approaching my 30th birthday, I felt I needed to own property. I decided it was time to buy a condo.

The truth was, it really was not time to buy a condo. The market was high. Artificially high. In order to find something in my price range, I would need to forgo the established neighborhoods I might have liked to live in, and instead investigate those that were "on their way up," as the real estate agents euphemistically phrased it. I also could not afford anything large enough for all my roommates to move in with me, even if they'd wanted to have me as a landlord, so it meant I would be leaving my good friends. And with mortgage payments being larger than the rent I'd been accustomed to paying, I would soon be banking less, while working at an ad agency, which is not the most stable of employment.

Nevertheless, I felt driven to buy a condo. And I felt I needed to do so before I turned 30. So, I dashed from open house to open house, visiting the towns that surrounded Boston (some of which I'd never previously set foot in), trying to find something I wanted to buy.

Finally, I saw a two-bedroom duplex in South Boston that had a small yard, off-street parking, and peeks of the downtown Boston skyline. It was conveniently located near a subway stop, so I could take mass transportation into town. And it was new construction, with a roomy layout and good-sized closets. I knew nothing about South Boston, nor did I know a single soul who lived there. But the clock was ticking, so I made an offer.

One month and two days before my 30 birthday, I closed on my condo. My friends threw me a birthday party in my new, yet sparsely furnished living room. And it seems like days after that, the housing bubble burst, and left my "up and coming" neighborhood a good distance from that noble goal, and my new condo considerably depreciated. However, I had met my personal goal, irrational as it may have been. Triggered by a temporal landmark, I had purchased property before I turned 30.

CASE STUDY
Using behavioral science to boost online student enrollment

Berklee Online, a division of Berklee College of Music, is the world's largest online music school, with a 97 percent student satisfaction rating. The online school attracts students from over 164 countries, including members of the famous Dave Matthews Band, Nine Inch Nails, and Phish. More than 75,000 students have turned to the successful school for online classes, courses, certificates, and degree programs.

But what do you do when competition in the online music education space starts to grow, and enrollment rates start to flatten? Debbie Cavalier, Senior Vice President of Online Learning at Berklee, and CEO and Co-founder of Berklee Online, and Mike King, Berklee Online's CMO, took a two-pronged approach. They commissioned a customer segmentation study to gain insights into the motivations and values of the school's applicants and students. And they hired me to consult with their marketing team, so the team could learn how to craft behavioral science-informed marketing messages for those segments.

Naturally, there were many behavioral science principles that I recommended they include in their messaging, in order to increase the effectiveness of their emails, social posts, landing pages, website copy, and ads. Some of my recommendations will be familiar to you if you've read the earlier chapters of this book. I suggested they continue to stoke the emotion (see Chapter 1) that surrounds pursuing a music degree, use loss aversion (see Chapter 2) to prompt response, and highlight the exclusive (see Chapter 3) opportunities that could only be found at Berklee Online.

Additionally, to help ward off the growing competitive threat, I recommended the team cite social proof (see Chapter 5) by underscoring their satisfied students, invoke the authority principle (see Chapter 10) by mentioning the many awards the online program had won and the singular quality of the faculty, and that they include the reason why (see Chapter 13) prospective students should consider earning their online degree from Berklee.

As you might have guessed given the topic of this current chapter, I also encouraged Berklee Online's marketing team to factor in certain temporal landmarks when creating their campaigns. After being introduced to the concept, the team did a great job of strategically identifying three different kinds of temporal landmarks they could work with. One type included more universal fresh start transition periods, such as the beginning of a year, season, month, or week. The second type was tied to their academic calendar, and used the beginning of new terms and new classes as points of demarcation. And the third type was episodic, based on key events that may or may not repeat, such as an upcoming tuition increase and the launch of the new online Master's degree program, both of which they could use as effective temporal landmarks.

When speaking with Debbie a couple of years later, I was happy to hear things were continuing to go well for their marketing team, and that their efforts were paying off. She made me smile when she said that whenever the team added behavioral science to the marketing copy, they'd say they had "Nancified" it! Even more important, Debbie reported that the work had become "more effective and engaging," and that they'd seen "improvements in overall campaign success." In fact, she said that "Today Berklee Online's enrollment numbers are more than double what they had been before working with Nancy Harhut. There are many reasons for this, but our adoption of behavioral science marketing principles is most certainly included." Now that is ending an engagement on a high note.

FIGURE 17.1 *Fresh starts spur behavior*

Berklee Online takes advantage of a temporal landmark in this email flagging the start of a new semester.

People put off behaviors when they perceive the payoff to be too distant

Marketers can use the fresh start effect by prompting their customers and prospects to see their past selves and their future selves as being separate. That is one critical component to using this tactic. You want someone to feel that who they were yesterday is not who they are today, and that the today person can accomplish more because of this transition point that they have hit.

However, there are times when this human tendency to separate the selves will work against a marketer. In those times, it is important for a marketer to help customers envision themselves in the future as being very much like the person they are in the present. Being able to do this will help a marketer overcome temporal discounting, which is the human tendency to devalue distant rewards.

Behavioral scientists have found that people can be very present focused, with a preference for instant gratification. If given a choice, your customers and prospects will likely choose sooner, albeit smaller rewards over larger, but later ones.

For this reason, it is not uncommon for them to know that they should do something because it's in their best interest, and yet fail to do it. Humans exhibit a distinct preference for putting off taking actions that have payoffs that are not immediate. It is a lot easier to spend $150 on dinner and a night out, which can be enjoyed in the present moment, than it is to bank that same amount of money to spend later, or to invest it in a retirement account, or to use it to buy something practical such as insurance, which has a future, and even uncertain, payoff. It's not that people don't believe they should save some of their paycheck, that they should put aside money for their retirement, or that they should have insurance. It's just that they delay these decisions because it's easier and more convenient to think that their future selves can take care of them.

MARKETERS MUST OVERCOME TEMPORAL DISCOUNTING

People often assume their future selves will have more discipline, more patience, more motivation, or simply will be in a more advantageous position to accomplish some of their goals. As a result, they put things off in favor of enjoying the present moment. Often, however, when the future does arrive, these same people regret their earlier decision and wish they had taken action sooner, when they had that chance. For example, when it comes time to retire, they wish they had systematically saved money during their working years. Or when they find themselves stuck in a job with no possibility of being promoted, they wish they had taken those college courses when they were younger, so they would have the skills that are required to advance in their career. However, humans are impatient in the moment.

As Carlos Abadi explains in his 2019 *Decision Boundaries* article, "Hyperbolic Discounting":

> … many people prefer $100 now to $110 in a day, but very few people prefer $100 in 30 days to $110 in 31 days. It appears people would rather wait 1 day for $10 if the wait happens a month from now. However, they prefer the

opposite if they must wait right now. More generally, the rate at which people discount future rewards declines as the length of the delay increases. This phenomenon has been termed hyperbolic discounting by psychologist Richard Herrnstein.

Abadi goes on to say, "Yet after a month passes, many of these people will reverse their preferences and now choose the immediate $100 rather than wait a day for an additional $10." People are inconsistent, and demonstrate curious and not completely rational behavior when dealing with time.

Research shows people see their future selves more as strangers

Stanford University researchers Hal Ersner-Hershfield, G. Elliott Wimmer, and Brian Knutson conducted studies that also demonstrate the curious way people relate to time (Ersner-Hershfield et al., 2008). They put study participants into an fMRI machine so they could view the participants' brain activity. Then they showed the participants a series of descriptive words, such as "honorable" and "funny," and asked them to indicate how closely that word described their present selves, their future selves (in 10 years), a current "other" (either Matt Damon for male participants or Natalie Portman for female participants), or a future version of that "other."

The most brain activity happened when people were evaluating their current selves, which is not unexpected, since people are more interested in themselves than in anyone else. What was telling, however, was that when research participants thought about their future selves, their brain activity was more similar to what they experienced when they thought about a current "other" than it was to when they thought about their current self.

As Becky Kane observed, when writing about the study in her article "Present Bias: Why you don't give a damn about your future self," "Put in practical terms, when thinking of yourself in a month or a year or a decade, your brain registers that person in ways similar to how it would register Taylor Swift or the mailman or the lady driving the car in the next lane over." People view their future selves more as strangers than as extensions of who they are today.

In her article, Kane also references an additional study about the effects of temporal discounting. This study involves a group of student research participants who were interviewed about their willingness to help tutor other students (Pronin et al., 2008). One group of students was asked to commit to tutoring during the current midterm period, a second group was asked to commit to tutor during the following midterm period, and a third group of student research participants was asked to estimate how much time they thought incoming freshmen could commit to tutoring.

The results reflect the Hershfield findings above. As Kane observes:

> Those asked how much time they would be willing to commit in the present said just 27 minutes on average while those asked to commit during the following midterm period responded with an average of 85 minutes. Even more compelling is the fact that the study found no statistically significant difference between the number of minutes students committed for their future selves and time committed for someone else entirely.

Again, people see their future selves as largely unrelated to their present selves.

However, in a fourth version of the experiment, researchers reminded some of the student participants that they would likely have the same time constraints in the next midterm period as they currently had. When these students were asked how much time they would be able to commit to tutoring during the following midterm period, their estimates were considerably lower. Helping those students see themselves in the future as being very much like who they were in the present made a difference.

MISTAKE

Providing people with the right information and emotional prompt, and assuming they will make good decisions about their future. Instead, marketers must also help people bridge the gap between their present and future selves.

Help customers see themselves as they currently are—just older

Overcoming the effects of temporal discounting requires a marketer to help bridge the gap between how a person sees themselves in the present, and how they imagine themselves in the future. Essentially, you need to convince your targets that they will be the same people they are today, but at a later date. One way you can do this is by using visuals. In 2012, the financial firm

Merrill Edge launched their Face Retirement campaign, which featured software that allowed people to upload a photo of themselves and age progress it, so they could see what they would look like 10, 20, 30 or more years down the road. According to a 2014 article in *Finextra*, nearly one million people used the tool, with 60 percent of them pursuing more information about retirement and planning for the future. The campaign went on to win a 2014 Effie Award for marketing effectiveness.

The Merrill Edge campaign was clearly compelling. However, if you need to counter the effect of temporal discounting, but worry that your marketing budget won't support the use of age progression software, you have other options. The words you choose can help you create the bridge between your target's present self and their future self.

In fact, in 2015, my colleagues and I worked with Dr. Aaron Reid, founder and CEO of Sentient Decision Science, to conduct some proprietary research into, among other topics, overcoming the effect of temporal discounting. The research included several industries and two generational groups. One aspect of the study explored how marketing copy could be used to offset the purchase-delaying effect that temporal discounting has on the acquisition of insurance. For research-savvy readers, the study involved implicit and choice-based conjoint research methods, emotional weighting, eye-tracking studies, and heat mapping. Put differently, it was sophisticated and thorough, and designed to measure authentic response, delivering results that were superior to traditional modeling efforts.

The research found that using language that prompted people to see themselves in the future as similar to who they currently were not only helped overcome temporal discounting, but also increased people's preferences for higher-premium insurance policies. So how exactly does this work? Let's say, for example, that you are a marketer of disability insurance, which pays people a portion of their income if an accident or illness prevents them from working. You could write copy that says:

> Even financially responsible people like you who are currently in good health
> can be the victim of circumstance, and get into an accident or contract
> an illness. If that happens, and you can no longer work, your bills—both
> the new medical ones and the ones you currently pay, such as your rent,
> credit card, utility, cable, and internet bills—could start to pile up. Now
> imagine owning insurance that could help you pay those bills, so you don't
> have to cut back or even risk going into debt. Just like today, you would feel
> on top of your finances.

The copy mentions expenses the target currently has, and helps them see that they'll want to be able to pay for those things in the future, even if something were to happen to them that prevented them from working. It also labels the target as financially responsible, and contrasts that with the unappealing notion of going into debt.

As Dr Reid observed at the conclusion of the study, "Simple, yet precise modifications to the language used to describe the situation, risks, and benefits related to insurance and investment decisions can significantly increase product consideration and likelihood to purchase." He went on to add, "Given the scientific experimental design, we can attribute causality to the specific behavioral economics-based copy changes" (Perkett, 2015).

CASE STUDY
Overcoming temporal discounting to prompt people to start saving for retirement

When you're young, it's easy to put off thinking you need to prepare for getting old. And when you're feeling cash-strapped, it's easy to put off new demands for the limited funds you do have. In both of these scenarios, those activities can be readily relegated to the future. So, when a financial firm came to HBT Marketing and asked us to help them increase enrollments into their retirement accounts, we knew we'd have to deal with temporal discounting.

When a marketer is first trying to convince someone to sign up for their company's 401(k) plan, there are some arguments that make a lot of sense. One of those is to show people how their contributions will accumulate over time. Small but regular investments can add up to quite a retirement nest egg. This is especially true if an employee starts to save early in their career. However, because of the effect of temporal discounting, it can be challenging to make this argument. People just discount the distant payoff, and prefer to spend the money they have now, thinking there will always be time later to start saving.

Another compelling argument can be made if the employer matches any of the employee's contributions. Those matches can be positioned as free money, akin to the employee getting a raise. However, the problem with that is, employees often see their own part of the contribution as a loss. Because their immediate take-home pay is effectively decreased, they are often too focused on that to appreciate the ultimate gains that opening a 401(k) account would bring.

As the team thought through the assignment, it became more and more clear that addressing temporal discounting would be key to crafting an effective campaign.

It was also clear that such an effort would need to occur prominently in the messaging. This thinking guided the team's language choice for the copy, which was slated to appear in email, direct mail, and Facebook ads. For example, in one execution, the copy encouraged the target to think about their current situation, and pointed out that even though they had to juggle many financial commitments, they were still in charge, and they made the decisions about when and where to spend their money. "Do you want retirement to change that?" the copy queried.

Another execution said, "You can make it happen, even if you have other responsibilities now." And a third execution urged the target to get started right away, so their money could grow. It read, "And then, just like today, you'll know you made some good choices for yourself and the people who depend on you." The copy built a bridge that helped the target envision themselves as they currently were, with the same preferences, obligations, and feelings, but in the future. And it worked. Our client saw a substantial 12 percent increase in new account openings.

Other examples of marketing that successfully negates the temporal discounting effect

As I study marketing examples, I often flag communications I see that represent good examples of behavioral science being used. These three struck me as particularly powerful:

- An online bank advertising certificates of deposits (CDs) ran messaging that suggested they had asked the future you if that person wanted more money, and that person had said yes. When the target reads that message, it's hard to disagree with it. Since most people would like more money now, it's not a stretch to think they'd also want more money in the future. As a result, it makes them receptive to the idea of getting a CD.

- A university ran messaging that began with the statement, "I am a future…", and then offered a selection of ways to complete it. Prospective students could find the phrase that best described them (future freshman student, future graduate student, etc.), which in turn helped them to see their future selves.

- A different university showed a video of their recent graduation ceremony and asked their target market if they could picture themselves on that same stage. By prompting them to envision themselves at commencement, they helped the target to create a bridge between their current and future selves.

How marketers can use temporal landmarks and temporal discounting to motivate behavior

- Send communications at the start of the week—or at the beginning of the weekend, depending on what you're marketing.

- Take advantage of holidays (see Chapter 16) because they can represent temporal landmarks.

- Look at how you can use non-holiday special days, such as Tax Day and back-to-school day. For example, a non-profit can encourage potential donors to sign up for automatic monthly contributions just after filing their income taxes, so they would have a larger charity write-off the following year.

- Time your B2B communications to use temporal landmarks such as the start of the fiscal year, the end of a quarter, and the beginning of a company's busy season.

- If you have the data, don't overlook personal landmarks, such as the anniversary of when someone bought a house, won an award, or adopted a pet.

- Remember that marketing certain products often requires overcoming temporal discounting. Some of these include diet and weight loss products, exercise equipment, smoking cessation aids, health and wellness products, college enrollments, insurance policies, retirement accounts, service upgrades, and repair and remodeling products.

- Allow customers to delay their payments. That way they experience the pleasure of immediate ownership while putting off the pain of paying.

- Offer instant gratification, including overnight shipping, immediate downloads, and ungated content.

- Discount your product by providing a mail-in rebate. The idea of saving money will prompt people to purchase right away, but some may not get around to requesting their rebate.

- Highlight ways you deliver immediate value, even if the ultimate value your product or service provides comes at a later date. For example, a company marketing an Individual Retirement Account (IRA) might emphasize that investment gains are tax-deferred until later, when they are withdrawn in retirement, so customers get a present-day tax advantage.

KEY TAKEAWAYS

1   Temporal landmarks are transition periods during someone's life. At these points, people feel that they've been granted a fresh start, and can leave behind all their prior shortcomings.

2   When your target hits a temporal landmark, they are often more open to trying new things, because they feel they have a greater likelihood of accomplishing them.

3   Marketers could benefit from timing their messages to coincide with temporal landmarks.

4   Temporal landmarks can be days that are marked on a calendar, such as holidays, and the start of years, seasons, months, and weeks. And they can be individual to a person, such as a birthday, anniversary, marriage, new home purchase, promotion, or retirement.

5   A temporal landmark can prompt your targets to see themselves as the "old me" (before the landmark) and the "new me" (after the landmark), viewing the two different selves as separate.

6   People prefer instant gratification, and have a tendency to discount distant rewards.

7   Your customers are likely to opt for smaller but sooner rewards and payoffs versus later, albeit larger ones. They do not like to wait.

8   Marketing certain products will require you to overcome temporal discounting, which can cause people to put off purchasing decisions until later. Often, they will opt for purchases they can enjoy in the moment versus spending or investing their money on products or services whose benefits can only manifest at a later date.

9   Marketers can overcome temporal discounting by helping their targets see the similarities between their present selves and their future selves. Without help, your target may have a hard time imagining how their future self will feel and what they would want their present self to do.

10 Marketers can build the bridge between their targets' present and future selves using appropriate imagery or language. The key is to get your targets to see themselves as they are, but in the future.

In conclusion

Marketers can capitalize on temporal landmarks, when people see themselves transitioning from their old selves to their new selves. During these transition periods, customers and prospects are more likely to try new products and services. Temporal landmarks include the start of seasons and weeks, as well as life events such as birthdays and new jobs.

Marketers of certain, future benefit products, however, must help prospective customers see themselves as the same in the future. They need prospects to feel they'll have the same desires and preferences in the future that they currently do, in order to prompt them to act now and not delay their purchase decisions.

References

Abadi, C (2019) Hyperbolic discounting, *Decision Boundaries*, 9 December, https://decisionboundaries.com/hyperbolic-discounting-2/ (archived at https://perma.cc/8XJQ-EBC2)

Alter, A and Hershfield, H (2014) People search for meaning when they approach a new decade in chronological age, *PNAS*, https://www.pnas.org/doi/10.1073/pnas.1415086111 (archived at https://perma.cc/Y7J9-XLAV)

Dai, H, Milkman, KL and Riis, J (2014), The fresh start effect: Temporal landmarks motivate aspirational behavior, *Management Science,* **60** (10), 2563–82, https://doi.org/10.1287/mnsc.2014.1901 (archived at https://perma.cc/U6ZK-PZGR)

Ersner-Hershfield, H, Wimmer, GE and Knutson, B (2009) Saving for the future self: Neural measures of future self-continuity predict temporal discounting, *Social Cognitive and Affective Neuroscience*, https://www.ncbi.nlm.nih.gov/pmc/articles/PMC2656877/ (archived at https://perma.cc/F23C-ZYM2)

Fried, C (2018) Behavioral nudges timed to certain days are effective motivator, *UCLA Anderson Review*, 6 June, https://anderson-review.ucla.edu/milestones/ (archived at https://perma.cc/Z9RD-88XD)

Kane, B (nd) Present Bias: Why you don't give a damn about your future self, and 3 strategies for achieving your long-term goals anyway, according to science [Blog] *Doist.com*, https://blog.doist.com/present-bias/ (archived at https://perma.cc/W4SN-RW3X)

Merrill Edge (2014) Merrill Edge Face Retirement app goes 3D, *Finextra*, 26 February, https://www.finextra.com/pressarticle/54111/merrill-edge-face-retirement-app-goes-3d (archived at https://perma.cc/7LNF-5HUX)

Perkett, C (2015) Wilde agency releases research study on behavioral economics, *PR.com*, 08 October, https://www.pr.com/press-release/640927 (archived at https://perma.cc/U8WJ-5KXR)

Pink, DH (2018) *When: The scientific secrets of perfect timing*, Riverhead Books, New York

Conclusion

You've finished reading the book. Now what? At this point, you're armed with at least 25 behavioral science principles that you can use to influence the behavior of your customers and prospects. Choose wisely. And test often.

Think about why people won't do what you want them to do. Identify the reasons that could be stopping them. Do they not know your company? Do they think they wouldn't use your product or service? Are they holding out for a better deal? Are they worried about getting someone else's buy-in?

Once you zero in on the potential barrier, review your newfound nuggets of behavioral know-how, and pick the principles most likely to neutralize those buying barriers. Test the top ones, including variations of them, to find what works best for you. And remember, even if your initial hypothesis doesn't pan out, each test delivers valuable knowledge—and gets you a step closer to your ultimate goal.

Don't forget to incorporate the best practices of your chosen marketing channel. Let data inform your decisions—and behavioral science ensure you serve them up in a brain-friendly way. Then look for the lifts in your response rates. As you've seen, some can register in the double- and triple-digit range. Others may deliver more incremental increases that, when added together, make the difference. You may well find that including more than one behavioral science trigger in your communications drives the best results.

Backed by science. Tested by marketers. Ready for you.

You can use these principles with confidence, knowing that they're backed by science and have been successfully employed by other marketers. More than that, behavioral science is currently applied in a variety of fields, including health, education, and public policy, to name just a few. When you introduce behavioral science to your marketing strategy and execution, you're relying on evidence-based research, rather than individual opinion. That alone delivers an immediate advantage.

And should you worry that advantage is unfair, remember that all the decisions that go into the development of your marketing campaign are designed to optimize it. You choose lists and media for their propensity to deliver response. You advertise prices that prospects will find appealing. You photograph your products to look attractive. Now you can create marketing messages designed for the way people will process them.

Marketers could easily begin to think of a fifth addition—"psychology"—to the four Ps of the marketing mix (product, place, price, promotion), if psychology only followed the alliteration! And just as you would not make unethical choices with the first four, you should use behavioral science responsibly, too. In doing so, it becomes one additional tool you have to increase your success.

Wield what science has proven about people's behavior in order to influence it

At the end of the day, marketers need to get people to make decisions. Behavioral scientists have studied how people do that. They've documented the shortcuts they take, the prompts they respond to, and the defaults they rely on. Savvy marketers are now in a position to use what science has proven about human behavior in order to influence it. Now that you understand how people really make choices, you can create marketing messages that are much more apt to get noticed, remembered, and responded to. All it takes is injecting some behavioral science.

You're ready to create more effective marketing—the kind that factors in the ways people instinctively behave. When you craft messages for how your target will receive them, it delivers an automatic advantage. And now that advantage is yours. Use it to drive the customer behavior you seek.

INDEX

Page numbers in *italic* denote information within figures.